Shadows of Tender Fury

SHADOWS of TENDER FURY

**The Letters and Communiqués
of Subcomandante Marcos and the
Zapatista Army of National Liberation**

**Translated by Frank Bardacke, Leslie López,
and the Watsonville, California,
Human Rights Committee**

**Introduction by John Ross
Afterword by Frank Bardacke**

**MONTHLY REVIEW PRESS
NEW YORK**

The illustrations in this edition are by the Mexican artist José Guadalupe Posada (1852-1913) and are from: *The Works of José Guadalupe Posada,* edited and with an introduction by Hannes Jähn, published in Germany by Zweitausendeins in 1976; and *Posada's Popular Mexican Prints,* selected and edited by Roberto Berdecio and Stanley Appelbaum, published in the United States by Dover Publications in 1972.

Library of Congress Cataloging in Publication Data

Marcos, subcomandante.
    [Correspondence. English. Selections]
    Shadows of tender fury : the letters and communiqués of
    Subcomandante Marcos and the Zapatista Army of National Liberation /
translated by Frank Bardacke, Leslie López and the Watsonville, California,
Human Rights Committee ; introduction by John Ross ; afterword by Frank
Bardacke.
    p. cm.
    ISBN 0-85345-918-5 (pbk.) : $15.00
    1. Marcos, subcomandante—Correspondence. 2. Revolutionaries—
Mexico—Chiapas—Correspondence. 3. Ejército Zapatista de Liberación
Nacional (Mexico). 4. Chiapas (Mexico)—History—Peasant Uprising, 1994.
5. Mexico—Politics and government—1988-
I. Bardacke, Frank. II. López, Leslie. III. Ross, John, 1938 Mar. 11- IV. Watsonville,
California, Human Rights Committee. V. Title.
F1256.M3613 1994
972'.750835'0922—dc20   94-39246
                                                      CIP

Monthly Review Press
122 West 27th Street
New York, NY 10001

Manufactured in the United States of America
10 9 8 7 6 5 4 3 2 1

CONTENTS

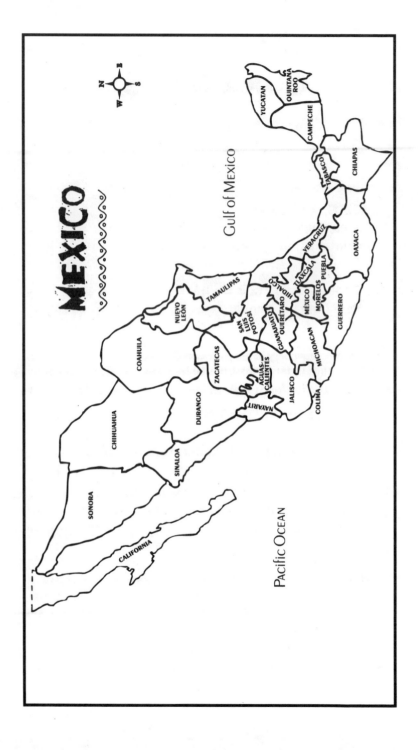

〜〜〜〜〜〜〜〜〜

THE EZLN, A HISTORY: MIRACLES, COYUNTURAS, COMMUNIQUÉS

JOHN ROSS

"My job is to make wars and write letters."
—Subcomandante Marcos in a letter to Carlos Monsiváis,
20 July 1994

THE MIRACLES

One day in January 1994, in the middle of the war for Chiapas, Dominga Hernández, a Tojolabal farm woman, went out to gather firewood up in the forest near her home on the Lomantán communal farm in the conflict-ridden municipality of Las Margaritas. Abruptly, Dominga found herself bathed in spectral light—*rayos lucentes*.... Was she under attack from the Mexican airforce, actively bombing the zone during those dangerous days?

The Holy Child was propped up against the oak tree and beckoned Dominga forward. "My child," instructed the Child, "do not let your heart be hard. The hour has come in which I will enter the poor. Take me to your home so I can be with my people. . . ." Now the *Niño* (a replica of the Baby Jesus) resides on an altar in Dominga's patio, attended by visitors and visionaries, flowers of Hesh, and smoldering fragments of fragrant copal incense. The Bishop of the San Cristóbal diocese, the notorious liberation theologian Samuel Ruiz, has sent his priests to investigate this new miracle, to confirm the apparition, and to watch for fresh signs.

The Child of Lomantán is not the first sign. In 1992, Virgins bathed in these same *rayos lucentes* were seen at Ixthuacán and Teopisca,

7

closer to the Bishop's bailiwick. The year 1992 marked five hundred years of indigenous resistance to the European invasion of the Americas, and among the Mayans of eastern Chiapas the appearances of Virgins and *Niños* and *rayos lucentes* seem to coincide with moments of maximum Indian rage.

The beginning of the eighteenth century was another highwater mark of indigenous rancor in the kingdom state of Chiapas. As Antonio García de León tells us in his monumental Hobsbawmian saga, *Resistance and Utopia* (Mexico City: Ediciones ERA, 1985), the years between 1697 and 1730 were fraught with miracles, divine revelations, and bloody rebellion. In 1712, Salvador Gómez, "La Gloria," an itinerant preacher from Cancuc, was taken up into the heavens and commended by the saints to form a new church and ordain his own priests. Back on the ground, he hooked up with María Candalaria, a prophetess to whom the Virgin of Rosario had recently appeared. The Army of the Virgin, 3,000 Mayans armed with machetes and hoes, marched from town to town, slaughtering priests and tax collectors and carrying the old saints back into the churches. The "Republic of the Tzeltales" was established at Cancuc and Ocosingo and twenty other communities and the towns renamed for Jerusalem and other Holy Land hotspots. The Gloria's army of the possessed and downtrodden advanced on the highland royal city now known as San Cristóbal and the colonials gathered in the Cathedral to pray for salvation. Their gods responded. The troops of the Spanish Crown came on like the cavalry just in the nick of time, routing the wild Indians and scattering the Army of the Virgin back into the lowlands. The royal horsemen rode them down, cutting off rebels' ears all the way to Cancuc, where the ringleaders of the insurrection were beheaded.

The Altos and the jungle of Chiapas have never lacked for prophets in the way they have lacked for land and bread and liberty. In 1868, three green stones fell from the sky at Tjazaljemel, near Chamula. The Tzotzil farm woman Augustina Gómez Checheb wrapped them in linen and placed them in a wooden box. Then the stones began to talk, and the *piedras parlantes* were yet another sign. Under the protection of the *cacique* (rural boss) of Chamula, Pedro Cuscat, Augustina spoke what the stones would have her say: take back the old saints and recover the land from the *criollos* of San Cristóbal by any means necessary. In

Chamula, the land is still measured in rows and not hectares, as scarce now as it was then.

Into this arcane dynamic stepped Ignacio Galindo, an outside agitator and wandering anarchist from Nayarit state and a veteran of the Yucatán War of the Castes, in which he had fought for the Mayans against the *criollo* landowners. Galindo was said to have been fond of floating around the highlands in a hot-air balloon, which is purportedly how he landed in Chamula. When the anarchist, his wife, and an assistant descended from the mountain, they were declared saints by the representatives of the embattled Chamulas. *Posh* (sugarcane alcohol) was consumed and agreements reached. An army was raised and Augustina Gómez Checheb's twelve-year-old brother crucified to assure success. The good burghers of San Cristóbal just down the valley sensed the rusty blades being drawn across their throats and summoned reinforcements. For days, the governor's troops held off the furious assaults of the Indians who, protected by their saints, declared themselves impervious to lead bullets. They were not. Galindo was captured, executed, his body cast upon the Plaza of San Cristóbal to rot and remind those who would yet plot revolutions of the fate of rebels, at least in this corner of the kingdom of Chiapas.

On January 1, 1994, a new army of prophets marched up from the lowlands right into that same plaza, decrying the cruel injustices of the landowning class and proclaiming the Indian Armageddon. The soldiers of this army came without faces or histories, as if, miraculously, they had landed in San Cristóbal, bathed in spectral lights, still another apparition from the heavens. Like most miracles, the debut of the Zapatista Army of National Liberation in the plaza of San Cristóbal in the first hours of the New Year 1994 was long in the making. And it is the making of this miracle, what the Mexican left loves to call the *coyuntura,* the "coming together," of distinct social and cultural moments and currents, in the jungle and the Altos of Chiapas, that is the true miracle of the Zapatista uprising.

THE *COYUNTURA*

The Zapatista base communities are concentrated in the Mayan Tzotzil-, Tzeltal-, Tojolabal-, and Chol-speaking regions leading into and within what remains of the Lacandon rainforest of southeastern Mexico, butt up against the Guatemalan border at the turn Chiapas takes north toward Tabasco and the Yucatán. The Mayan coffee and corn farmers who have carved out their plots from the jungle here are not native to these lands. Their *ejidos* (rural communal production units) are rooted in distinct migrations from other regions of Mexico and Chiapas, campesinos expelled from their communities because of land and religious disputes. The migrants began pouring into the Lacandon in the 1960s, encouraged by the government to cut down the forests and sow the land. The "Southern Agrarian Frontier" served as a safety valve to siphon off the potential explosiveness of southern Mexico's displaced indigenous farmers, a reserve of the poorest of the poor far from the center of power where the dispossessed could find gainful employment and even feed their families with the fruits of their labor.

The Promised Land did not work out quite that way. The cattle ranchers came with their gangs of heavily armed "white guards" and seized the best land in the valleys. The trees were cut down and the soil gave out. The settlers, who had come from their home communities years before, infused with pioneer spirit and schooled in the legends of biblical exoduses, grew resentful at a government that would not heed their petitions to certify their *ejidos* or provide them with bank credits and which stole their votes every election to maintain the Institutional Revolutionary Party (PRI) eternally in power. The harsh realities of life in this frustrated paradise kept the pot boiling from generation to generation.

The *cañadas,* the canyons funneling down toward the floor of the jungle, were right in the crosshairs of the colonization. Clashes with the pale-faced, stetsoned ranching class made for a volatile atmosphere: as early as the mid-1970s, armed *guerrilleros* were operating in the area. The *ejidos* organized and fought the ranchers, fought government decrees that sought to evict them from the jungle, fought the loggers who tried to swindle them out of their trees, fought the trees for a little room to grow their corn in, fought the environmentalists who wanted to protect the disappearing Lacandon, fought each other over boundaries and politics. Much of the ferment was focused in feisty Tzeltal and Tojolabal villages, where the *ejido* assembly, or the "assembly of the pueblo," was the determining authority. In these spaces the pioneers had won from their natural and class adversaries, the collective administration of community affairs flourished. The assemblies made the decisions and there were few native *caciques,* as in other indigenous regions in the state and the country. The oppressors in the *cañadas* were always plainly marked: the *finqueros* and ranchers, the *caxtlanes* (whites) of Ocosingo, Las Margaritas, Altamirano, Comitán, and San Cristóbal. Today, the *cañadas* are the stronghold of the Zapatista Army of National Liberation.

Social tensions in the Lacandon did not go unnoticed. The government which had first lured the settlers into the Lacandon now tried to cut off the flow into the forest, was rebuffed, and then sent in the National Campesino Confederation (CNC) and the National Indigenous Institute (INI) to put out the fire. The Church, with Bishop Samuel Ruiz as beacon, brought the lamp of liberation theology to the *ejidos.* Not to be left behind, the Mexican left came to the Lacandon too, often in pursuit of electoral clientele. Particularly notable among the Marxist missionaries were the brigades of young radicals dispatched from industrial cities like Monterrey and Torreón by the Política Popular movement, a Maoist-oriented network of *colonos* (urban squatters) and students who wielded substantial grassroots power in the north of Mexico during the presidency of Luis Echeverría (1970-1976). With their proletarian rhetoric and political constructs built from the bottom up—their own version of the communal assembly—Política Popular was soon branching south. Brigadistas were sent to Chiapas as early as 1978. Often, they teamed up with Samuel Ruiz's Jesuits and Dominicans to organize the *cañadas* and other sectors of the Lacandon into alliances of *ejidos.*

Marcos tells us he came to the *cañadas* as part of a brigade from the north in 1983, announced to the startled Tzeltales that he and his comrades were there to form an army, and headed for the caves in the hills—if you need us, we'll be up there, they pointed. Soon, the young men of the region, and the young women too, were going to the mountain to train, to learn Spanish and how to use a weapon.

Down below on the *ejidos,* self-defense squads were organized to keep the "white guards" out of communal lands and before long, because protecting just one *ejido* is not enough, alliances were formed—the roots of the Zapatista army. The outside agitators and the Indian farmers grew close, their agreement about the primacy of the communal assembly meshed, and the EZLN as a political formation took seed.

The growth of the Zapatista Army of National Liberation (EZLN) was nourished by PRI government authoritarianism and economic havoc, largely the result of the International Coffee Organization's decision to allow the price of coffee to float on the world market in 1990. The crash of coffee prices was compounded by a ban on all timber-cutting in the state, imposed by the heavy-handed governor, Patrocinio González Garrido, a prohibition that made economic survival for the Mayans of the Lacandon a precarious assumption. The neoliberal Salinas government's revision of Article 27 of the Mexican Constitution, the provision that institutionalized the agrarian reform for which EZLN namesake Emiliano Zapata was martyred, ended the distribution of land to the land-poor, encouraged the sale and privatization of the *ejido,* and made continued tenancy on the land the settlers had won from the jungle even more tenuous. The impending North American Free Trade Agreement threatened to take the Mayan "Men of Corn" out of the Mexican corn market. In late 1992, the Zapatista community assemblies gave the General Command a year in which to prepare the war. The *coyuntura* was closing.

THE COMMUNIQUÉS

The Zapatista Army of National Liberation entered San Cristóbal a few minutes past midnight on January 1, 1994 ("We were late as usual," explains Marcos), pronounced the "Declaration of the Lacandon Jungle" from the balcony of the government palace, sacked the town hall, slapped up their proclamation of war on all the walls of the old royal city, attacked a nearby military installation, and fought their way over the mountains, back down to their base in the jungle. For the first twelve days of the war, the EZLN and the Mexican military skirmished, the air force bombed suspect Zapatista communities, and the civilian population suffered grievously. The government issued daily bulletins, grew truculent and conciliatory at the same time. Salinas offered pardons to the rebels if they would give up their weapons and unmask their leaders. The military and the electronic media labeled the Zapatistas "transgressors of the law" and "foreigners" and "professionals of violence." But the government also proposed a cease-fire and peace negotiations.

To all these overtures, the EZLN's voice remained muted. Since the

Declaration of the Lacandon Jungle, the rebels had not uttered a word and the silences were unnerving. Who were those masked men and what exactly did they want? Then on Sunday morning, January 9, a group of Tzotzil men in the highland village of San Andrés Larrainzar approached ace reporter Epigmenio Ibarra and asked him if he knew the editor of the crusading *El Tiempo* newspaper down in San Cristóbal. The communiqué published the next day in Amado Avendaño's eight-sheeter was the first of many to flow from Zapatista territory under the pen and through the voice of Subcomandante Marcos. The "Sup" has not been stilled since. Cognoscenti speak of over 400 communiqués and letters in a year that, at this writing, still has 100 days left. My eyes have seen a diskette.

EZLN communiqués are either formulated by the Clandestine Revolutionary Indigenous Committee-General Command (CCRI-GC) under Marcos' signature, or are issued directly by Marcos, sometimes as postscripts to CCRI-CG declarations—there is little question that Marcos drafts both species of epistle. The first communications were written on a manual typewriter, a battered Olivetti portable. They were slow in arriving and their tardiness in transit sometimes impeded the delicate dialogue between the General Command and government peace negotiator Manuel Camacho Solís. Now the technology is state-of-the-art, a laptop and a printer. An ever resourceful chain of couriers moves the messages first to the diocese from which they are distributed to the national "pluralistic" daily *La Jornada,* to *El Financiero*—Mexico's *Wall Street Journal,* to the long-lived critical weekly *Proceso,* and to *El Tiempo,* Avendaño's wretchedly ink-less, sometimes-daily that has been defending the local indigenous population for a quarter of a century against the racism of the "authentic coletos," San Cristóbal's light-skinned ruling clique. The Zapatistas' outlets get their communiqués into print within twelve hours of their arrival and they are often translated and on the Internet by the next morning. The EZLN's communications network is thus extremely effective in delivering the rebels' message to hundreds of thousands of Mexicans quickly. But despite the speed of outreach, deciphering what it is Marcos and the EZLN are trying to say often occupies fans, journalists, and government intelligence agents for hours.

Since publication of the first communiqués, Marcos' stature as a litterateur has expanded concentrically. His outrageous irony and *encabronado* (figuratively, "like a furious cuckold") tone, studded with colloquialisms that punch right through to the point (sooner or later) has earned him a heavy readership on the left and dozens of pirated volumes in Mexico and beyond. The Sup's poetry has transformed him into a cult hero as much as has his "pestilent" (his word) ski-mask. The little we have seen of Marcos' formal poetry (which he says he saves exclusively for *el sexo feminino*) seems stilted and deliberately obfuscated—his real poetry is in his prose . . . and in his motion. A live performance brings the two together. Watching Marcos declaim, his quick-tongued words swooping and plunging, cracking with emotion, world-weary and sad, then suddenly pounding into insistently hopeful cadences and ending only when his breath does, incites a veteran San Francisco poet like myself to snap his fingers and urge a reprise.

The Subcomandante's career as a man of letters took a fascinating turn in preparation for the National Democratic Convention held August 8 and August 9 in the depths of the Lacandon jungle. Firing off invitations to famous writers left and right, Marcos entered into literary correspondence with the magnum novelist Carlos Fuentes and with Carlos Monsiváis, the elegant, eminently urban chronicler of civil society—"Marcos has read more Carlos Monsiváis than Carlos Marx," Carlos Fuentes once observed. Also invited by the Sup to the Zapatista zone in letters styled in the prose of their destinees: Eduardo Galeano, Noam Chomsky, the Polish journalist Ryzward Kapuscinsky (*The Soccer War*), and Elena Poniatowska ("Tinísima"), to whom the Subcomandante penned a mash note in archaic Castillian. Visitors to the EZLN encampment are often led by the Sup into labyrinthian discussion of the work of Julio Cortazar, Borges, García Márquez, and other notables of the Latin Boom.

But aside from Marcos' literary pretensions, the EZLN letters frame an amazing chapter in recent Mexican history. The communiqués in this volume span an apocalyptic season on this side of the border—from the war in the jungle, Mexico's first armed uprising in twenty years, to the peace talks in San Cristóbal, the Gran Guignol in the Cathedral of Paz where the Bishop and the government sat at the same table with ski-masked, heavily armed guerrillas. The letters then take us from the discussion of the government's 32-point offer in the Zapatistas' communal assemblies to the still-murky assassination of the PRI's hand-picked presidential candidate Luis Donaldo Colosio at the other end of the country, in Tijuana. From that traumatic moment, the communiqués turn toward the "Second Declaration of the Lacandon Jungle," the rejection of the government's peace offer, and the accompanying convocation of the National Democratic Convention at which the Zapatistas pledged to lay aside their weapons and follow "civil society" in peaceful resistance to the impending, inevitably fraud-tainted August 21 presidential elections. What you have here is history so fresh that it pulsates on the page.

The designation of the Zapatistas as the first post-modern Latin guerrilla formation has been confirmed by the intellectual greats and near-greats so often that it must be true. Certainly, their rhetoric is devoid of Cold War cant. While the socialist models and their armed, revolutionary expressions were crashing all around them, Marcos and his band survived and grew, borrowing a little from here and there but ultimately just staying tuned to their own people. The objective conditions, the fall of the coffee prices, the revision of Article 27, kicked in in good time. The *coyuntura* locked and the miracle was made manifest. Then these words began.

The Zapatistas' armed audacity and poetic vision have won them an international constituency. But, on the homefront, one senses that it is their selflessness that attracts acolytes. The EZLN's lack of interest in taking state power but rather in making the state accountable to the *pueblo* is a vision the rebels have inherited from their namesake, the incorruptible revolutionary Emiliano Zapata, assassinated by his government April 10, 1919, at the Chinameca hacienda in Morelos state, where he had been lured on the promise of receiving guns and ammunition. Despite Zapata's long heroic struggle, what Mexicans most remember about this martyred revolutionary is his betrayal at the hands of the government.

It was that betrayal that was so much on the Zapatistas' minds as they tried to decide whether or not to go up to San Cristóbal and sit at the peace table with the "bad government" back in February. The CCRI, through Marcos' pen, agonized over their fears of a new Chinameca and then declared, in a typical give-away-the-store-to-the-people flourish, "Para nosotros, nada! Para todos, todo!" ("For us, nothing! For everyone, everything!").

These letters repeatedly make that point.

—Mexico City
September 1994

THE ZAPATISTAS IN THEIR OWN WRITE

A NOTE FROM THE TRANSLATORS

This book contains a complete set of communiqués from the Zapatista Army of National Liberation (EZLN), as they appeared in the Mexican press between January 1 and June 10, 1994, as well as Marcos' speech to the National Democratic Convention on August 8. The communiqués include formal declarations of principles and demands, military directives, diplomatic maneuvers, statements of solidarity with other groups, open letters to Mexican citizens, stories for children, poems, and all manner of political polemics. They are printed here in chronological order.

The eloquence of these communiqués is partly responsible for what success the Chiapan Zapatistas have had up until now. These open letters helped to put pressure on the federal government to negotiate with the EZLN. They created deep sympathy and support for the Zapatistas throughout much of Mexico, and made the author of most of the communiqués, Subcomandante Insurgente Marcos, "el Sup," a national celebrity.

The communiqués were written in many different voices. Number 1, Marcos' own introduction to Chiapas, is written as a guide for tourists. Many of the early military reports, diplomatic notes, and letters of solidarity are written in diplomatic language, as the EZLN was struggling to be formally recognized as a belligerent force by the federal government, and the language of the letters is meant to underscore the official nature of the EZLN organization. Many of the communiqués are written in a Spanish that has the feel of indigenous languages. And, finally, some of Marcos' more personal letters and stories are written in the idioms of Mexico City's streets and universities.

We have done our best to deliver all these different Spanish voices in English translation. Mark Twain, in his explanatory note to *Huckleberry Finn,* says that he "pains-takingly" used several different dialects in his text, and that he makes "this explanation for the reason that without it many readers would suppose that all these characters were trying to talk alike and not succeeding." We would like to make a similar claim. Most of the time, when the language seems strange, it is not because we have made some kind of mistake; we meant it to be that way.

Here are some particular notes on the translation:

—Words that appear in English in the original are denoted by italics inside quotes, like this, *"but of course."*

—Words followed by an * are explained in the Glossary at the end of the book.

—We left the words "compañero" and "compañera," "campesino" and "campesina," "Subcomandante Insurgente," "Señor," and *"vale"* in Spanish. The only one that might cause confusion is "campesino." Its closest meaning in English is "peasant," not farmworker. *"Vale"* is discussed in the Glossary.

—Marcos' description of guerrilla training and the story of the plumed tapir in the Prologue are parodies of Latin American guerrilla diaries and magic realism. The sense of parody was nearly impossible to translate, and absolutely impossible if the English reader is not familiar with the works that are being spoofed.

—The initials CCRI-CG of the EZLN stand for Comité Clandestino Revolucionario Indígena, Comandancia General del Ejército Zapatista de Liberación Nacional, or as it might be translated in English, the Revolutionary Indigenous Clandestine Committee—General Command of the Zapatista Army of National Liberation.

—We translated *hermanos* as "brothers and sisters" rather than just brothers, giving the Sup the benefit of the doubt.

—The phrase "bad government" comes from *mal gobierno* and the way it is used here sounds peculiar in Spanish too. We think it is an echo of the language used by the original Zapatistas.

—The informal return address of the Zapatistas, "Desde las montañas del sureste mexicano," we translated as "From the mountains of the Mexican Southeast," rather than the more fluid "From the mountains of southeastern Mexico," because we believe that the Zapatistas were insisting that their part of the world constitutes a distinct section of their country.

—We do not know to whom "Votán" refers in the "Votán Zapata" honorary title in communiqué number 57. We would like to believe that he is a Mayan version of Prometheus.

—Near the beginning of Marcos' convention speech, he says, "Por nuestro moderno systema de computo hemos hecho la cuenta y llegado a la conclusión que somos un chingo." The first part is easy and can be translated as, "Using our sophisticated system of computation, we have counted and come to the conclusion . . . " but what to do with "somos un chingo"? "There are a fuck of a lot of us here" was the first choice, although the grammarians among us held out for "There are a fucking lot of us here." The real problem, however, is that "somos un chingo" is not as strong as "a fuck of a lot of us" nor as pale as "a hell of a lot of us." "A shitload of us" was how the translator of Omar Cabezas' *Fire from the Mountain* handled a similar problem, but we didn't much like the shift from a vulgar sexual reference to a scatological one. In general, Marcos' written language is more polite than his spoken language, so we chose "a hell of a lot" for this written translation of the speech. We do not mean to bowdlerize Marcos, and made no similar choice elsewhere in the book.

This translation was the work of a group of people from the Watsonville, California, Human Rights Committee ("Neltiliztli"): Fernando Alcantar, Ricardo Carvajal, Olga Díaz, Lucina Jiménez, Arturo López, and the two of us. We also had help from people outside our Committee: Samuel López, Caitlin Manning, Jerry Rosenfield, David Sweet, and Sarah Young. We consulted other translations of a few of the communiqués, published in *Monthly Review, Resist!,* by Barbara Pilsbury of *Equipo Pueblo,* and by the NY Transfer News Collective.

Ted Bardacke, a reporter living in Mexico City, collected the originals from *La Jornada,* and sent them to us.

We alone are responsible for all the errors in the final text. May the Sup forgive us.

—Frank Bardacke and Leslie López

PROLOGUE:
SUBCOMANDANTE MARCOS
INTRODUCES HIMSELF

June 30, 1994

To all the large, medium-sized, small, marginal, pirate,
buccaneer, and etcetera presses who are publishing the
communiqués and letters of the EZLN and have written
asking for a prologue for your respective publications, or
have requested an exclusive of some kind or other.

From Subcomandante Insurgente Marcos
EZLN General Headquarters
Mountains of the Mexican Southeast
Chiapas, Mexico

I received your request for a kind of prologue or introduction to
the book that is being published by _____ (note:
fill the empty space with the name of the large, medium-sized, small,
marginal, pirate, buccaneer, etcetera publishing house which has
asked for this exclusive introduction) containing the communiqués,
letters, and other materials of the EZLN.

As far as I can see, my reputation for being a scatterbrain is not
sufficient to dissuade you from sending me questions and problems

about publications, prologues, and other equally absurd things. So I am going to answer, ad hoc, your questions about such transcendent problems. And there is nothing better for this purpose than to tell you a little story that happened to us many moons ago.

It was 1986. I left our base camp with a column of combatants on a short exploratory march. All my boys were novices; the majority of them had been with us for less than a month and they were still arguing about what was the worst part of trying to adapt: the diarrhea or the nostalgia. The two "veterans" in the group had been with us for two and three months, respectively. So there I was, sometimes dragging them, sometimes pushing them, through their political and military training. Our mission was to open a new route for our military maneuvers and to train the recruits in the tasks of exploration, marching, and setting up camp. The work was hard because there was not enough water and we had to ration what we had taken with us from the base camp. So survival practice was added to the training, as the lack of water made cooking difficult. The maneuvers were to last four days, with approximately one liter of water per person, per day, and only *pinole* with sugar to eat. An hour after we left the base we found that our route took us through some steep, difficult hills. The hours passed and we ascended and descended hills on paths that would frighten the most experienced mountain goats.

Finally, after seven or eight hours of non-stop up and down, we arrived at the top of a hill where I decided to set up camp, as the afternoon was beginning to give way to twilight shadows. The water ration was distributed, and most of the recruits, despite my warnings to save a little liquid for the *pinole*, "burned their ships" and immediately chugged down their whole ration, as they were very thirsty, and the psychological effect of knowing the water was rationed only made their anxiety worse. When the time came to eat, they saw the consequence of their foolishness: no matter how much they chewed, they were unable to swallow—without water they were not able to get the *pinole* with sugar to go down their throats. There were two hours of such silence that we could clearly hear the crunching between their teeth, and the sounds from their throats when they finally managed to swallow a piece of the sugared corn dust. The next day, having learned their lesson, they all saved a part of their water ration for their morning *pinole*. That day we left on the maneuver at 09:00 hours and returned at 16:00, so it was seven hours of walking and cutting paths, going up and down hills, without any water except what we sweat.

We spent three days like that; on the fourth, the weakness of the whole group was evident. During the meals (?), the sado-masochism that seems to characterize insurgents appeared: between bites of *pinole* and little sips of water, we began to talk about taquitos, tamales, cakes, steaks, soft drinks, and other things that could only make us laugh because our bodies didn't have enough water to cry. To top it off, the day we were going to return to our base, we found a nearby river, and that night the mountain mischievously honored us with a strong downpour which soaked us before we managed to get under cover. We did not lose our good humor and we swore endlessly at the roof, the rain, and the jungle, and all their respective kin. But really this was all part of the training and was not surprising. The work was completed, in general the people responded well, although one person nearly fainted carrying his load up a particularly difficult hill.

All of this is nothing but the "scenery" for the story I want to tell you. On one of these days of exploration, we returned to the camp, as always, completely wiped out. While the rations of *pinole* and water were being distributed, I turned on the short-wave radio to catch the evening news, but out of the radio came only the strident song of parrots and macaws. I then remembered a work by Cortazar (*Ultimo Round? El Libro de Manuel? Historias de Cronopios y de Famas?*) that talks about what would happen if "things-were-out-of-place." But I didn't let such a small incident bother me, as I was accustomed to seeing in these mountains things as apparently absurd as a little deer with a red carnation in its mouth (probably in love, because if not, why a *red* carnation?), a tapir with violet ballet shoes, a herd of wild boar playing cards and, with their teeth and hooves, tapping out the rhythm of "we will break down the house to see Doña Blanca . . . ." "As I say, I wasn't much surprised and I moved the dial looking for another station, but there wasn't anything but the songs of the parrots and macaws. I changed to the medium-wave mode, with the same results. Without losing hope, I took the apparatus apart to find the scientific reason for this toneless song.

When I opened the back of the radio, I found the logical and dialectical cause of this irregular transmission: a bunch of parrots and macaws flew out, screaming with joy at regaining their freedom. I managed to count 17 parrots, 8 female macaws and 3 males, as they all scrambled out. After a rather tardy self-criticism for not having cleaned the apparatus, I prepared to give it the maintenance it required. As I was taking out the feathers and droppings (and even the skeleton of a little parrot that the others had taken care to give a Christian burial, and above whose tomb shined a carefully made cross and a stone with the inscription in Latin? *Requiescat in Pace*), I found a little nest with a little gray egg, speckled with green and blue, and beside it was a little envelope, that—with barely concealed eagerness—I quickly opened. It was a letter, addressed "To whom it may concern." In a tiny script, the little parrot had written her sad and melancholy story.

She had fallen in love with a young and elegant macaw (so said the letter) and he loved her back (so said the letter). But the other parrots, concerned about the purity of their race, did not approve of such a scandalous romance and absolutely prohibited the parrot from seeing the handsome young macaw (so said the letter). And so the great love that united the couple (so said the letter) obliged them to see each other clandestinely, behind one of the transistors of the radio. As "a macaw is fire, and a parrot dry wood, along came the Devil and told them they should" (so said the letter) and soon one thing led to another and this little egg that I now had in my hands was the forbidden fruit of their illicit relation. The parrot requested (so said the letter) that whoever should find the egg should protect it and support it until the little one would be able to take care of itself (so said the letter), and finally there was list of maternal recommendations for care, and a tearful lament for her cruel fate, etcetera (so said the letter).

Overwhelmed by the enormous responsibility of becoming an adopted father and cursing the impulse that led me to clean the radio, I tried to find moral and material support from one of my combatants, but all of them were already asleep, probably dreaming of mountain springs of coffee with milk and rivers of coca-cola and lemonade. Following the often cited maxim that "There is no problem so big that you can't walk away from it," I abandoned the egg, putting it by the side of my hammock, and got myself ready to enjoy a well-de-served rest. It was useless; my guilt feelings (deep down, very deep down, I actually have a good and noble soul) would not let me sleep and soon I picked up the little egg and found a comfortable spot for it on my belly. At midnight, a very unfortunate hour, it began to move. At first I thought it was my stomach protesting the lack of food, but no, it was the little egg that was moving and beginning to break. With an inexplicable maternal instinct I made myself ready to witness the sacred moment when I would become a mother . . . I mean . . . a father. And how great my surprise to see come out of the shell neither a macaw nor a parrot, not even a baby chicken or a little dove. No, what came out of the shell was . . . a little tapir! Seriously, it was a little tapir with green and blue feathers. A plumed tapir! In a moment of clarity (which now come to me less and less often) I understood the true meaning of this sordid little story: the crux-of-the-matter-as-I-don't-know-who-said. "Eureka!" I screamed, exactly-as-had-screamed-I-can't-remember-who-either.

What had happened was the parrot was "double dealing," that is, she had a liaison with a tapir, they sinned, and she was trying to frame the macaw. But everything had now fallen apart, given the radio problems and all the other etceteras. "They are all the same," I sighed. Having figured out the mystery, the only thing left was to decide what the hell I was going to do with the bastard tapir . . . And I am still trying to decide. For the time being I carry her hidden in my knapsack and give her a little of my food. I don't deny that we like each other, and my maternal instinct (excuse me, paternal) has given way to a insane passion toward the tapir, who throws me ardent glances which don't have very much to do with polite gratefulness but rather with a badly controlled passion. My problem is severe: if I fall into temptation, I will not only commit a crime against nature, but also incest, because, after all, I am her adopted father. I have thought about abandoning her, but I can't, she is more powerful than I. In short, I don't know what the hell to do . . .

As you can see, I have too many problems here to be able to attend to yours. I hope that now you will understand my continued silence in regard to the questions that you insist on putting before me. Of course, the CCRI-CG of the EZLN approves your request, and gives you permission to publish the materials and to write some kind of prologue or introduction. You're welcome.

Vale,* and as-you-can-find-out-who-said, "Books are friends that will never betray you." *Salud,* and please send me a veterinary manual for wild animals of the tropics.

> From the mountains of the Mexican Southeast
> Subcomandante Insurgente Marcos
> Mexico, June 1994

A FORGETFUL P.S.: Yes, I seem to have forgotten the purpose of all this: an introduction or prologue to the book of communiqués called: "From the First to the Second Declaration of the Lacandon Jungle" or I don't know what you are going to call the damned book from _____ Press. (Note once again: Fill the space with all the appropriate names, publishing houses, etcetera, etc.)

And so it happens, I imagine, that something ought to be said to the readers of this book. Taking advantage of the fact that there is a respite between airplanes, tapirs, and communiqués, I write this letter disguised as a postscript:

To the readers of this book who are going to know
     what it is called
From Supmarcos
June 1994

This book contains the communiqués of the EZLN from the First Declaration of the Lacandon Jungle to the Second Declaration of the Lacandon Jungle, that is, from December 31, 1993, to June 10, 1994. It also brings together a series of letters that present and then reiterate some of the principal political and ideological positions of the Zapatista Army of National Liberation.

It is worthwhile to speak a little about the procedure used to produce the communiqués of the Revolutionary Indigenous Clandestine Committee-General Command of the EZLN. All the communiqués signed by the CCRI-CG of the EZLN were approved by the members of the committee, sometimes by all the members, sometimes by their representatives. The writing of the texts was one of my jobs, but the communiqués themselves are produced in two different ways:

One is that the members of the committee, or a collective of the committee, see the need to make a pronouncement about something, that is, "to say their word." First, the principal points of what is going to be said are proposed and debated, and then they order me to write it up, using the debate as my general orientation for what to say. Later I present the written communiqué, they revise it, take out some things, add some others, and, finally, approve it or reject it.

The other method is that, on the arrival of information from far off parts or confronted by a fact that I think merits it, and seeing the value of commenting on it, I propose to the committee that we send out a communiqué. I then write it and present it as a proposal. It is discussed and approved or rejected.

Did I say "rejected"? Yes, even though the current circumstances contribute to the appearance that Subcomandante I. Marcos is the "head" or "leader" of the rebellion, and that the CCRI is just the "scenery," the authority of the committee in the communities is indisputable. It is impossible to sustain a position there without the support of the leadership of this indigenous organization. I have made various proposals for communiqués that were rejected, some for being "too hard," others for being "too soft," and some others because "they confuse things, rather than clarifying them." Also, some communiqués were sent out despite my objections. It is not worth citing examples, but the correctness of the judgment of my compañeros on the committee has been demonstrated throughout these six months of war.

There are also texts that I often write to introduce the communiqués. I am more "loose" in these, but the committee keeps a close eye on them too. More than one of my "Letters of Introduction" has merited a reproof from members of the CCRI-CG.

It took a long time for the communiqués to arrive, and they arrived irregularly. The "untimely" nature of our pronouncements is something we have tried to remedy, with no success whatsoever. The speed with which some of the communiqués reached the press was due to lucky circumstances that, unhappily, were never a result of anything we planned.

Nevertheless, I believe that the lack of "speed" of the Zapatista answers are understandable to most of the readers who now are face to face with this book. What you probably cannot understand is the complex and anonymous heroism of the couriers who carried, from our lines to the cities, these white pages with black letters that spoke our thought. There are various anecdotes about these anonymous

Zapatistas who risked all to cross enemy lines time and again, wearing out their mounts, with their feet destroyed by the cold and the rain in January and February, and by heat and thorns in the later months. These routes of misery and oblivion, the ancient tracks and steep trails, carried, from the mountains to the asphalt, the Zapatista words of dignity and rebellion. As of now these messengers have not faced cameras or tape recorders, have not received letters or been interviewed, there have been no testimonies as to the *"sex appeal"* of their anonymity, no recognition for their efforts to make *our word, their word,* reach other ears. This is a good place to recognize them for their silent—and effective—work.

I spoke in a letter that appears in this book about the reasons we delivered our word to some particular media for publication in their pages or for broadcast on their radio stations. I will not push it too hard, but a word should be said about the part these media played. The honest press made ways for Zapatista thought to appear in the pages of newspapers and magazines, and in some radio broadcasts. I believe that whatever the outcome of our collective desire for dignity, the honest press will feel, always, the satisfaction of having fulfilled their duty.

There is something else about this passionate moving of words, something that does not appear in any postscript or any communiqué. It is the anxiety, the uncertainty, the galloping questions that assault us every time one of the couriers leaves with one, or several, communiqués. Questions and more questions fill up our nights, accompany us on our rounds to check the guards, sit beside us on some broken tree trunk looking at the food on the plate, are carried in the hand that divides up the provisions, and move in the feet that walk back and forth. "Were these words the best ones to say what we wanted to say?" "Were they the right words at this time?" "Were they understandable?" We were never satisfied with any communiqué at the time it was sent.

In general, we make an effort to differentiate between the communiqués of the CCRI-CG and the introductory letters. While the first were written in capital letters and signed by the committee, the second are in capital and small letters, and signed by "Subcomandante Insurgente Marcos." We believe that both types did the job they needed to do. What their future will be in this book form is uncertain, but the word of those who speak the truth will always find its way.

There is something more to say about the Zapatista "editorial line." We follow the motto: "Now or maybe never." Given the conditions of war and isolation in which we find ourselves, we don't "measure" what we say and we try to throw it all out at once . . . because every communiqué could be the last one.

That is why from the first communiqués on, the position and ideas of the EZLN have been defined, and repeated, continually. This anxious word forever stumbling all over itself comes out of a situation which can only be understood by those who find themselves now, or have been, in the same circumstances.

On the one hand, we cannot give ourselves the luxury of lying. One becomes spontaneous when living on the thin edge of war, and we have discovered that lying requires at least a little bit of planning. On the other hand, we have not been able to "measure out" our word, and look for the "opportune moment" to say it, nor wait cunningly for conditions to be just right. The clearest examples of this Zapatista "editorial line" are the letters of the January 18, 1994 ("Who must ask for pardon and who can grant it," number 13) and January 20, 1994 ("The sup will take off his mask, if Mexico takes off its mask," number 14). The one of January 20 (the one which presents the result of the trial of Absalón Castellanos Domínguez) seen from a distance, and after everything that has happened, could appear exaggerated—and that is the way it seems to me now. But at that moment, face to face with the typewriter, anxiety moved my fingers, and it seemed to me that there was no other way to say what I had to say. This is not a question of pessimism or optimism, it is something more . . . more . . . more immediate, a spontaneous and unadorned judgment of the dramas that were happening to us, and those that might happen.

I am sorry if I am disillusioning someone with this "horrible" secret, but we never planed beforehand what we were going to say, nor the form in which we were going to say it. We had, and we have, a clear understanding of who we are and who we are not, what we can do and what we cannot, and what we ought to do and what we ought not. From this general standard, or from this foundation, the letters and communiqués were sent out, in the same way we walked in the mountains: one worries about the step one is taking, and does not plan the next step; it is enough to know that you are still walking, and later . . . later . . . there might never be a later.

There is also in these letters and communiqués the constant presence of death. I know that this has bothered more than one reader, but on this side of the war, in the same way that one says "book," "weapon," or "love," one says "death," and so it must be written. I remember as I was writing one letter, I told myself to stop insisting on this theme, but I remind you of what I explained above about the "Zapatista editorial line." Later, when I reread that letter in the newspaper, it turned out to be one of the most gloomy I had written. In short, since we don't write to please, but rather to explain, one is able to put aside these worries about writing what one believes respectable people would want one to write.

Vale. Health and a good appetite, reading is nourishment which, fortunately, never fills one up.

I don't know if all that I have pointed out here will help or hurt the rereading of the materials that are compiled in this book. I tried, as much as possible, to write a communiqué about the communiqués, a letter about the letters. I see, with pleasure, that once again the Zapatista "editorial line" has imposed itself on me, and that what I have written about these letters is only what has occurred to me right now. Therefore, on the improbable chance that another introduction will be needed later, and that bad luck marks me out to do it again, I will put the date, hour, and place on this prologue, so that the readers will know that I finished writing this one before dawn on the morning of June 28, 1994, that the watch on my left wrist read 02:30 hours, it was raining hard, and that a good while ago Tacho told me he was going to sleep. The place, for a change, is

From the mountains of the Mexican Southeast
Subcomandante Insurgente Marcos
Mexico, June 1994

P.S. about the P.S.'s: Of course a little digression about the postscripts should go in a postscript. It happens that one feels that something has remained between the fingers, that there are still some words that want to find their way into sentences, that one has not finished emptying the pockets of the soul. But it is useless, there will never be a postscript that can contain so many nightmares . . . and so many dreams . . .

• 1 •
CHIAPAS:
THE SOUTHEAST IN TWO WINDS,
A STORM, AND A PROPHECY

To *La Jornada*

Dear Sirs,

Now that Chiapas has exploded in the national consciousness, many diverse authors have dusted off their *Illustrated Larouse* and their *Unknown Mexico*, and their disks of statistics from INEGI* and FONAPO,* or even the classic texts of Bartolomé de las Casas. Eager to do our part to quench this thirst for knowledge about the situation in Chiapas, we are sending you a piece of writing that our compañero Subcomandante Insurgente Marcos completed in the middle of 1992. His purpose was to waken the conscience of some compañeros who were then thinking of joining our struggle.

We hope this material will win a place in some supplement or section of your prestigious newspaper. The rights of authorship belong to the insurgents; they will feel paid in full by seeing something about their history circulate nationally. Perhaps other compañeros will be inspired to write about their states and regions, hoping that other prophecies, like the one of Chiapas, will come true.

—Press Office
National Zapatista Liberation Army (EZLN)

CHAPTER 1
THE FIRST WIND

The one from above tells how the almighty government was so touched by the misery of the indigenous people of Chiapas, that it gave them hotels, jails, a military barracks, and a military airport. And also tells how the beast feeds on the blood of the people, and other unhappy and unfortunate events.

Suppose you live in the north, center, or western part of the country. Suppose you believe the old injunction of Sectur [Ministry of Tourism] to "See Mexico First." Suppose you decide to get to know the southeast of the country, and suppose that in the southeast you choose the state of Chiapas. Suppose that you drive (getting here by air is not only expensive but improbable, a fantasy: in the entire state there are only two "civilian" airports and a military one). Suppose you take the Transístmica Highway. Suppose that you ignore the Federal Army barracks on the highlands above Matías Romero and you go on to Ventosa. Suppose you don't notice the government ministry's immigration checkpoint (which makes one think one is leaving one country and entering another). Suppose you take a left, and move decisively toward Chiapas. A few kilometers ahead you will leave Oaxaca and find a large sign which reads, "Welcome to Chiapas."

Did you find it? Good, let's suppose so. You got here (to this southeast corner of the country) by one of the three existing roads: the road from the north, the one along the Pacific coast, or the one you supposedly have just taken. But the natural wealth that leaves these lands doesn't travel over just these three roads. Chiapas is bled through thousands of veins: through oil ducts and gas ducts, over electric wires, by railroad cars, through bank accounts, by trucks and vans, by ships and planes, over clandestine paths, third-rate roads, and mountain passes.

And what tribute does this land continue to pay to various empires? Oil, electric energy, cattle, money, coffee, bananas, honey, corn, cocoa, tobacco, sugar, soy, melons, sorghum, mamey, mangos, tamarind, avocados, and Chiapan blood flows out through a 1,001 fangs sunk into the neck of southeastern Mexico. Billions of tons of natural resources go through Mexican ports, railway stations, airports, and road systems to various destinations: the United States, Canada, Holland, Germany, Italy, Japan—but all with the same destiny: to feed the empire. The dues that capitalism imposes on the southeast corner of the country ooze out, as they have since the beginning, mud and blood.

A handful of businesses, among them the Mexican state, take the wealth of Chiapas and in exchange leave their mark of death and disease: in 1989, the financial fang got a filling worth 1,222,699,000,000 pesos [$407,566,000], and only left behind 616,340,000,000 [$205,433,000] in credit and works. More than 600,000,000,000 pesos [$200,000,000] went to the stomach of the beast.

In Chiapas there are eighty-six fangs of Pemex sunk into the municipalities of Estación Juaréz, Reforma, Ostuacán, Pichucalco, and Ocosingo. Every day they suck out 92,000 barrels of petroleum and 516.7 billion cubic feet of natural gas. They take the gas and oil and leave the trademark of capitalism: ecological destruction, agricultural waste, hyper-inflation, alcoholism, prostitution, and poverty. The beast is not satisfied, and extends its tentacles to the Lacandon jungle: eight oil fields are now under exploration. The jungle is opened with machetes, wielded by the very same campesinos whose land has been taken away by the insatiable beast. Trees fall and dynamite explodes in lands where only the campesinos are prohibited from felling trees to plant crops. Every tree a campesino cuts can cost him a fine worth ten day's salary and send him to jail. Poor people cannot cut down trees, but the oil company, more and more in the hands of foreigners, can. The campesino cuts a tree in order to live, the beast cuts to plunder.

Chiapas also bleeds coffee. Eighty-seven thousand Chiapans work in the coffee industry; 35 percent of Mexico's coffee production comes from this region. Forty-seven percent of that is sold on the national market, the other 53 percent is exported, primarily to the

United States and Europe. More than 100,000 tons of coffee leave Chiapas to fatten the bank accounts of the beast: in 1988, a kilo of *pergamino* coffee was sold abroad at an average price of 8,000 pesos [$2.50], but the producers in Chiapas were paid 2,500 pesos [about $.80] a kilo or less.

After coffee, the second most important loot is cattle. Three million head a year await the butchers and small group of middlemen who send them to the refrigerators of Arriaga, Villahermosa, and Mexico City. The impoverished people of the *ejidos*[*] are paid 1,400 pesos [about $.44] a kilo for the beef, while the middlemen get ten times that much.

The tribute that capitalism extracts from Chiapas has no historical parallel. Fifty-five percent of the nation's hydroelectric power comes from this state, as well as 20 percent of all the electric energy. Nevertheless, only a third of all Chiapan houses have electricity. Where do the 12,907 kilowatts produced annually by hydroelectric plants in Chiapas go?

Despite the current popularity of ecology, Chiapan forests continue to be destroyed. From 1981 to 1989, 2,444,700 cubic meters of precious woods, conifers, and tropical trees were taken from Chiapas and sent to Mexico City, Puebla, Veracruz, and Quintana Roo. In 1988 the exploitation of the forest produced 23,900,000,000 pesos [almost $8 million] in profit, 6,000 percent more than in 1980.

Seventy-nine thousand Chiapan beehives are fully integrated into the European and American honey market. Two thousand seven hundred and fifty-six tons of honey and wax produced every year in the countryside are converted into dollars that the people of Chiapas will never see.

Half of the corn produced here goes to the national market. Chiapas is one of the largest producers of corn in Mexico. Sorghum goes mostly to Tabasco. Ninety percent of the tamarind goes to Mexico City and other states. Two-thirds of the avocados are sold outside Chiapas, and all of the mamey. Sixty-nine percent of the cocoa goes on the national market, and 31 percent goes to the United States, Holland, Japan, and Italy. The vast majority of the 451,627 tons of bananas are exported.

WHAT DOES THE BEAST LEAVE, IN EXCHANGE FOR EVERYTHING IT TAKES?

Chiapas, with 75,634.4 square kilometers, some 7,500,000 hectares, is the eighth largest state in Mexico. It has 111 municipalities, organized for plunder into 9 economic regions. It is home to 40 percent of the nation's plant varieties, 36 percent of its different kinds of mammals, 34 percent of its amphibians and reptiles, 66 percent of its bird species, 20 percent of its varieties of fresh water fish, and 80 percent of its butterfly species. Exactly 9.7 percent of the nation's rain falls on Chiapas. But its greatest wealth is its 3.5 million people, two-thirds of whom live and die in the countryside. Half of the people do not have potable water, and two-thirds have no sewage systems. Ninety percent of the people in rural areas have little or no money income.

For a state that produces petroleum, electric energy, coffee, wood, and livestock for the hungry beast, the Chiapan transportation system is a grotesque joke. Only two-thirds of the municipalities have paved roads; 12,000 rural communities depend solely on mountain trails hundreds of years old. Since the time of Porfirio Díaz,[*] the railroad lines have followed the demands of the capitalist looters and not the needs of the Chiapan people. The line that follows the coast (there are only two lines—the other crosses the northern part of the state) dates from the beginning of the century and its carrying capacity is limited by the old Porfirista bridges that cross the canyons of the southeast. The one port, Puerto Madero, is used exclusively by the beast, to ship out what it has robbed.

Education? The worst in the country. Seventy-two out of every one-hundred children do not finish the first grade. Half of the schools go no higher than the third grade, and half of them have only one teacher to teach all the courses. The true drop-out figures are even higher, as the children of the indigenous people are forced to enter the system of exploitation in order to help their families survive. In every indigenous community it is common to see children carrying corn or wood, cooking or washing clothes, during school hours. Of the 16,058 schoolrooms in Chiapas in 1989, only 96 were in indigenous areas.

Industry? Look at it this way: 40 percent of Chiapan "industry" consists of milling corn and building wood furniture. The largest industries (.2 percent of the total) are petroleum and electricity, now owned by the Mexican government, but soon enough they will be in the hands of foreigners. Medium-sized industries (.4 percent of the total) are primarily sugar mills, and fish, flower, quicklime, milk, and coffee operations. About 94.8 percent of Chiapan firms are very small businesses.

Health? Capitalism leaves its mark: 1.5 million Chiapans have no medical services whatsoever. There are .2 clinics for every 1,000 people, five times less than the national average; there are .3 hospital beds for every 1,000 Chiapans, three times less than the rest of Mexico; there is one operating room for every 100,000 people, two times less than in the rest of the country; there are .5 doctors and .4 nurses for every 1,000 persons, two times less than the national average.

Health and nutrition go hand in hand with poverty. Fifty-four percent of the Chiapan population is malnourished, and in the mountains and jungles 80 percent of the people are hungry. Standard diet for a campesino is coffee, corn, tortillas, and beans.

And that is what capitalism leaves in payment for what it takes.

This part of Mexican territory annexed itself to the young, independent republic in 1824, but was not included on national maps until the petroleum boom reminded the country that it had a southeast. (Eighty-two percent of Pemex's petrochemical installations are in the southeast; in 1990, two-thirds of public investment in Chiapas was in energy.) But this state does not just respond to the fashions of six-year presidential terms; its experience with plunder and exploitation goes back hundreds of years. Chiapan veins have always bled the very same loot: wood and fruit, livestock and men—all headed for the metropolis. Just like the banana republics of the past, but now at the peak of neoliberalism and "libertarian revolutions," the southeast continues exporting natural resources and manual labor, and, as it has for five hundred years, still imports the primary product of capitalism: misery and death.

One million indigenous people live in these lands and share with mestizos* and ladinos* a troubling nightmare: five hundred years after the "meeting of two worlds," indigenous people have the option to die of misery or repression. The program to improve the lives of the poor, this little stain of social democracy blowing through the state of Mexico which Salinas de Gortari calls PRONASOL,* is a cruel joke that brings tears of blood to the eyes of those who, under these suns and rains, are barely able to survive.

WELCOME!
YOU HAVE ARRIVED IN THE POOREST
STATE OF THE COUNTRY: CHIAPAS

Suppose that you continue driving and from Ocosocoatla you go down to Tuxtla Gutiérrez, the state capital. Don't plan to stay long, Tuxtla Gutiérrez is just a big warehouse for the state's products. Part of our wealth passes through here to wherever the capitalists decide. Don't delay, just barely touch the lips of the bloody maw of the monster. You pass Chiapas de Corzo, ignoring the Nestle's factory, and begin climbing into the mountains. What do you see? You must have entered another world: an indigenous one. Another world, but the same one in which millions of other people in our country suffer.

This indigenous world is made up of 300,000 Tzeltales, 300,000 Tzotziles, 120,000 Choles, 90,000 Zoques, and 70,000 Tojolabales. Even the federal government acknowledges that only half of these people are illiterate.

Continue on the interior mountain road and you arrive at what is called the Chiapan highlands. Here, five hundred years ago, the many indigenous peoples were lords and masters of the earth and water. Now they are still numerous, but masters only of poverty. Go on, and you reach San Cristóbal de las Casas, which used to be the capital of Chiapas until some intra-bourgeois squabbles one hundred years ago took away the dubious distinction of being the capital of the poorest state in Mexico. No, don't delay here either: if Tuxtla Gutiérrez is just a big warehouse, San Cristóbal is just a big marketplace. By thousands of different routes, the Tzotziles, Tzeltales, Choles, Tojolabales, and Zoques bring capitalism its tribute: wood, coffee, livestock, weavings, crafts, fruit, vegetables, corn . . . and they also take something away: sickness, ignorance, mockery, death. In the poorest state in Mexico, this is the poorest region.

Welcome to San Cristóbal de las Casas, a "Colonial City" say the mestizos, though the majority of the people are indigenous. Welcome to the great marketplace, the pride of PRONASOL. Here you can buy or sell anything—except the dignity of the indigenous people. Here everything is expensive—except death. But don't stay long, keep going up the road, appreciating what has been built for the tourists: in 1988 Chiapas had 6,270 hotel rooms, 139 restaurants, and 42 travel agencies; this year 1,058,098 tourists left 250,000,000,000 pesos [$83,000,000] in the hands of restaurant and hotel owners.

Did you add it up? Yes, that's right. While there are seven hotel rooms for every 1,000 tourists, there are .3 hospital beds for every 1,000 Chiapans.

Fine, forget the figures and move on, taking care to avoid the three lines of cops in camouflage berets trotting along the side of the road. Pass by the police station and continue along, passing hotels, restaurants, and fancy stores, and then move on to the Comitán exit. Leaving the "bowl" of San Cristóbal, right along the same road you will see the famous grottos surrounded by lush forests. Do you see that sign? No, you are not mistaken, this natural park is administered by . . . the army! Without letting go of your confusion, continue on . . . What do you see? Modern buildings, nice homes, paved roads . . . Is it a university? Workers' housing? No, look carefully at the sign next to one of the cannons: "General Barracks, Military Zone 31." With that painful olive-green image still in your eye, you arrive at the crossroads and decide not to go to Comitán. Thus you avoid the pain of seeing, some meters ahead on the hill they call "The Foreigner's," North American military personnel operating, and teaching their Mexican counterparts to operate, a radar station.

You decide that it is better to go to Ocosingo, as ecology and other nonsense is all the fashion these days. Look at the trees, take a deep breath . . . now do you feel better? Yes? Then keep on looking to your left because if you don't, at the 7-kilometer mark you will see a magnificent edifice with the noble SOLIDARITY[*] logo on the front. Don't look, I tell you, turn your head away, you don't want to know that this new building is a . . . jail. (Evil tongues say that this is one of PRONASOL's main gifts to the people: now the campesinos don't have to go all the way to the capital to be put in jail.)

Don't get discouraged. The worst will always be hidden: too much poverty would scare the tourists. Continue on down to Huixtan, up to Oxchuc, check out the beautiful waterfall at the headwaters of

Jataté River, which runs through the Lacandon jungle. Pass by Cuxuljá, and instead of taking the Altamirano detour, drive on to Ocosingo: "The Door to the Lacandon Jungle."

Okay, wait here for a while. Take a quick trip around the city . . . The main points of interest? Well, the two big buildings at the entrance to town are whorehouses, the next one is a jail, and across the street is the church. Next is the office of the ranchers' association, followed by the Federal Army barracks, the state police office, the city hall, and finally Pemex headquarters. The rest of the buildings are little houses all on top of each other that rattle and shake as the giant trucks owned by Pemex and the richest ranchers pass by. Well, what's it seem like to you? A hacienda from the time of Porfirio Díaz? But that period ended seventy-five years ago!

No, you better not go down this third-rate road all the way to San Quintín, across from the Montes Azules reserve. Don't go down to where the Jataté and Perlas rivers cross, or walk for eight hours for three consecutive days to arrive at San Martín, a small poor *ejido*. Nor would you want to get close to the big shed of rusted, corrugated metal that is falling to pieces. What is it? Well, sometimes a church, sometimes a school, sometimes a meeting place. Right now it is a school, as it is 11 in the morning. Don't get close, don't look inside, don't see the four groups of children brimming with worms and lice, half naked, taking classes from the four young indigenous people who act as teachers for a miserable wage which they won't get unless they make the same three-day walk that you were just urged not to try. What grade does this school go to? The third, with a little hallway the only division between the "classrooms." And, finally, ignore the posters on the wall, the only thing that government has sent to these children, posters for the prevention of AIDS.

Instead, let's return to the paved road. (Yes, I know even it is in bad shape.) Let's leave Ocosingo and continue admiring these lands . . . The owners of the land? Yes, big ranchers. Production: cattle, coffee, corn . . . Did you see the National Institute of Indigenous Peoples? Yes, right there on the way out of town. Did you see the fine pickup trucks? They are given on credit to indigenous campesinos. Because of ecological considerations, they only use unleaded gasoline . . . But there is no unleaded gas in Ocosingo. A small detail . . .

But you are right, the government is worried about the campesinos. Sure, the evil tongues say that there are guerrilla fighters in the mountains and that the money from the government is only to buy the loyalty of the indigenous people, but those are just rumors, probably from people who are trying to discredit PRONASOL . . . What? the Civil Defense Committee? Oh yes. It is a group of heroic ranchers, businessmen, and union sell-outs who organize "white guards" to threaten and evict people. But didn't I just say that the Porfiriato ended seventy-five years ago?

We better move on . . . at the next intersection take a left. No, don't go to Palenque. Instead, let's go on, let's go by Chilón. It is beautiful, isn't it? Yes, Yajalón . . . very modern, it even has a gas station . . . look, there is the bank, and the city hall, the police station, the ranchers' association, and the army. Are we on another hacienda? Let's leave and not visit the other big modern buildings on the outskirts of town, on the road to Tilba and Sabanilla. Then we won't have to see the handsome sign, SOLIDARITY, which graces the entrance of . . . another jail.

Good, we got to the crossing, now on to Ocosingo . . . Palenque? Are you sure? Okay, let's go. Yes, it is a beautiful land. And there are the ranchers. Correct: cattle, coffee, wood. Look, we are arriving at Palenque. A quick visit through the city? Those are hotels, over there restaurants, over here city hall, the troopers, army barracks, and over there . . . What? No, never mind, I know what you are going to say. Don't say it . . . Tired? Okay, let's stop for a while. Don't you even want to see the pyramids?

No, okay. How about Xi'Nich? It is something different. A march of indigenous people. They are going all the way to Mexico City. Uh-huh, walking. How far is it? 1,106 kilometers. Results? Their petitions were received. Yes, just that.

Are you still tired? Okay, let's wait here some more. How about Bonampak? The road is very bad. Let's go anyway, we will take the scenic route . . . Over there is the military reserve, and here is the navy, and now the state police, and at last the government ministry.

Is it always like this? No, sometimes you run into campesino protest marches.

Had enough? Do you want to go home? Other places? In what country? Mexico? You will see the same thing; the colors, languages, landscape and names will change, but the people, the exploitation, the misery and death are the same. Just look carefully. Yes, in all the states of the republic.

So long and good luck. If you need a tourist guide don't forget to call me, I am at your service. Oh, and one other thing. It won't always be like this. Another Mexico? No, the same one. I am talking about something else—how other breezes begin to blow, how another wind is rising.

CHAPTER 2

Tells the deeds of the apprentice viceroy governor, of his heroic combat against the progressive clergy, and his good fortune with the feudal lords of cattle, coffee, and business. And reveals other events equally fantastic.

Once upon a time there was a chocolate viceroy with a peanut nose. The apprentice to the viceroy, Governor Patrocinio González Garrido, in the manner of the old monarchs introduced by the Spanish Crown at the time of the Conquest, has reorganized Chiapan geography. The formal designation of space as either urban or rural is a rather sophisticated exercise of power, but when done with the clumsiness of Sr. González Garrido it reaches exquisite levels of stupidity. The viceroy has decided that the cities, with their services and facilities, should be for those who already have everything. And he decides, does the viceroy, that the masses are fine outside, in the great outdoors, and that the only indoor place they deserve is in the jails, which should not be too comfortable. So the viceroy has decided to build the jails outside the cities, so that the unwanted and offending multitude will not be close enough to disturb the fine gentlemen.

Jails and barracks are the main public works that this governor has brought to Chiapas. His friendship with the big ranchers and the powerful businessmen is no secret to anyone, nor is his hostility toward the three dioceses that regulate the Catholic life of the state. The diocese of San Cristóbal, with Bishop Samuel Ruiz at its head, is a constant bother to the reorganizing project of González Garrido. Wishing to modernize the absurd structure of exploitation and plunder which reigns in Chiapas, Patrocinio González is often tripped up by the stubbornness of the religious and secular people who preach and live the Catholic option for the poor.

With the sanctimonious applause of the Tuxtla bishop, Aguirre Franco, and the silent approval of the bishop of Tapachula, González Garrido inspires and supports the "heroic" conspiracies of ranchers and businessmen against the members of the San Cristóbal diocese. But "Don Samuel's teams," as some people call them, are not made up of inexperienced believers: before Patrocinio González even dreamed of governing this state, the diocese of San Cristóbal de las Casas preached the right to freedom and justice. For one of the most retrograde parts of the bourgeoisie in the country, the ranch owners, the words "freedom" and "justice" can mean only one thing: rebellion. And these patriotic and religious ranchers and businessmen know how to stop rebellions: the existence of well-paid armed "white guards," trained by members of the Federal Army, the public security police, and state troopers is well known to the campesinos. It is these white guards who insult, torture, and shoot them.

A few months ago, the priest of Simojovel, Joel Padrón, was arrested. Accused by the ranchers of inciting and participating in land occupations, Father Joel was taken by state authorities and confined in Cerro Hueco, the jail at the state capital. Support from Mexico City and mobilizations by members of the diocese of San Cristóbal (the dioceses of Tuxtla and Tapachula were conspicuous in their absence) managed to win Father Padrón's freedom.

While thousands of campesinos marched in Tuxtla Gutiérrez demanding the release of the priest, the ranchers of Ocosingo sent their resplendent white guards to evict the campesinos who were occupying some farms. At Momoma, four hundred men, armed by the ranchers, attacked and beat people, burned houses, whipped indigenous women, and, with a shot in the face, killed campesino Juan. After the eviction, the white guards, mostly cowboys from the big ranches and small businessmen proud to be on an excursion with the land-owning lads, raced through the region in pickup trucks supplied by the bosses. Openly displaying their weapons, drunk and stoned, they shouted, "The ranchers' association is number one!" and warned everybody that this action was only a beginning. The municipal authorities of Ocosingo and the soldiers stationed there were impassive spectators at this triumphant parade of armed hoodlums.

In Tuxtla Gutiérrez close to 10,000 campesinos marched for the liberation of Joel Padrón. In a corner of Ocosingo, Juan's widow by herself buried the victim of the proud ranchers. There was no march, no prayer, no petition of protest about the death of Juan. This is Chiapas.

Recently, Viceroy González Garrido was the protagonist in a new scandal, made public only because the victims had the resources to denounce him. With the consent of the viceroy, the feudal gentlemen of Ocosingo organized a Citizen Defense Committee, whose intent was to institutionalize the *neoporfirista** white guards to better protect order in the Chiapan countryside. Nothing would have happened if it hadn't been for the discovery of a plot to assassinate the priest Pablo Ibarren and the nun María del Carmen, as well as Samuel Ruiz, the bishop of the diocese. The Citizen Defense Committee gave the priest and nun a time limit to leave the municipality, but the radical elements of the committee clamored for the "more drastic solution" that would have included Bishop Ruiz. The plot was exposed by a part of the Chiapan press that is still honest and was picked up by the national media. There were retractions and lies, and the viceroy declared that he maintained good relations with the church, and named a special prosecutor to investigate the case. The investigation came up with nothing, and "the flood waters returned to the river bed."

About the same time, government agencies released some chilling statistics: in Chiapas 14,500 people die a year, the highest death rate in the country. What causes most of these deaths? Curable diseases: respiratory infections, gastroenteritis, parasites, malaria, scabies, breakbone fever, tuberculosis, conjunctivitis, typhus, cholera, and measles. Evil tongues say that the figure should be higher than 15,000 dead per year because the deaths in the marginalized zones that make up the majority of the state are not counted. In the four year reign of Patrocinio González Garrido, more than 60,000 Chiapan people have died, most of them poor.

The viceroy directs, and the feudal gentlemen behind him command, a war against the people that is more subtle than simply dropping bombs on them. There is nothing in either the local or national press about this series of assassination plots that have taken so many lives (and stolen so much land) that it seems as if we were still living in the times of the Conquest.

The Citizen Defense Committee continues recruiting, and holds meetings to convince both the rich and the poor of the city of Ocosingo that they must organize and arm themselves so that the campesinos won't be able to enter the city and, respecting neither the rich nor the poor, destroy everything. The viceroy smiles his approval.

CHAPTER 3

Tells how the viceroy had a brilliant idea and put it into practice, and also tells how the empire decreed the death of socialism, and enthusiastically took on the job of broadcasting that good news, bringing joy to the powerful, consolation to the faint-hearted, and indifference from everybody else. It also tells how the people say that Zapata has not died. And other upsetting facts.

The viceroy is worried. The campesinos refuse to applaud the institutionalized plunder that is now written into Article 27 of the Constitution.* The viceroy is in a rage. The exploited are not happy being exploited. They refuse to humbly line up to receive the handouts that PRONASOL sprinkles over the Chiapan countryside. The viceroy has run out of patience, and consults his advisors. They tell him again an old truth: jails and troops are not enough to dominate a people, you also have to dominate their thoughts. The viceroy paces uneasily through his superb palace. He stops, he smiles, he writes . . .

STATION XEOCH: Rap and lies for the campesinos.

Ocosingo and Palenque, Cancuc y Chilón, Altamirano y Yajalón, the indigenous people are celebrating. The peons and small property owners, the campesinos without land, and the impoverished *ejiditarios* are happy because they have received a new gift from the almighty government. They now have a local radio station that reaches, finally, the furthest corners of eastern Chiapas. The programming is most appropriate: marimba music and rap proclaim a brand new world. The Chiapan countryside is modernizing. XEOCH transmits from the municipal seat of Ocosingo, 600 megahertz AM, from 4 a.m. to 10 p.m. The news has been milled before it is broadcast: religious "subversives" are preaching "confusion" among the campesinos, abundant credit is available (somehow it never gets to the indigenous communities), and there are new public works (that nobody has seen anywhere). The arrogant viceroy also finds the time to transmit his threats over XEOCH so that everyone will remember that the people are not only controlled through lies and rap, but that there are also jails and troops, and a penal code that is the most repressive in the country. The code penalizes all displays of popular discontent: rioting, rebellion, inciting rebellion, mutiny, etc. The careful cataloguing of crimes in the articles of this law are proof that the viceroy concerns himself with doing things right.

There is nothing to struggle for. Socialism is dead. Long live resignation, reformism, modernity, capitalism, and a whole list of cruel etceteras. The viceroy and the feudal gentlemen dance and laugh joyfully in their palaces, big and small. Their rejoicing is disturbing to a few independent thinkers who live around here. Incapable of understanding, they fall into unhappy breast beating. It is true, they say, why struggle? The correlation of forces is unfavorable. It is not the right time . . . we have to keep waiting . . . perhaps years . . . watch out for political adventurers. We have to be sensible. Let nothing happen, neither in the countryside nor the cities, let everything continue as it is. Socialism is dead. Long live capital. Radio, television, and the newspapers proclaim it, and some ex-socialists, now sensibly repentant, repeat it.

But not everybody listens to the voices of hopelessness and resignation. Not everyone has jumped onto the bandwagon of despair. Most people continue on; they cannot hear the voice of the powerful and the faint-hearted as they are deafened by the cry and the blood that death and misery shout in their ears. But in moments of rest they hear another voice, not the one that comes from above, but rather the one that comes with the wind from below and is born in the heart of the indigenous people of the mountains, a voice that speaks of justice and liberty, a voice that speaks of socialism, a voice that speaks of hope . . . the only hope in this earthly world. And the very oldest among the old people in the villages tell of a man named Zapata who rose up for his own people and in a voice more like a song than a shout, said, "Land and Freedom!"

And these old folks say that Zapata is not dead, that he is going to return. And the oldest of the old also say that the wind and the rain and the sun tell the campesinos when they should prepare the soil, when they should plant, and when they should harvest. They say that hope also must be planted and harvested. And the old people say that now the wind, the rain, and the sun are talking to the earth in a new way, and that the poor should not continue to harvest death, now it is time to harvest rebellion. So say the old people. The powerful don't listen, the words don't reach them, as they are made deaf by the witchery that the imperialists shout in their ears. "Zapata," repeat the youth of the poor, "Zapata," insists the wind, the wind from below, our wind . . .

CHAPTER 4
THE SECOND WIND—THE ONE FROM BELOW

Tells how, in the southeast of the country, dignity and rebellion are related, and how the ghost of Jacinto Pérez[*] runs with raccoons through the mountains of Chiapas. It also tells how patience is running out, and other events that people do not want to admit but will have their consequences.

The Chiapan people were born, dignified and rebellious, made brothers and sisters to the other exploited people of the country, not by the Act of Annexation of 1824, but rather through a long chain of abuses and revolts. Since the time that vestments and armor conquered these lands, dignity and revolt have lived and spread under these stormy skies.

Collective work, democratic thought, and majority rule are more than just a tradition among indigenous people; they have been the only way to survive, to resist, to be proud, and to rebel. These "bad ideas" (in the eyes of the big landowners and businessmen) go against the grain of the capitalist precept, "a lot in the hands of the few."

It has been said, quite wrongly, that the rebellion of the people of Chiapas has its own tempo, which does not correspond to the rhythms of the nation. It is a lie. The exploited Chiapans' special genius is the same as that of the exploited in Durango, or the Bajío,[*] or Veracruz: to fight and to lose. If the voices of those who write history are not accurate, it is because the voice of the oppressed does not speak . . . not yet. There is no historical calendar, national or regional, which records all the rebellions and protests against this bloody system, imposed and maintained by force throughout every region of the country.

In Chiapas, the voice of rebellion is heard only when it shakes up the little world of the powerful. It is then that the ghost of the indigenous barbarian Jacinto Pérez resounds through the walls of the government palaces, and the powerful must rely on hot lead, traps, tricks, and threats. If the rebellions of the southeast lose, as they lose in the north, the center, and east, it is not because they lack numbers and support, it is because wind is the fruit of the earth, and it has its own season, and matures not in books filled with regrets but rather in the breasts of those who have nothing more than their dignity and their will to rebel. And this wind from below, the wind of rebellion and dignity, is not just a response to the wind imposed from above, it is not just a brave answer, but rather it carries within itself something new. This wind promises not only the destruction of an unjust and arbitrary system; it is, above all, a hope that dignity and rebellion can be converted into dignity and freedom.

How will this new voice be heard in our lands and throughout the country? This hidden wind, content for now to blow through the mountains and the glades, without yet going down into the valleys where money commands and lies govern, how can it grow?

This wind, born below the trees, will come down from the mountains; it whispers of a new world, so new that it is but an intuition in the collective heart.

CHAPTER 5

Tells how the dignity of the indigenous people began to make its voice heard and how short a time that voice lasted, and also tells how the voices of the past are repeated today, and how the Indians will begin to walk again, together with other dispossessed marchers, but this time with surer steps, in order to take what belongs to them. And how death's music, which now plays only for those who have nothing, will play for others too. And also tells

other amazing things that happen, and, according to some, must happen.

The indigenous Xi'Nich ("March of the Ants") made by the campesinos of Palenque, Ocosingo, and Salto de Agua demonstrates the absurdity of the system. These indigenous people had to walk 1,106 kilometers in order to be heard; they went to the capital of the republic so that federal authorities would get them an interview with the viceroy back in Chiapas. They arrived in Mexico City just when capitalism was painting a terrifying tragedy in the sky above Jalisco [an underground explosion of natural gas, which killed hundreds in Guadalajara]. They arrived in the old capital of New Spain, now Mexico City, five hundred years after a foreign nightmare was imposed on these lands. They came and listened to all the honest and noble gentlemen in the capital—and there still are some—and they listened to the voices that today oppress not only the southeast but the north, center, and east of the country. They walked back the same 1,106 kilometers with their pockets full of promises. Nothing happened . . .

In the municipal seat of Simojovel, the campesinos of the CIOAC were attacked by people hired by the local ranchers' association. The campesinos of Simojovel have decided to end their silence and respond to the big ranchers. Campesino hands surround the municipal seat and let no one enter or leave without their consent. The Federal Army returns to their barracks, the police retreat, and the feudal gentlemen scream for blood so that order and respect may return to the state. Negotiating committees come and go. The conflict seems to resolve itself, the matter subsides, and an apparent calm returns.

In the town of Betania, on the outskirts of San Cristóbal de las Casas, indigenous people are regularly detained and fined by the state police for cutting wood to use in their homes. The police are only complying with their duty to protect the environment, they say. Some indigenous people decide to end their silence and kidnap three state troopers. Not stopping there, they take over the Pan-American Highway and cut off communication to the east of San Cristóbal. They take the tied-up troopers to the Ocosingo and Comitán cross-roads, and demand to speak to the viceroy before they will unblock the road. Business is bogged down, tourism collapses. The noble *coleta*[*] bourgeoisie pull the hair out of their venerable heads. Negotiating committees come and go. The conflict seems to resolve itself, the matter subsides, and an apparent calm returns.

In Marqués de Comillas, a municipality of Ocosingo, the campesinos cut wood to survive. The state police detain them and requisition the wood for the benefit of their commander. The indigenous people decide to end their silence and they take the police vehicles and make the agents prisoners. The government sends out security forces, and they are also taken prisoner. The indigenous people hold onto the police trucks, the wood, and the prisoners. Finally, they turn the cops loose. There is no answer from the government. The indigenous people march to Palenque to demand a solution to the dispute, and the army suppresses the march and arrests the leaders. The campesinos hold onto the trucks. Negotiating committees come and go. The government releases the campesino leaders, and the campesinos release the trucks. The conflict seems to resolve itself, the matter subsides, and an apparent calm returns.

In the municipal seat of Ocosingo, 4,000 indigenous campesinos march from different points in the city to the ANCIEZ. Three of the marches converge on the municipal palace. The president of the municipality does not know what is happening and flees; a calendar left on the floor of his office shows the date: April 10, 1992. Outside, the indigenous campesinos of Ocosingo, Oxchuc, Huixtan, Chilón, Yajalón, Sabanilla, Salto de Agua, Palenque, Altamirano, Margaritas, San Cristóbal, San Andrés, and Cancuc dance in front of a giant image of Zapata, painted by one of them. They recite poems, sing, and speak. They are the only ones there to listen. The large landowners, the big businessmen, and the police are all closed up in their houses and businesses, and the garrison seems to be deserted. The campesinos shout that Zapata lives and that their struggle continues. One of them reads a letter to Carlos Salinas de Gortari accusing him of destroying the agrarian reform won by Zapata, of selling out the country through the North American Free Trade Agreement, and of returning Mexico to the time of Porfirio Díaz. They forcefully declare that they do not recognize Salinas' changes of Article 27 of the Constitution. At two in the afternoon the demonstration dissolves, the matter subsides, and an apparent calm returns.

Absalo is an *ejido* in the municipality of Ocosingo. For a long time, campesinos there have taken land that legally and naturally belongs to them. Three leaders of their community have been taken prisoner and tortured by the government. The indigenous people decide to end their silence and seize the road between San Cristóbal and Ocosingo. Negotiating committees come and go. The leaders are released. The conflict seems to resolve itself, the matter subsides, and an apparent calm returns.

Antonio dreams that the land that he works belongs to him. He dreams that his sweat earns him justice and truth; he dreams of schools that cure ignorance and medicines that frighten death. He dreams that his house has light and that his table is full; he dreams that the land is free, and that his people reasonably govern themselves. He dreams that he is at peace with himself and with the world. He dreams that he has to struggle to have this dream, he dreams that there has to be death so that there might be life. Antonio dreams and wakes up . . . now he knows what he has to do. He sees his wife squatting to poke the fire, he hears his son crying, he looks at the sun greeting the east, and he smiles as he sharpens his machete.

A wind comes up and everything stirs. Antonio rises, and walks to meet the others. He has heard that his desire is the desire of many, and he goes to look for them.

The viceroy dreams that his land is agitated by a terrible wind, and that everything rises up; he dreams that all he has stolen has been taken away from him, he dreams that his house is destroyed and his government overthrown. He dreams and he doesn't sleep. The viceroy goes to the feudal gentlemen and they tell him that they are dreaming the same thing. The viceroy can't rest, he goes to his doctors, and among them they decide that he is suffering from Indian witchcraft, and only blood will free him of its spell; so the viceroy orders murder and imprisonment and the building of more jails and barracks, but his dreams continue to keep him awake.

In this country everyone dreams. Now it is time to wake up.

THE STORM

It will be born out of the clash between the two winds, it will arrive in its own time, the coals on the hearth of history are stoked up and ready to burn. Now the wind from above rules,

but the one from below is coming, the storm rises . . . so it will
be . . .

THE PROPHECY

When the storm subsides, when the rain and the fire leave the
earth in peace again, the world will no longer be the world, but
something better.

—The Lacandon Jungle
August 1992

• 2 •
DECLARATION OF THE LACANDON JUNGLE: TODAY WE SAY "ENOUGH"

To the People of Mexico

Mexican brothers and sisters,

We are the product of five hundred years of struggle: first against
slavery; then in the insurgent-led war of Independence against Spain;
later in the fight to avoid being absorbed by North American expan-
sion; next to proclaim our Constitution and expel the French from our
soil; and finally, after the dictatorship of Porfirio Díaz refused to fairly
apply the reform laws, in the rebellion where the people created their
own leaders. In that rebellion Villa and Zapata emerged—poor men,
like us.

We are denied the most elementary education so that they can use
us as cannon fodder and plunder our country's riches, uncaring that
we are dying of hunger and curable diseases. Nor do they care that
we have nothing, absolutely nothing, no decent roof over our heads,

no land, no work, no health, no food, no education. We do not have the right to freely and democratically elect our own authorities, nor are we independent of foreigners, nor do we have peace or justice for ourselves and our children.

But *today we say enough!* We are the heirs of the people who truly forged our nation, we are the millions of the dispossessed, and we call on all of our brothers and sisters to join us on the only path that will allow us to escape a starvation caused by the insatiable ambition of a seventy-year-old dictatorship, led by a small inner clique of traitors who represent ultra-conservative groups ready to sell out our country. They are the same people who opposed Hidalgo and Morelos, those who betrayed Vicente Guerrero,* those who sold more than half of our country to the foreign invader, those who brought a European prince to govern us, those who formed a dictatorship of *científicos porfiristas,** those who opposed the Petroleum Expropriation, and those who massacred the railroad workers in 1958 and the students in 1968—they are all the very same ones who today take everything from us, absolutely everything.

After we tried to do everything legally possible, based on our Magna Carta, to stop all this, as a last hope we invoke that same document, our Constitution, Article 39, which says:

"National sovereignty resides, essentially and originally, in the people. All public power emanates from the people, and is constituted for the benefit of the same. *The people have, at all times, the inalienable right to alter or modify the form of their government."*

Therefore, as per the terms of our Constitution, we send this declaration to the Mexican Federal Army, one of the basic pillars of the dictatorship under which we suffer. This army is controlled exclusively by the party in power, headed by the federal executive office, which is today unlawfully held by the illegitimate head of state, Carlos Salinas de Gortari.

Congruent with this *Declaration of War,* we ask other *Powers of the Nation* to take up the fight to depose the dictator and restore legitimacy and stability to this nation.

We also ask that international organizations and the International Red Cross observe and regulate any combat involving our forces so as to protect the civilian population; we declare that we are now, and always will be, subject to the Laws of War of the Geneva Convention, which defines the EZLN as a belligerent force in our struggle for liberation.

The Mexican people are on our side; we are patriots and our insurgent soldiers love and respect our tricolored flag; we use red and black on our uniforms, the same colors working people use when on strike; on our flag are the letters *"EZLN,"* *Zapatista Army of National Liberation,* and we always carry that flag into battle.

We reject, in advance, any and all efforts to discredit the just cause of our struggle by accusing us of being drug traffickers, or drug guerrillas, or bandits, or whatever other characterizations our enemies might use. Our struggle is in accordance with our constitutional rights and our goal is justice and equality.

Therefore, and in accordance with this Declaration of War, we give the military forces of the Zapatista Army of National Liberation the following orders:

First. Advance to the capital of the country, defeat the Mexican Federal Army, protecting and liberating the civilian population along your liberating march, and permit the liberated peoples to elect, freely and democratically, their own administrative authorities.

Second. Respect the life of all prisoners and turn over any wounded to the International Red Cross for medical attention.

Third. Initiate summary judgments against the soldiers of the Mexican Federal Army and the political police who have taken courses or have been advised, or trained, or paid by foreigners either inside or outside our country; those who are accused of treason; and those who repress or mistreat the civilian population or assault the public welfare.

Fourth. Form new ranks with all Mexicans who show an interest in joining our just struggle, including those enemy soldiers who give up without fighting our troops and who swear to follow the orders of the General Command of the *Zapatista Army of National Liberation.*

Fifth. Ask for the unconditional surrender of enemy barracks before making war against them.

Sixth. Suspend the plunder of our natural resources in all the areas controlled by the *EZLN.*

PEOPLE OF MEXICO. We, men and women, upright and free, are conscious that the war we now declare is a last resort, but it is also just. The dictatorship has been waging an undeclared genocidal war against our communities for many years. We now ask for your committed participation and support for this plan of the people of Mexico who struggle for *work, land, housing, food, health, education, independence, freedom, democracy, justice, and peace.* We declare that we will not stop fighting until we win these basic demands of our people, forming a free and democratic government.

Join the insurgent forces of the Zapatista Army of National Liberation.

General Command of the EZLN
The year 1993

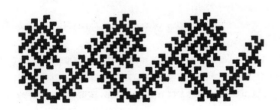

• 3 •
"HERE WE ARE, THE FOREVER DEAD . . ."

**Communiqué from the CCRI-CG of the EZLN
January 6, 1994**

**"Here we are, the forever dead, dying once again,
but now in order to live."**

To the people of Mexico
To the people and governments of the world

Brothers and sisters,

On January 1 of this year, our Zapatista troops began a series of political-military actions whose primary objective was to inform the Mexican people and the rest of the world about the miserable conditions in which millions of Mexicans, especially us, the indigenous people, live and die. With these actions we also let the world know of our decision to fight for our most elementary rights in the only way that the governmental authorities have left us: armed struggle.

The serious poverty that we share with our fellow citizens has a common cause: the lack of freedom and democracy. We think that authentic respect for the liberties and democratic will of the people are the indispensable prerequisites for the improvement of the economic and social conditions of the dispossessed of our country. For this reason, at the same time that we unfurl the banner of improving the material conditions of the people of Mexico, we demand freedom and democracy by calling for the resignation of the illegitimate government of Carlos Salinas de Gortari and the formation of a government of democratic transition, which would guarantee fair elections at all levels of government throughout the country.

We reiterate that both our political and economic demands are now in effect, and we will try to unite all the Mexican people and their independent organizations around them so that, through varied forms of struggle, a national revolutionary movement will be born with a place for all kinds of social organizations whose honest and patriotic goal is a better Mexico.

Since the beginning of our war of liberation we have not only been subject to military attacks from various repressive governmental bodies and the Federal Army, but we have also been slandered by the state and federal governments and by some of the mass media who are trying to undermine our struggle and deceive the Mexican people. They claim that our struggle is led by foreigners, professionals of violence, and shadowy, anti-patriotic interests who are only seeking personal gain. Due to these lies and slander, we, the EZLN, feel obligated to say the following:

First. Our EZLN does not have a single foreigner in our ranks or in our leadership bodies, and has never received help or training from revolutionary movements of other countries or from foreign governments. The news that Guatemalans, trained in a neighboring country, are fighting in our ranks has been invented by the federal government to discredit our cause. We have never had, nor do we have now, any connection with the FMLN of El Salvador or the URGN of Guatemala, or with any other armed movement in Latin America, North America, Europe, Africa, Asia, or Australia.

We did not learn our military tactics from Central American insurgent movements, but rather from Mexican military history: from Hidalgo, Morelos, Guerrero, Mena; from the resistance to the Yankee invasion in 1846-1847; from the popular response to the French intervention; from the great heroic feats of Villa and Zapata; and finally, from the indigenous struggles of resistance throughout the history of our country.

Second. Our EZLN does not have any connection to authorities of the Catholic church, nor to those of any other creed. We have not received orientation or direction or ecclesiastic structural support, either from the Diocese of the state of Chiapas, or from any papal representative, or from the Vatican, or from anyone. Those who fight in our ranks are primarily Catholics, but we are also people of other beliefs and religions.

Third. The commanders and the troops of the EZLN are mostly indigenous people of Chiapas, because the indigenous are the poorest and most dispossessed of Mexico, but also, as now can be seen, because they are the most dignified. We are thousands of indigenous people up in arms, and behind us are tens of thousands of people in our families. Add it up: we amount to many thousands of indigenous people in struggle. The government says that this is not an indigenous uprising, but we think that if thousands of indigenous people have risen up in struggle, then it must be an indigenous uprising.

In our movement there are also Mexicans of varied social origins and from different states of our country. They agree with us and have united with us because they are opposed to the exploitation that we suffer. Just as these non-indigenous Mexicans have united with us, more will do so in the future because our struggle is national and not limited to the state of Chiapas. Currently, the political leadership of our struggle is completely indigenous. One hundred percent of the members of the indigenous revolutionary clandestine committees in the combat zones belong to the Tzotzil, Tzeltal, Chol, Tojolaba, and other ethnic groups. It is true that not all the indigenous people of Chiapas are with us, because there are still many brothers and sisters under the influence of the deceiving ideas of the government. Nevertheless, we are already thousands of people, and that must be taken into account. We use ski-masks and other methods of hiding our faces as an elementary security precaution and as a vaccine against *caudillismo.**

Fourth. We have a variety of armaments and military equipment, whose number and quality we did not, for obvious reasons, publicly display to the media or to the civilian populations in the municipalities that we took on the first and second of January. We gathered these arms and equipment little by little, and prepared our forces silently during the last ten years. The "sophisticated" means of communication that we possess can be bought in any import store in the country. In order to get the arms and equipment, we never resorted to robbery, or kidnapping, or extortion; we have always maintained ourselves from what we have been given by humble and honest people throughout Mexico. And because we never fell into banditry to fill our treasury, the repressive apparatus of the state never even knew we existed during our ten years of careful and serious preparation.

Fifth. Some ask why we decided to begin now, if we were prepared before. The answer is that before this we tried other peaceful and legal roads to change, but without success. During these last ten years more than 150,000 of our indigenous brothers and sisters have died from curable diseases. The federal, state, and municipal governments' economic and social plans do not even consider any real solution to our problems, and consist of giving us handouts at election times. But these crumbs of charity solve our problems for no more than a moment, and then, once again, death returns to our houses. That is why we think no, no more, enough of this dying useless deaths, it would be better to fight for change. If we die now, we will not die with shame, but with the dignity of our ancestors. Another 150,000 of us are ready to die if that is what is needed to waken our people from their deceit-induced stupor.

Sixth. The conditions of "reconciliation" that the federal government is trying to impose on us are unacceptable to our organization. We will not lay down our arms until the demands that we made at the beginning of our struggle are met. Rather, as conditions for the beginning of a dialogue, we propose the following:

(1) Recognition of the EZLN as a belligerent force.

(2) A cease-fire by both parties throughout the war zone.

(3) The withdrawal of federal troops from all communities, with full respect for the human rights of the rural population. The return of the troops to their home garrisons in various parts of the country.

(4) Cessation of the indiscriminate bombing of the rural population.

(5) On the basis of the three previous conditions, the formation of a national mediation commission.

Our troops are committed to respect these conditions if the government troops will do the same. If not, our troops will continue to fight on, until they reach Mexico City.

Our EZLN reiterates that we will continue to observe the laws of war established by the Geneva Convention with respect to the civilian population, the Red Cross, the press, the wounded, and enemy soldiers who surrender to our troops.

We are making a special call to the North American people and government. We call on the people to initiate actions in solidarity with our compatriots; we call on the government to suspend all economic and military aid to the Mexican federal government: it is dealing with a dictatorship that does not respect human rights, and any aid would be used to massacre the people of Mexico.

Mexicans: The military balance sheet up to January 5 shows the following results:

(1) Zapatista casualties: 9 dead and 20 badly wounded being taken care of in our field hospitals; an indeterminate number of slightly wounded who have returned to their combat posts; 12 missing in action. We have not included in this count our soldiers who were wounded and then, in cold blood, illegally executed with a shot in the head by officials of the Federal Army. The number of our compañeros who were killed in this way has not been determined as our troops are still fighting in Ocosingo.

(2) Enemy casualties (including police and federal soldiers): 27 dead, 40 wounded, and 180 prisoners who surrendered to our forces and were later released in good condition. There are at least 30 more federal soldiers dead, but that number is not confirmed. These losses, together with an undetermined number of wounded, occurred January 4 in the mountains to the south of San Cristóbal de las Casas, when bombs dropped by planes of the F.A.M. [Mexican Federal Army] fell on trucks carrying federal soldiers.

(3) Enemy war matériel destroyed or damaged: 3 F.A.M. attack helicopters (one in the municipal seat of Ocosingo, and two others at San Cristóbal de las Casas); 3 F.A.M. armed planes (all three at San Cristóbal de las Casas); 15 radio patrols; 15 transport vehicles; 4 state Judicial Police torture centers.

(4) Prisoners liberated: 230 from four jails which were attacked by

our forces (2 in San Cristobál de las Casas, 1 in Ocosingo, and 1 in Margaritas).

(5) War matériel captured: approximately 207 weapons of varied caliber (M-16, G-3, M-2, grenade launchers, shotguns, and pistols) and an undetermined amount of ammunition; 1,266 kilograms of dynamite; 10,000 TNT detonators; more than 20 transport vehicles; an undetermined number of radio communication systems used by the police, army, and air force.

To the national and international press:

We call to the attention of the honest national and international press the genocide that the federal armed forces are carrying out in the municipalities of San Cristóbal de las Casas, Ocosingo, Altamirano, and Margaritas, as well as on the roads in the surrounding areas, where they are indiscriminately killing civilians and then later presenting the bodies as EZLN casualties. Some of the Zapatistas that the army claims to have killed still enjoy perfect health. The attitude of the federal troops in these cities contrasts with that of our forces, who are careful (as the civilians of these cities can testify) to protect innocent lives. Most of the destruction of public and private buildings that has been attributed to Zapatista forces was done by the federal troops when they entered the four municipalities.

To the Federal Army:

The present conflict unmasks, once again, the face of the Federal Army and reveals its true character and purpose: indiscriminate repression, the violation of all human rights, and the total lack of military ethics and honor. The Federal Army's murders of women and children in the combat zone show the world an army out of control. We call on the officers and troops of the army to refuse to carry out orders to exterminate civilians and to summarily execute the wounded and prisoners of war, and instead to maintain your own military honor and ethics. We reiterate our invitation to you to abandon the ranks of the bad government and to join the just cause of the people, who, as you yourselves have seen, only want to live in peace with justice or to die with dignity. We have respected the lives of the soldiers and police who have surrendered to our forces, while you take pleasure in summarily executing the wounded Zapatistas, unable to fight, who fall into your hands or those who surrender. If you begin to attack our families and do not respect the wounded and prisoners, we will begin to do the same.

To the people of Mexico:

Finally, we call all workers, poor peasants, teachers, students, progressive and honest intellectuals, housewives, professionals, and all independent political organizations to join our struggle in your own way using your own methods, so that we can win the justice and freedom that all Mexicans desire.

We will not turn in our arms!
We want justice, not pardon or charity!

From the mountains of the Mexican Southeast
CCRI-CG of the EZLN, Mexico
January 1994
(Signed) Subcomandante Marcos

• 4 •
"OUR VOICE BEGAN ITS JOURNEY CENTURIES AGO . . ."

**Communiqué from the CCRI-CG of the EZLN, Mexico
January 11, 1994**

**"Our voice began its journey centuries ago
and will never again be silenced."**

To the people of Mexico
To the peoples and governments of the world

Brothers and sisters,

We have learned that our January 6, 1994, communiqué has already been published, at least in part, in the national and international press. New things have happened between January 6 and today, January 11, 1994, so, once again, we say our words so that others may hear.

First. One of the things that happened is that Sr. Aguilar Talamantes, candidate for president of the republic from the so-called Cardenista Front of National Reconstruction Party, in a public act in the city of San Cristóbal de las Casas, declared that he was offering his party as the "peaceful branch" of the EZLN and that he, Aguilar Talamantes, was nominating himself as the EZLN's candidate for the presidency of the republic. We, the members of the CCRI-CG of the EZLN, have analyzed these declarations and we think it's right to speak to this matter, and what we say is this:

The EZLN did not rise up in arms in order to support one or another candidate for the presidency of the republic. The EZLN doesn't seek the victory of any party; the EZLN seeks justice, freedom, and democracy so that the people can elect the person who best suits them, and so that this decision, whatever it may be, will receive the respect and understanding of all Mexicans and everybody else. The EZLN asks that the government, of whatever party, be a legitimate government, resulting from a truly free and democratic election, and that it meet the most urgent needs of our Mexican people, especially the needs of us, the indigenous peoples.

The EZLN respectfully rejects the proposals of the Cardenista Front of National Reconstruction Party to represent itself as "the peaceful branch" of the EZLN, and of Sr. Aguilar Talamantes to be the EZLN's candidate for the presidency of the republic. We say, too, once and for all, that we reject any other nomination or self-nomination to speak for us; our voice began its journey centuries ago and will never again be silenced.

On the other hand, we greet and welcome all attempts and proposals, made in good faith and honesty, for mediation between the EZLN and the federal government.

Second. To our proposal to open the dialogue by initiating a cease-fire on both sides, the Federal Army answered by bombing rural communities in the towns of Ocosingo, Las Margaritas, and Altamirano. The belief, in some sectors of the government, that it is possible and desirable to reach a military solution to the conflict through the total extermination of our EZLN is gaining ground among those who rule the country. We reiterate our willingness to dialogue, with the stipulations indicated in the January 6 communiqué. But it seems that this disposition toward dialogue on the part of the EZLN has been mistakenly interpreted by the military authorities of the government as a sign of weakness. Nothing could be further from the truth: to proposals for dialogue, we respond with willingness to dialogue; to indiscriminate attacks and bombings, we respond with our guns. If the government continues trying to deceive the public, saying that our fall and elimination are close, well that's the government's business—it has deceived before and now everyone is paying for the lies. But we know that our struggle will never end, not even with the last drop of blood of the last one of our combatants. If the federal government is inclined to be paid in blood for our demands for justice, freedom, and democracy, we will not hesitate to pay the price.

If there are no indications that the willingness to dialogue on the part of the federal government is anything more than lying words, in the next few days we will give orders to all our active and reserve forces to attack all the cities they find within their reach. We do not doubt that the cost will be high, but they keep forcing us down this road.

Third. In the past few days we've learned of various terrorist attempts on civilian targets in different parts of the country. These attempts are being attributed to members of our EZLN. The CCRI-CG of the EZLN declares that the Zapatista troops fight against police and the Federal Army and not against parking lots in commercial centers. Zapatista troops will not attack any civilian targets.

Fourth. On January 10, 1994, the federal government announced changes in the department of state and other federal departments. It announced that Patrocinio González Blanco Garrido, the secretary of state and former governor of Chiapas, was leaving office and named Manuel Camacho Solís as Peace Envoy to resolve the Chiapas conflict. The EZLN hereby declares that it doesn't know Sr. Camacho Solís, but if this man has an honest and true desire to seek a just political solution to the conflict, we welcome his nomination and reiterate to him our willingness to dialogue on the terms expressed in the January 6, 1994 communiqué.

Fifth. The CCRI-CG of the EZLN declares that documents sent by the EZLN will be valid and recognized by all Zapatista combatants only if they have the signature of compañero Subcomandante Insurgente Marcos.

From the mountains of the Mexican Southeast
Mexico, January 1994

• 5 •
"HOPE ALSO LIVES IN OUR HEART"

CCRI-CG of the EZLN, January 12, 1994

"Hope also lives in our heart."

To the people of Mexico
To the peoples and governments of the world

Brothers and sisters,

Today, January 12, 1994, we learned that Sr. Carlos Salinas de Gortari, in his role as Supreme Commander of the Federal Army, ordered a cease-fire of federal troops. The secretary of national defense added that they would continue with air and land patrols, that they would not abandon the positions that they currently occupy, and that they would impede the movement of our combatants.

The CCRI-CG of the EZLN hails this decision of Sr. Salinas de Gortari and sees it as a first step toward initiating the dialogue between the warring parties.

The conditions proposed by the CCRI-CG of the EZLN in its January 6, 1994, communiqué as requirements for initiating the dialogue have not been totally fulfilled. However, Carlos Salinas de Gortari's declaration is a beginning.

In return, the CCRI-CG of the EZLN, the collective and supreme leader of rebel Zapatista troops, hereby orders:

First. All regular, irregular, and urban command units of the various branches and services of the EZLN are ordered to suspend all offensive operations against federal troops and the positions that said troops now occupy.

Second. All regular, irregular, and urban command units of the various branches and services of the EZLN are ordered to maintain the positions they now occupy and respond firmly and decisively if they are attacked by Federal Army troops by land or air.

Third. The EZLN's offensive cease-fire order will be carried out the moment that this communiqué is received, and until then the CCRI-CG of the EZLN will maintain itself as it considers to be prudent and necessary.

Fourth. We will under no circumstances turn in our weapons nor surrender our forces to the bad government. This cease-fire is intended to alleviate the situation of the civilian population in the combat zone, and to open channels of dialogue with all progressive and democratic sectors of Mexico.

Our struggle is righteous and true; it is not a response to personal interests, but to the will for freedom of all the Mexican people and of the indigenous people in particular. We want justice and we will carry on because hope also lives in our heart.

From the mountains of the Mexican Southeast
CCRI-CG of the EZLN

• 6 •
"NO LONGER WILL WE LIVE ON BENDED KNEES"

**Communiqué from the CCRI-CG of the EZLN, Mexico
January 13, 1994**

**"We want peace with justice, respect, and dignity.
No longer will we live on bended knees."**

To the people of Mexico
To the peoples and governments of the world

Brothers and sisters,

In the past few days, various statements have been made concerning the people who might form part of a mediation commission to arrive at a political solution to the current situation in the combat zones in the southeast of Mexico. A supposed communiqué, erroneously attributed to the EZLN, published by the national daily *La Jornada*, proposed as intermediaries the following people: the Bishop of San Cristóbal de las Casas, Chiapas, Sr. Samuel Ruiz García; the Guatemalan indigenous woman and Nobel Prize winner Rigoberta Menchú; and the journalist Julio Scherer, editor of the magazine *Proceso*. Other voices and proposals have been heard but we have not put in our word until now. We think it's time to make public our thinking on this subject:

In order to be accepted by the CCRI-CG of the EZLN, the members of the mediation commission should meet the following requirements:

First. They must be Mexicans by birth. We think problems among Mexicans should be resolved by Mexicans, without outside involvement, even if the foreigners might be honest, upright men and women.

Second. They must not belong to any political party. We don't want our righteous struggle to be used by any party for its own electoral advantage, nor do we want the heart of our cause to be misinterpreted.

Third. Publicly, they must maintain a neutral stance in relation to the current armed conflict. That is, they must be in favor of neither the federal government nor the EZLN, and they must not be part of the organizational structure of either.

Fourth. They must be sensitive to the serious social problems that plague our country, and especially to the suffering of the indigenous people of Mexico.

Fifth. They must be recognized by the public as honest and patriotic.

Sixth. They must make a public commitment to make every effort to achieve a decent political solution to this armed conflict.

Seventh. They must form this National Mediation Commission in order to mediate between the government and the EZLN.

The CCRI-CG of the EZLN believes that the Bishop of the Diocese of San Cristóbal de las Casas, Sr. Samuel Ruiz García, fulfills the above-mentioned requirements, and we hereby formally invite him to participate, as a patriotic Mexican (and not as a religious authority, since this is not a religious problem) in the future National Mediation Commission.

The CCRI-CG of the EZLN asks Mexican society to propose its best men and women to form part of this commission, whose principal mission would be to find a political solution to the conflict. If these men and women fulfill the requirements mentioned above, the EZLN will welcome their participation on the National Mediation Commission and will listen attentively and respectively to the commission's voice and heart.

From the mountains the Mexican Southeast
CCRI-CG of the EZLN

• 7 •
"THE MOUTH OF THE POWERFUL LIES ONCE AGAIN"

Communiqué from the CCRI-GC of the EZLN, Mexico January 13, 1994

"The mouth of the powerful lies once again."

To the people of Mexico
To the peoples and governments of the world

Brothers and sisters,

Today, January 13, 1994, at approximately 1:30 p.m., troops of the Federal Army violated the cease-fire ordered by the federal executive, Carlos Salinas de Gortari, when they attacked a Zapatista unit at a place near the community of Carmen Pataté, in the municipality of Ocosingo, Chiapas. Federal troops, transported in ten army trucks, with the support of armed helicopters and planes, tried to penetrate our positions and were repelled by Zapatista rifles. Then federal troops began to arrest civilians who live in communities close to the battle, no doubt intending to retaliate against these noncombatants or in order to present them as captured Zapatista soldiers, as they have done before.

In yesterday's communiqué, the CCRI-CG of the EZLN answered Sr. Carlos Salinas de Gortari's gesture of decreeing a cease-fire on the part of federal troops by ordering Zapatista troops to cease all offensive fire. In that communiqué we ordered our troops not to initiate offensive action and only to respond if they were attacked by troops of the bad government. With today's aggressive act by federal troops on the Zapatistas, the supposed good will of the federal government to seek a political solution to the conflict remains in serious doubt. The EZLN reiterates its willingness to dialogue, but it is not willing to let itself be fooled. Either Sr. Salinas de Gortari is lying, or the Federal Army is not willing to follow orders from the executive branch of the federal government.

The CRIC-CG of the EZLN alerts the people of Mexico and the peoples and governments of the world not to allow themselves to be misled by the declarations of the federal government, which, as today's events show, are words of deceit.

From the mountains of the Mexican Southeast
CCRI-CG of the EZLN
Mexico, January 1994

· 8 ·
LETTER TO BILL CLINTON
AND THE PEOPLE OF THE U.S.A.

January 13, 1994

To Mr. Bill Clinton
   President of the United States of North America
To the North American Congress
To the people of the United States of North America

Sirs,

We address you to inform you that the federal government of Mexico is using the economic and military aid that it receives from the people and government of the United States of North America to massacre the indigenous people of Chiapas.

We wonder if the United States Congress and the people of the United States of North America approved this military and economic aid to fight the drug traffic or to murder indigenous people in the Mexican Southeast. Troops, planes, helicopters, radar, communications technology, weapons and military supplies are currently being used not to pursue drug traffickers and the big kingpins of the drug mafia, but rather to repress the righteous struggle of the people of Mexico and of the indigenous people of Chiapas in the Southeast of our country, and to murder innocent men, women, and children.

We don't receive any aid from foreign governments, people, or organizations. We have nothing to do with national or international drug trafficking or terrorism. We organized ourselves of our own volition, because of our enormous needs and problems. We are tired of so many years of deception and death. It is our right to fight for a dignified life. At all times we have abided by the international laws of war and respected the civilian population.

The support that the North American people and government offer the Mexican federal government does nothing but stain your hands with indigenous blood. Our desire is the same as the rest of the world's peoples: true freedom and democracy. And for this passion we are willing to give our lives. Do not cover your hands with our blood by being accomplices of the Mexican government.

From the mountains of the Mexican Southeast
CCRI-CG of the EZLN
Mexico, January 1994

• 9 •
"WAR IS A MATTER OF POLITICS"

For the national newspaper *La Jornada*
For the national newspaper *El Financiero*
For the local newspaper *El Tiempo* of San Cristóbal de las Casas

January 13, 1994

Sirs,

I now address myself to you. The CCRI-CG of the EZLN has sent out a series of communiqués to the national and international press. The compañeros of the CCRI-CG of the EZLN have asked me to look into, once again, the form in which these documents arrive at their destinations and become public knowledge. We are approaching you to see if it is possible to bring these documents into the public domain by way of your newspapers. They contain our position statements concerning the events that occurred between January 7 and January 13, 1994. I clarify this point because, in order to get to you, the package of documents has to travel for days along ancient trails and steep dirt roads, through mountains and valleys, pass war tanks, military vehicles, and thousands of olive-green uniforms—in other words, these letters must get through the complete war arsenal with which they try to intimidate us. They forget that war is not a matter of weapons or of large numbers of armed men, but of politics. Anyway, the point is that these documents and this letter will take a few days to reach your hands, if, in fact, they do arrive.

We're still all right; in these documents we reiterate our willingness to dialogue toward a fair solution of the conflict. Other than that, we have been pretty much immobilized by all the military paraphernalia with which the federal government is trying to cover up the giant sewer of injustice and corruption that our actions have uncovered. The peace that some are now seeking was always war for us; it seems that the great lords of land, business, industry, and money are bothered that the Indians are going to die in the cities and stain the streets that until now were dirtied only by the wrappings of imported products. They prefer that the Indians continue to die in the mountains, far away from good consciences and tourists. It will not be like that anymore: the prosperity of the few cannot be based on the poverty of the many. Now the comfortable will have to share our fate, for better or worse. They had the chance before to open their eyes and do something to stop the enormous historic injustice that the country imposed on its original inhabitants, but they didn't see the Indian as anything other than an anthropological object, a curiosity for tourists, part of a *"Jurassic Park"* (is that how it's spelled?), which, luckily, would disappear with a NAFTA that includes them only as disposable waste, because the death of those in the mountains doesn't matter much.

They are all guilty, from the top federal functionaries down to the last corrupt "indigenous" leader, who, not freely elected by the Chiapan people, passes himself off as a governor. Guilty are the mayors concerned more with decorative projects and tightening their relationships with important men than governing their people, and all levels of functionaries who deny health, education, land, housing, services, fair work, food, justice, and above all, respect and dignity to those who, before them, populated these lands. They forgot that human dignity is not the birthright of only those who have their primary needs satisfied; those who have nothing material also have a right to that which makes us different from things and animals: dignity. But it's fair to acknowledge that in the middle of this sea of indifference there were, and are, voices raised in alarm about what these injustices might bring. Among these voices was, and is, that of honest journalism, which still exists, nationally and locally. In short, as I must be boring some people, it seems that you already have enough problems trying to convince the Federal Army to let you do your journalistic work. To put it simply, then, what we want is peace with dignity and justice.

They don't frighten us with their tanks, planes, helicopters, their thousands of soldiers. The same injustice that has us without highways, roads, and basic services now turns against them. We don't need highways; we've always journeyed on steep trails and dirt tracks. Not even with all the federal soldiers would they be able to close all the roads on which our misery used to travel and our rebellion now travels. Nor do the lies of the press and television affect us. Perhaps they forget the *real* percentages of illiteracy in the state of Chiapas? How many homes do not have electricity, and therefore television, in these lands?

If the nation lets itself be misled again by these lies, at least one of us will always remain to wake it up again. The Clandestine Revolutionary Indigenous Committees are indestructible; they have had a chain of command since they were formed. If one falls, another will take its place, and future replacements will get ready. They will have to wipe out everybody, absolutely everybody, to stop us by military methods. And always they will have to live with the doubt as to whether there is one of us left somewhere who might start up everything all over again.

I will not distract you any longer. I hope that the "description" of "Comandante Marcos" hasn't brought mishap to more "innocent people" (double or nothing that with this "description" they're going to end up arresting the actor who plays "Juan Diablo" in the soap opera *Wild Heart* on the channel—*"but of course"*—"of the stars"). A question: Will all this at least serve to teach Mexicans to say "Chiapas" instead of "Chapas" and "Tzeltales" instead of "Setsales"?

Your health and a hug, if there is still a place and a way for that.

Subcomandante Insurgente Marcos

• 10 •
FEDERAL ARMY CONTINUES TO VIOLATE CEASE-FIRE

**Communiqué from the CCRI-CG of the EZLN
January 17, 1994**

To the people of Mexico
To the people and governments of the world

We are sending this message to the national and international press to denounce new violations of the cease-fire by federal troops.

On January 16, 1994, at approximately 11:30 am, 35 troop transport vehicles, carrying about 400 Federal Army soldiers, assaulted the municipal seat of Oxchuc and arrested more than 12 civilians, unjustly accusing them of being part of our EZLN. The CCRI-CG of the EZLN denounces the Federal Army for taking on judicial duties that do not belong to it, and for terrifying the civilian population. The superior, abusive attitude of the Federal Army when it assaults the civilian population constitutes a flagrant violation of the cease-fire ordered by their supreme commander on January 12, 1994. The night of January

16, 1994, Mexican air-force planes bombed small communities near the town of Monte Libano, in the municipality of Ocosingo. Violations of the cease-fire continue to affect the civilian population.

Our troops are obeying orders of the CCRI-CG of the EZLN to cease all offensive fire against the Federal Army. We continue to be willing to dialogue in search of a just solution to this conflict, but it is our obligation to protect the civilian population in the combat zone and therefore we announce that if the Federal Army continues to violate the cease-fire, we will reconsider the orders to our troops to stop all offensive fire.

We ask that the compliance of all federal troops with the cease-fire be monitored by members of the federal government, since these repeated violations may ruin the process of dialogue that has recently begun.

From the mountains of the Mexican Southeast
CCRI-CG
Mexico, January 1994
Subcomandante Marcos

• 11 •

MESSAGE TO SAMUEL RUIZ GARCÍA AND MANUEL CAMACHO SOLÍS

**Communiqué from the CCRI-CG of the EZLN, Mexico
January 18, 1994**

To Sr. Samuel Ruiz García
    National Mediation Commissioner
To Sr. Manuel Camacho Solís
    Envoy for Peace and Reconciliation in Chiapas

The CCRI-CG of the EZLN respectfully addresses you to say the following:

First. Through the media we have heard that Salinas de Gortari has proposed an amnesty law to Congress.

Second. As we declared in the third point of our January 13, 1994, communiqué to Sr. Manuel Camacho Solís, "all proposals for dialogue or other matters that the federal government wants to take up with us, should be sent through Sr. Samuel Ruiz García, Bishop of the Archdioceses of San Cristóbal de las Casas. Only communications that we receive through Samuel Ruiz García will be considered valid by us; all others will be ignored." We have not received any written communication about the above-mentioned "amnesty law," and therefore we are not able to say anything official about its contents.

Third. From what we have managed to learn from the media about the "amnesty law," we can only say that, in general, we think it is premature, and that the dialogue process should first consider the political and social causes that produced our movement.

Fourth. We sincerely ask that the dialogue process continue at its own time and pace, just as Sr. Manuel Camacho Solís has publicly requested on several occasions.

Fifth. We remind you that the previous conditions for beginning a dialogue for a just political solution of the conflict have not been completely met, as the Federal Army remains outside its garrisons and continues to violate the cease-fire, threatening our forces and the civilian population.

Sixth. We think that the process you two have begun is leading to justice and respect. We salute your effort and we reiterate our willingness, for the good of our people and the whole nation, to listen and to keep open all possible channels of communication.

Respectfully,
From the mountains the Mexican Southeast
CCRI-CG of the EZLN
Mexico, January 1994
Subcomandante Marcos

• 12 •
MESSAGE TO
MANUEL CAMACHO SOLÍS

**Communiqué from the CCRI-CG of the EZLN
January 18, 1994**

To Sr. Manuel Camacho Solís
    Envoy for Peace and Reconciliation in Chiapas

Sr. Camacho Solís,

The CCRI-CG of the EZLN addresses you again:

We have attentively and respectfully heard your words on the radio in response to our letter dated January 13, 1994. We need to think hard and analyze some of the things you said in order to say what we truly believe. Our complete response to what you are trying to do will have to wait for some time, since we have not yet received a written communication and we only have what you said on the radio. Nevertheless, in general we see great value in your answer and we salute the spirit of your words. Therefore, the CCRI-CG of the EZLN declares:

First. The CCRI-CG of the EZLN officially recognizes Sr. Manuel Camacho Solís as the Envoy for Peace and Reconciliation in Chiapas.

Second. The CCRI-CG of the EZLN recognizes Sr. Manuel Camacho Solís as a faithful mediator, and we will receive all of his words and thoughts attentively and respectfully; we will analyze them honestly and carefully, and we will answer them formally and truthfully.

Third. The CCRI-CG of the EZLN, in keeping with its official recognition of Sr. Manuel Camacho Solís as Envoy for Peace and Reconciliation in Chiapas, guarantees him free movement within the territories under the control of the EZLN, and guarantees that his person and effects will be fully respected by Zapatista troops.

Respectfully,
From the mountains the Mexican Southeast
CCRI-CG of the EZLN
Mexico, January 1994
Subcomandante Marcos

• 13 •
"WHO MUST ASK FOR PARDON AND WHO CAN GRANT IT?"

To the national weekly *Proceso*
To the national newspaper *La Jornada*
To the national newspaper *El Financiero*
To the local newspaper *El Tiempo*, San Cristóbal de las Casas

January 18, 1994

Sirs,

I ought to begin with a few apologies (a bad beginning, my grandmother would say). Because of a mistake by our press office, we did not send my last letter to the weekly *Proceso*. I hope the people at *Proceso* will understand this oversight, and that they will receive this note without rancor, resentment, or re-etcetera.

First, I would like to direct your attention to the enclosed communications from the EZLN. They refer to repeated violations of the cease-fire by the Federal Army, the offer of amnesty by the federal government, and the appointment of Camacho Solís as the Envoy for Peace and Reconciliation in Chiapas.

I believe that you have already received the documents we sent you on January 13. I don't know what reaction those documents will provoke, or what the response of the federal government will be to our demands, so I don't make reference to them in this letter. Up until today, January 18, 1994, the only thing we have heard about is the federal government's formal offer of pardon to our troops.

Why do we have to be pardoned? What are we going to be pardoned for? Of not dying of hunger? Of not being silent in our misery? Of not humbly accepting our historic role of being the despised and the outcast? Of having picked up arms after we found all other roads closed? Of not having paid attention to the Chiapas Penal Code, one of the most absurd and repressive in history? Of having demonstrated to the rest of the country and the entire world that human dignity still lives, even among some of the world's poorest peoples? Of having been well prepared before we began our uprising? Of having carried guns into battle, rather than bows and arrows? Of being Mexicans? Of being primarily indigenous people? Of having called on the people of Mexico to struggle, in all possible ways, for that which belongs to them? Of having fought for freedom, democracy, and justice? Of not following the example of previous guerrilla armies? Of not giving up? Of not selling out? Of not betraying ourselves?

Who must ask for pardon and who can grant it? Those who for years and years have satiated themselves at full tables, while death sat beside us so regularly that we finally stopped being afraid of it? Those who filled our pockets and our souls with promises and empty declarations?

Or should we ask pardon from the dead, our dead, those who died "natural" deaths of "natural causes" like measles, whooping cough, breakbone fever, cholera, typhoid, mononucleosis, tetanus, pneumonia, malaria, and other lovely gastrointestinal and lung diseases? Our dead, the majority dead, the democratically dead, dying from sorrow because no one did anything, because the dead, our dead, went just like that, without anyone even counting them, without anyone saying, "ENOUGH!" which would have at least given some meaning to their deaths, a meaning which no one ever sought for them, the forever dead, who are now dying again, but this time in order to live?

Must we ask pardon from those who have denied us the right and ability to govern ourselves? From those who lack respect for our customs, our culture, and ask us for papers and obedience to a law whose existence and moral basis we do not accept? Those who pressure us, torture us, assassinate us, disappear us for the serious "crime" of wanting a piece of land, neither a big one nor a small one, but a simple piece of land on which we can grow something to fill our stomachs?

Who must ask for pardon and who can grant it?

The president of the republic? State officials? Senators? Representatives? Governors? Mayors? Police? The Federal Army? The great gentlemen of banking, industry, commerce, and land? Political parties? Intellectuals? *Galio* and *Nexus?* The mass media? Students? Teachers? People in the neighborhoods? Workers? Farmworkers? Indigenous people? Those who died uselessly?

Who must ask for pardon and who can grant it?

Well, that is all for now.

Good health and a hug, and in this kind of cold weather you should be thankful for both . . . (I believe), even though they come from a "professional of violence."

Subcomandante Insurgente Marcos

82

• 14 •

THE SUP WILL TAKE OFF HIS MASK, IF MEXICO TAKES OFF ITS MASK

To the national weekly *Proceso*
To the national newspaper *La Jornada*
To the national newspaper *El Financiero*
To the local newspaper *El Tiempo*, San Cristóbal de las Casas

January 20, 1994

Sirs,

We tried to get close to you, hoping to make personal contact with Sr. Camacho Solís, but we had to back off as a result of heavy pressure from the Federales.[*] Thus our letters are late again. I enclose here another series of communiqués: one addressed to other Chiapan indigenous organizations, another to the people of Mexico, one more about the continuing trial of General Absalón Castellanos Domínguez (which I just received from the Zapatista Tribunal of Justice), and the last one to Samuel Ruiz García and Manuel Camacho Solís. Thanks in advance for seeing to it that they are published.

Time is short and the gates are closing. It is getting difficult to send you things to let you know more about us than just ski-masks, wooden rifles, spears, and "the terrible goat horns" [machine guns with magazines shaped like goat horns]. Protected by the so-called "cease-fire," the *federales* are weaving an apparatus of military intelligence and repression that will allow them to make a spectacular hit against us, and thereby hide their stupidity in combat and their abuses of the civilian population. The Mexican army is tempted to use "commando" military actions to find our central command group and destroy it. We foresaw such a plan years ago. If they are successful in destroying our central command, nothing fundamental will change: through our chain of command and the omnipresence of the Clandestine Committees of Indigenous Revolutionaries, we will eventually rise up again after any attack, no matter how spectacular or crushing it may appear.

Well, I finally got a few hours to read a few of the publications that someone was good enough to send me (the arrival of subscriptions or people selling newspapers in the mountains of the Southeast is as improbable as an empty seat in the Mexican City metro during rush hour). I now realize—from way up here—that the ski-masks and the "obscure" intentions of the Zapatistas have provoked great anguish among you. I have abused you, consciously, by pulling you into this dialogue. Nevertheless, I believe that this correspondence, though ill-timed and inconvenient, has been good for everyone.

Now the horizon is beginning to darken and every line could be the last one. So, at the risk of abusing you again, I would like to take this opportunity to touch upon some matters, however briefly. Thank you if you read them, and even more thanks if you publish them. Up here, it is a bad time, and we could be near the end.

I have the honor to have as my superiors the best men and women of the various ethnic groups: Tzeltal, Tzotzil, Chol, Tojolabal, Mam, and Zoque. I have lived with them for over ten years and I am proud to obey and serve them with my arms and soul. They have taught me a lot more than what they now teach the country and the whole world. They are my commanders and I will follow them down any path they choose. They are the collective and democratic leadership of the EZLN, and their acceptance of a dialogue is as true as their fighting hearts and their concern about being tricked once again.

The EZLN has neither the desire nor the capacity to bring together all the Mexican people around its own project. But it has the capacity and the desire to add its weight to the national force that inspires the people of our country to fight for justice, democracy, and freedom.

If we have to choose between paths, we will always choose the path of dignity. If we can find the way to a dignified peace, we will follow the road that leads to it. If a dignified war is our only choice, we will grab our weapons and fight it. If we can find a life of dignity, we will continue to live. If, on the other hand, dignity means death, then without hesitation we will go to meet it.

What the EZLN is seeking for the indigenous people of Chiapas, every honest organization in the whole country should seek for all

Mexicans. What the EZLN is seeking with weapons, all honest organizations should seek with their own forms of struggle.

We will not take the country hostage. We do not want, nor do we have the capacity, to impose our ideas on civil society through armed force (in the same way that the current government, through the force of arms, imposes its own project on the country). We will not obstruct the upcoming election.

When an armed political force (like the Mexican federal government) asks another armed political force (like the one from the EZLN) to turn in their guns, that means, in political and military terms, a request for unconditional surrender. In exchange for this unconditional surrender, the federal government offers us the same as always: an adjustment of internal accounts, a package of declarations, some promises, and more bureaucratic dependency.

We are suspicious of the request "to lay down our weapons." Mexican and Latin American history teaches us that those who turn in their arms, trusting the "forgiveness" of their pursuers, end up mutilated by some death squad or political faction or the government. Why shouldn't we believe the same will happen here?

We think that revolutionary change in Mexico is not just a question of one kind of activity. It will come, strictly speaking, from neither an armed revolution nor an unarmed one. It will be the result of struggles on several fronts, using a lot of methods, various social forms, with different levels of commitment and participation. And the result will not be the triumph of a party, organization, or alliance of organizations with their particular social programs, but rather the creation of a democratic space for resolving the confrontations between different political proposals. This democratic space will have three fundamental premises that are already historically inseparable: the democratic right of determining the dominant social project, the freedom to subscribe to one project or another, and the requirement that all projects must point the way to justice.

Revolutionary change in Mexico will not follow a strict calendar; it could be a hurricane that hits after a long period of quiet, or a series of social battles that slowly destroy the forces opposed to them. Revolutionary change in Mexico will not be under the sole command of only one homogenous group and its great leader; rather leadership will be shared by various groups that change over time but that all rotate around a common goal: the utopia of democracy, freedom, and justice which will or will not be the new Mexico. There will be social peace only if there is justice and dignity for everyone.

The current peace process is driven not by the political will of the federal government or by our supposed political-military force (which is still a mystery to most people), but rather by the firm action of what is called Mexican civil society. And the future actions of Mexican civil society, not the will of government or the force of our arms, will determine the possibilities of democratic change in Mexico.

Epilogue: "Ski-masks and other masks"

Why so much scandal about the ski-masks? Isn't Mexican political culture a "culture of hidden faces"? But in order to put a stop to the growing anguish of those who are afraid (or who wish) that some "komrade" or cartoon villain might be the one who appears from behind the ski-mask and the "prominent nose" (as *La Jornada* calls it) of the "sup" (as the compañeros say), I propose the following: I am willing to take off my mask if Mexican society takes off the foreign mask that it anxiously put on years ago. What will happen? The predictable: Mexican civil society (excluding the Zapatistas who know him—in image, thought, word, and action—perfectly well already) will learn, with some disappointment, that "sup-Marcos" is neither a foreigner nor as handsome as the "media affiliate" of the PGR* has been saying. But when Mexican civil society takes off its own mask it will realize, with much greater impact, that it has been sold an image of itself that is fake, and that the reality is more terrifying than people supposed. If we show each other our faces, the big difference will be that the "sup-Marcos" always knew what he looked like, while civil society will have to wake up from the long and lazy dream that "modernity" imposes on everything and everybody. "Sup-Marcos" is ready to take off his ski-mask; is Mexican civil society ready to take off its mask? Don't miss the next episode of this story of masks and faces, affirmed and denied (if the planes, helicopters, and olive-green masks allow it).

That is all—but a lot is missing. This could be the final episode of a very short exchange of letters between the ski-mask with a prominent nose and some of the best of the honest Mexican press.

Greetings and sorry I cannot give you a hug because it could raise jealousy and suspicion.

Subcomandante Insurgente Marcos

• 15 •
EZLN CONDITIONS AND AGENDA OF DIALOGUE

**Communiqué of the CCRI-CG of the EZLN, Mexico
January 20, 1994**

To Samuel Ruiz García,
  Nationally Appointed Mediator
To Manuel Camacho Solís,
  Envoy for Peace and Reconciliation in Chiapas

Sirs,

The CCRI-CG of the EZLN addresses you once again to say the following:

First. We have not yet received any written communication about the so-called "amnesty law," and therefore we are still unable to comment on it. But whatever its contents might be, we want to tell you that the "amnesty law" does not affect, nor will it affect, our willingness to dialogue for a just political solution to the current conflict. That is to say, we are not limited in any way by that "law," and independent of it, we will continue forward in the dialogue process. As the "law" does not prevent us from sitting down and discussing a political solution to our struggle, let's continue the dialogue process.

Second. After the January 18, 1994, letter from Manuel Camacho Solís, we have not received any other written communication from the Commission for Peace and Reconciliation in Chiapas. We remind you that only written communications that come through Samuel Ruiz García will be considered valid by us.

Third. The CCRI-CG carefully read the letter, dated January 18, 1994, from Manuel Camacho Solís, the Envoy for Peace and Reconciliation in Chiapas. We have a question about this letter. What does the federal government believe that we represent in the dialogue? A belligerent force? A political force? We need to know this in order to know what guarantees we will have about the dialogue process and about the government's compliance with any agreements that might eventually come from the dialogue. It is not clear how we are seen by Sr. Manuel Camacho Solís in his letter of January 18, 1994.

Fourth. The CCRI-CG of the EZLN declares that we hold absolutely no hostages. We have only one prisoner of war, General Absalón Castellanos Domínguez, whose release is now being processed and who you will hear more about at the opportune time. When General Absalón Castellanos Domínguez is released, we will have under our power no prisoners and no hostages—neither soldiers, nor policemen, nor civilians. All have been set free.

Fifth. The CCRI-CG of the EZLN has now been informed through the media that the Federal Army has withdrawn from the civilian zones it had occupied and has regrouped in its garrisons.

Sixth. The CCRI-CG of the EZLN declares that from January 17, 1994, until today, we have not registered a single violation of the cease-fire by federal troops.

Seventh. The CCRI-CG of the EZLN declares that all previous conditions have been met for beginning the dialogue of the Commission for Peace and Reconciliation in Chiapas, and we urge Manuel Camacho Solís and Samuel Ruiz García to begin work to open a true public dialogue with clear guarantees for the protection of the life, liberty, and free transit of those who might be nominated by the CCRI-CG of the EZLN to personally attend the dialogue meetings.

Eighth. Once Manuel Camacho Solís and Samuel Ruiz García have guaranteed the life, liberty, and free transit of the Zapatista delegates, we propose that the first point of the dialogue should be to establish by mutual agreement the agenda for the discussion and the time that it will begin.

Ninth. The CCRI-CG of the EZLN proposes the following agenda for the discussion:

(1) Economic demands. Everything regarding the grave material conditions of life which we, the indigenous people of Chiapas, suffer. The current situation, and the road to immediate and long- term solutions.

(2) Social demands. Everything regarding what we, the indigenous people of Chiapas, suffer: racism, marginalization, lack of respect, expulsion from our land, attacks against our culture and traditions, etc. The current situation and the road to a definitive solution.

(3) Political demands. Everything regarding the lack of legal space for real participation by us, the indigenous people of Chiapas and all Mexicans, in national political life. The current situation and the road to an immediate solution.

(4) The end to all hostilities and violent confrontations. Guarantees for both sides in the conflict.

We wait for your written answer to this letter.

From the mountains of the Mexican Southeast
CCRI-CG of the EZLN
Mexico, January 1994
Subcomandante Marcos

• 16 •
EZLN RESPECTS ALL FORMS OF HONEST STRUGGLE

**Communiqué from the CCRI-CG of the EZLN
January 20, 1994**

"The land that gives life and struggle belongs to all of us."

To our indigenous brothers and sisters in other organizations
To the people of Mexico
To the people and governments of the world

We address you, indigenous brothers and sisters of other independent and honest organizations of Chiapas and all of Mexico. We, the indigenous people of the CCRI-CG of the EZLN, speak to you in order to say the following:

First. We, the Zapatistas, have always respected and will continue to respect different honest and independent organizations. We have not obligated anyone to enter our struggle. All who have entered have done so of their own free will.

Second. We respect your form of struggle; we salute your independence and honesty, as long as they are authentic. We have taken up arms because they left us no other choice. You have our support if you continue on your own road, because we are struggling for the same thing, and the land that gives life and struggle belongs to all of us.

Third. Our form of armed struggle is just and true. If we had not lifted our rifles, the government would never have worried about the indigenous people of our lands and we would now continue to be not only poor, but forgotten. Now the government is very worried about the problems of indigenous people and campesinos, and that is good. But it was necessary for Zapatista rifles to speak so that Mexico could hear the voice of the poor people of Chiapas.

Fourth. We will continue respecting you and your forms of struggle. We invite you, your organizations, and your own independent forms of struggle to join in our heartfelt hope for freedom, democracy, and justice.

All organizations united in the same struggle!

From the mountains of the Mexican Southeast
CCRI-CG of the EZLN
Mexico, January 1994
Subcomandante Marcos

• 17 •
OUR FLAG JOINS OTHER FORCES UNDER THE MEXICAN FLAG

Communiqué from the CCRI-CG of the EZLN, Mexico
January 20, 1994

"We want all those who walk with truth, to walk together."

To the people of Mexico
To all honest and independent people, civil organizations,
    and democratic politicians of Mexico
To the peoples and governments of the world

Brothers and sisters,

The worthy struggle of the soldiers of the EZLN has received the sympathy of different people, organizations, and sectors of Mexican and international civil society. These progressive forces, through their honorable actions, have opened the possibility of a just political solution to the conflict that darkens our skies. Neither the political will of the federal executive nor the glorious military actions of our soldiers have been decisive in this turn of events. What have been crucial are the public demonstrations in the streets, mountains, and the media by many organizations, and by the honest independent people who are part of what is called Mexican civil society.

We, Mexico's last citizens and first patriots, have understood since the beginning that our problems, and those of the entire nation, can only be resolved through a national revolutionary movement with three principal demands: freedom, democracy, and justice.

Our form of struggle is not the only one; for many it may not even be an acceptable one. Other forms of struggle exist and have great value. Our organization is not the only one, for many it may not even be a desirable one. Other honest, progressive, and independent organizations exist and have great value. The Zapatista Army of National Liberation has never claimed that its form of struggle is the only legitimate one. It's just the only one we were left. The EZLN salutes the honest and necessary development of all forms of struggle that will lead us to freedom, democracy, and justice. The EZLN has never claimed its organization to be the only truthful, honest, and revolutionary one in Mexico, or even in Chiapas.

In fact, we organized ourselves this way because we were not left any other way. The EZLN salutes the honest and necessary development of all independent and progressive organizations that fight for freedom, democracy, and justice for the entire nation. There are, and will be, other revolutionary organizations. There are, and will be, other popular armies. We do not claim to be the one and only true historical vanguard. We do not claim that all honest Mexicans can fit under our Zapatista banner. We offer our flag. But there is a bigger and more powerful flag that can shelter us all. The flag of the national revolutionary movement can cover the most diverse tendencies, opinions, and different types of struggle, as long as they are united in a common desire and goal: freedom, democracy, and justice.

The EZLN calls on all Mexicans to unfurl this flag: not the flag of the EZLN, not the flag of the armed struggle, but the flag of all thinking beings, the flag that represents the reason and understanding of our people, the flag of freedom, democracy, and justice. Under this great flag our Zapatista flag will wave, under this great flag our rifles will be raised.

The struggle for freedom, democracy, and justice is not only the task of the EZLN, it is the task of all Mexicans and all honest, independent, and progressive organizations—each one on its own ground, each one with its own form of struggle, each one with its own organization and ideas.

All who walk in truth should walk together on a single path: the one that leads to freedom, democracy, and justice.

Our struggle did not end, nor was our cry silenced after we said, "Enough," on January 1, 1994. There is still more to go, the paths are different but the desire is one: Freedom! Democracy! Justice!

We will continue to struggle until we win the freedom that is our right, the democracy that is our reason, and the justice that is our life.

From the mountains of the Mexican Southeast
CCRI-CG
Mexico, January 1994

• 18 •
THE ZAPATISTA WOMEN'S UPRISING

To the national newspaper *La Jornada*
To the local newspaper *El Tiempo*
 of San Cristóbal de las Casas, Chiapas

January 26, 1994

Sr. Alvaro Cepeda Neri
 The column "Conjeturas"
 La Jornada, Mexico, D.F.
From Subcomandante Insurgente Marcos
 The mountains of the Mexican Southeast Chiapas

Sr. Cepeda Neri and family,

I acknowledge the receipt of your letter published in *La Jornada* on January 24, 1994. We thank you for your thoughts. Here we are well. Helicopters and airplanes come and go, draw near, look at us, we look at them, they pull away, come back again, and so it goes, day and night. The mountain protects us; the mountain has been our compañera for many years.

I would like to tell you about some things that happen around these parts that will surely never come out in the newspapers or magazines, as such publications are not interested in ordinary, everyday events. But there is, believe me, a daily heroism that makes possible the flashes of light which, now and then, illuminate our apparently mediocre national history.

A few hours ago I met with some members of the CCRI-CG. We argued about how to choose the delegates for the dialogue with the Commission for Peace and Reconciliation in Chiapas. Afterward we were looking at some newspapers that had arrived here (late, of course). The journalists' notes and comments provoked a lot of different reactions among us.

Javier, a Tsotzil who speaks deliberately as he searches for just the right word, read today about what happened in Tlalmanalco,* in the state of México. Indignant, he approached me and said, "We must invite these people to come here with us." I began to explain that we couldn't make such an invitation because those people are in a political party and we are not able to intervene in the internal affairs of other organizations, and besides it is very far away, and the reserve troops won't let them pass, and there wouldn't be enough beans for everybody, and on and on. Javier patiently waited for me to finish. Then he said to me, quite seriously, "I am not talking about the people of PRD." And he added, "I am talking about the police who beat them up." Squatting, he decrees, sentences, orders: "Invite those cops to come here. If they are true men they will come and fight us. Let's see if it is the same thing to fight us as it is to beat up innocent and peaceful people. Tell them, write that we will teach them to respect humble people."

Javier continued squatting before me, waiting for me to begin to write the letter to the state of Mexico's riot police. I didn't know what to do—at just that moment a guard told us that some newspapermen were coming and that they wanted to talk to someone. I excused myself from Javier to see who ought to speak to the newspaper people. The invitation to the riot police is still pending.

Now it is Angel, a Tzeltal whose great pride is that he finished Womak's book about Zapata ("It took me three years. I suffered, but I finished it," he says every time someone dares to doubt his prowess). He comes up behind me, brandishing a newspaper in his left hand (in his right hand he has an M-1). "I don't understand the words of this man," he protests to me. "He uses hard words, and it is not clear where he is going. It seems that he understands our struggle, but then it seems that he doesn't."

I look at the newspaper and Angel shows me a column by editor "x." I explain to Angel what the man is saying: that it is true that there is poverty in Chiapas, but it is not possible that indigenous people could have been so well prepared and could have risen up with a plan, that indigenous people always rise up spontaneously without a plan; and that means that foreigners and foreign countries are taking advantage of the poverty of indigenous people to speak badly of Mexico and its president, and that the EZLN may be among the indigenous people, but it doesn't represent them.

Angel started to jump around, so furious he couldn't manage to speak sensibly, his words—a mixture of Tzeltal dialect and Spanish—tripping all over each other. "Why do they always think we are like little children?" He throws the question in my face; I almost spill the half-cooked rice that a new cook has made "especially for the Sup." He calms down a little when I give him his plate of rice. "Why, according to them, are we not able to think for ourselves, or come up with a good plan, or put up a good fight?" I know the question is not for me; Angel knows the question is not for me; Angel knows well that the question is for the improbable *señor* who wrote the "profound article." We both know, Angel and I, that this and other questions will remain unanswered. "Perhaps intelligence only drops into the head of a *ladino*. Perhaps when our grandparents were around they couldn't think well either." Angel asks and asks. No one responds; no one ever will.

Susana, a Tzotzil, is angry. A while ago people were making fun of her. Some others from the CCRI-CG were saying that the first uprising of the EZLN in March 1993 was her fault. "I'm angry," she says to me. While I am trying to figure out what is going on, I hide behind a rock. "The compañeros say it was my fault that the Zapatistas rose up last year." I begin, cautiously, to come closer. After a while I discover what it is all about.

In March 1993, the compañeros were debating what later would be called the "Revolutionary Laws."* It was Susana's job to go to dozens of communities to speak to groups of women and get their thoughts on the "Laws of Women."* When the CCRI-CG met to vote on the laws, they got reports, one by one, from commissions on justice, agriculture, war taxes, the rights and obligations of people in struggle, and women. Susana read the proposals that she had put together from the thoughts of thousands of indigenous women.

She began to read, and as she progressed, the CCRI-CG assembly began to get more and more upset. You could hear people talking among themselves. Comments in Chol, Tzeltal, Tzotzil, Tojolabal, Mani, Zoque, and Spanish jumped from one side of the crowd to another. Susana didn't give in and continued attacking everyone and everything. "We don't want to be obligated to marry anyone we don't want to marry. We only want to have those children we can take care of and love. We want the right to be leaders in the community. We want the right to say what we think and to be respected. We want the right to study, and we even want the right to learn how to drive cars."

She went on until she was finished. When she was done there was a heavy silence. The "Laws of Women" that Susana had just finished reading meant a true revolution for indigenous communities. The women of the CCRI-CG were still receiving the translation—in their own dialects—of what Susana had said. The young men looked at one another; they were nervous and upset. Without planning to do so, the translators finished almost simultaneously and the compañeras delegated to vote began to applaud and talk among themselves.

It can't be said that the "Laws of Women" were approved unanimously. One Tzeltal delegate commented: "The good thing is that my woman doesn't understand Spanish . . . " A Tzotzil who was an infantry major and an official was on his back immediately: "You're screwed anyway because we are going to translate it into all the dialects." The compañero lowered his gaze. The women delegates were singing, the young men were scratching their heads. Prudently, I declared a recess.

This was the story, according to what Susana was telling me now, that came out when someone from the CCRI-CG read an article by some journalist saying that the proof that the EZLN was not authentically indigenous was that indigenous people couldn't possibly get it together to start their uprising on the 1st of January. Someone, as a joke, said that the 1st of January had not been the first uprising, rather it had been in March 1993. They were teasing Susana and she left with a bruising, "Oh, go fuck yourselves!" in Tzotzil that no one dared to translate. It's true. The first uprising of the EZLN was in March 1993 and it was led by the women Zapatistas. They suffered no losses and they won. A story from our part of the world.

In the middle of the night, Pedro, a Chol with a big mustache, comes up to me with a burning piece of pine in his right hand. He sits by my side. He says nothing while the light from the burning pine shines in his black eyes. "We have to go to Mexico City," he says to himself and to me. I start to scratch my head, thinking of the orders that would have to be given to begin the march, the routes we would follow, the losses we would suffer, the early morning entries into the cities, and the asphalt roads.

Pedro interrupts my thoughts. "City people say that Chiapas is different from other parts of Mexico, that here it is bad but that in the rest of Mexico it is okay." I look at him; he doesn't turn to look at me, but hands me the newspaper that he has in his hand. I look for my flashlight and begin to read an article that Pedro points out: the article says that our struggle is destined to fail because it is not a national struggle, and it is not national because our demands are local, indigenous.

"That's a poor argument," Pedro says. "Even poorer than we are. What we want is justice, but also freedom and democracy. And this man thinks that he isn't poor even though he is not truly able to elect his own governors. They feel sorry for us—the poor little people."

The pine burns between us. Pedro understands, I understand, the night understands . . . " The people in Mexico City don't understand. We have to go to Mexico City," Pedro says, as light from the burning pine illuminates his right side. The morning cold bites hard. A guard shouts, "Stop. Who lives?" "Our country," answers the other voice, and something warm happens among us.

Well, Señor Cepeda Neri, I wanted to use this letter to tell you this and some other things. But that is all for now. We hope that you and your family are well and healthy. Until next time—a rather improbable suggestion.

Health and respect to you and yours. *Vale.*
From the mountains of the Mexican Southeast
Subcomandante Insurgente Marcos

P.S.: Javier just came up to me enthusiastically to ask if this is the letter of invitation to the riot police of the state of México. I told him no, that it is for a journalist. "Ah," he says, disappointed. But he adds, forcefully, "Tell them not to forget us, that our truth is also theirs." *Vale.*

• 19 •
WE HAVE AN OPEN-DOOR POLICY

**Communiqué from the CCRI-CG of the EZLN
January 29, 1994**

To the national and international press

Sirs,

The CCRI-CG of the EZLN respectfully addresses you in order to propose the following:

First. As is generally known, the dialogue for peace between the EZLN and the federal government is about to begin, although the date and exact place are yet to be determined. There are already fundamental agreements about the talks between the CCRI-CG of the EZLN and the Envoy for Peace and Reconciliation in Chiapas. A few details have to be finalized and some previous agreements made concrete, but the basic questions are settled.

Second. We know that your job is to inform the people of Mexico and the world about what is happening at this stage of our just war against oppression, injustice, and lies.

Third. Some of the media have refused to report objectively what has happened in our state. Some have gone out of their way to rage against our cause and the indigenous people of Chiapas; we have never asked the media to become spokesmen for the EZLN, but we consider objective reporting to be their obligation, as well as a right of the whole society.

Fourth. We have an open-door policy to that part of the media that—as far as we can tell—carries out its job objectively, without taking the side of any group or party.

Fifth. Therefore, the CCRI-CG of the EZLN declares that all of the print media, regardless of political affiliation or ideological orientation, can cover the dialogue for peace and reconciliation. As far as television coverage is concerned, the EZLN will veto the presence only of the private national networks, Televisa* and Televisión Azteca. The first because it doesn't need to look for news, as it invents it and dresses it up as it pleases and according to its own interests. The second because its reporters have shown a lack of professionalism by offering money to our soldiers so that they will grant interviews. All the rest of the national and international television networks will be accredited without any problems from the EZLN.

Sixth. Accreditation of the press by the EZLN will take place through the Nationally Appointed Mediator, Sr. Samuel Ruiz García, at the hour, date, and place chosen by him.

Seventh. The EZLN wishes to make a special invitation to the following members of the media:

(1) Newspapers: *La Jornada, El Financiero, Tiempo* (of SCLC), *El Norte de Monterrey, New York Times, Washington Post, Los Angeles Times, Le Monde, Houston Chronicle.*

(2) Magazines: *Proceso, Siempre, Mira.*

(3) Television networks: Canal 6 de Julio, Multivisión, Canal 11, CNN.

(4) International news agencies: AP, UPI, AFP, Reuters, Prensa Latina.

(5) Radio stations: Radio Educación, WM (from SCLC), XEVA (from Tabasco), Radio Red, Grupo Acir.

Eighth. The EZLN declares that to the fullest extent possible we will pay special attention to the reporters from the above-named media.

Ninth. The EZLN reserves the right to give interviews or make declarations to whatever members of the media approach us.

Respectfully,
From the mountains of the Mexican Southeast
CCRI-CG of the EZLN

• 20 •
EZLN WILL RELEASE GENERAL CASTELLANOS AND WITHDRAW TROOPS

Communiqué from the CCRI-CG of the EZLN
January 31, 1994

Sr. Samuel Ruiz García, Nationally Appointed Mediator
Sr. Manuel Camacho Solís, Envoy for Peace and Reconciliation

Sirs,

The CCRI-CG again addresses you in order to say the following:

First. We received the letter from Envoy Camacho Solís dated January 29, 1994, with reference to the release of General Absalón Castellanos Domínguez. We have verified that the thirty-eight prisoners we talked about have been released from jail. General Absalón Castellanos Domínguez is in perfect health and knows that he will be let go soon. The release of General Absalón Castellanos is now under way and will be completed soon.

Second. We received the letter dated January 29, 1994, about the establishment of free (or gray) zones. We completely agree with the entire proposal of the Envoy for Peace and Reconciliation in Chiapas with reference to this point.

Third. In recognition of the clear intention of the Envoy for Peace and Reconciliation in Chiapas to ease the serious situation faced by the civilian population in the areas of conflict, the CCRI-CG of the EZLN will order, as soon as possible, the withdrawal of Zapatista troops from the following *ejidos:* San Miguel in the municipality of Ocosingo and Guadalupe Tepeyac in the municipality of Las Margaritas. The withdrawal of our troops will take place at the moment that the International Red Cross takes control of these free or gray zones and installs camps for humanitarian aid.

Respectfully,
From the mountains of Mexican Southeast
CCRI-CG of the EZLN

• 21 •
"WE HAVE ONLY ONE FACE . . ."

**Communiqué from the CCRI-CG of the EZLN
January 31, 1994**

"We have only one face and among us but a single thought. Our word walks with the truth. In life and in death we will continue our journey. As yet there is no pain in death, but rather hope in life. Choose."

To the people of Mexico
To the people and governments of the world

Brothers and sisters,

The CCRI-CG of the EZLN has carefully reviewed the letter of January 29, 1994, sent to us by the Envoy for Peace and Reconciliation, Sr. Manuel Camacho Solís.

The letter of the Envoy for Peace is not all that we were hoping for, but it does reflect a sincere concern and interest in achieving significant advances toward the dignified peace we all desire.

Our dissatisfaction comes from the following points in the letter of the Envoy for Peace:

(1) Recognition of the EZLN as a "political force in formation" is not satisfactory to us, as the federal government continues to avoid its responsibility to recognize our organization as a binding party in the eventual agreements reached by this dialogue. The EZLN is not begging for recognition from the federal government. The EZLN is a political and military reality—regionally, nationally, and internationally. The EZLN has offered the federal government the opportunity to resolve, through dialogue, the current conflict. The federal government is resisting any recognition of the EZLN. Therefore we declare that as of today we will urgently make contact with international organizations in order to achieve recognition of our EZLN as a "belligerent force," and to put ourselves under the protection of all international treaties.

(2) The EZLN rejects the elimination from the agenda of all questions about national politics. We are not trying to force national agreements, but we have the right to make our opinions known about diverse aspects of public life in Mexico, as all members of the EZLN are Mexicans by birth.

Therefore, we propose that questions of national public life be included in the agenda as points for discussion only, and that the Commission for Peace and Reconciliation in Chiapas agrees to hear our thoughts about the political direction of our country.

(3) The supposed commitment of Sr. Carlos Salinas de Gortari to the "choice for democratic politics" in the coming electoral process was made clear when—with the election still to come—he explicitly supported one, and only one, of the candidates for the presidency of the republic.

(4) The EZLN declares that the Envoy for Peace and Reconciliation in Chiapas, Manuel Camacho Solís, has always addressed us in a respectful and dignified manner. The EZLN deeply laments the recent change in tone of the Envoy for Peace and Reconciliation. When our ancestors were surrounded on the outskirts of Grijalva and the Spanish troops demanded their political and spiritual submission, rather than betray themselves they threw themselves into the river. We, heirs

to the struggle of our Chiapan grandparents, have no choice but to honor this lesson in dignity. We suffered "hardening" a long time ago; before we were silent, now we speak. The undignified and disrespectful peace in which we live continues to be, for us, an undeclared war of the powerful against our peoples. The federal government lies when they speak of us. There is nothing worse than to see ourselves humiliated again. No attack on our people could be greater than what, over a long period of time, the federal government has already done. There could be no greater rupture in our communities than the indigenous deaths that the federal economic programs offer us. There is no poverty greater than an enslaved spirit. The mouths of the powerful are filled with disrespect when they refer to us. We have lived and died without security for the last 501 years. The powerful have always had an armed force. What has changed? The dilemma is not "peace with democracy or a hardening of positions." The true choice for us is a dignified peace or a dignified war.

(5) The CCRI-CG urges the Envoy for Peace and Reconciliation in Chiapas and the federal government to make a serious and committed effort for the dignified peace that we all hope for.

(6) The EZLN will continue to abide by the cease-fire, just as we and the Federal Army have respected it since January 17. We emphatically deny that our troops looted ranches in the municipalities of Ocosingo, Altamirano, and Margaritas.

(7) The dominant attitude of the federal government has been to force us to our knees before talking to us. In contrast to this government position, many sectors of what is called Mexican civil society have been honestly concerned that this dialogue for peace and dignity actually take place. In consideration of these calls from the Mexican people, we say: We will accept the invitation of the Envoy for Peace and Reconciliation to a true and just public dialogue under the terms that we have listed in the attached, confidential proposal.

(8) As a recognition of the serious and committed efforts for peace with justice and dignity made by the Nationally Appointed Mediator, Samuel Ruiz García, and the Envoy for Peace and Reconciliation in Chiapas, Manuel Camacho Solís, the CCRI-CG of the EZLN declares the following:

First. Our troops are under orders, as of February 2, to leave the positions they now occupy in the *ejidos* of San Miguel (municipality of Ocosingo), and Guadalupe Tepeyac (municipality of Las Margaritas) so that these areas will become gray zones under the control of the International Red Cross, which will set up camps for the distribution of humanitarian aid.

Second. If the work for peace and reconciliation moves in a good direction, other positions occupied by EZLN troops will be given up to the International Red Cross for the development of more camps for the distribution of humanitarian aid.

Third. During the first round of talks for peace and reconciliation, the CCRI-CG of the EZLN will order the temporary dismantling of all the Zapatista roadblocks in the areas controlled by the EZLN, permitting the free movement of civilians only. No civilians will be bothered by our troops, who will maintain mobile guards and patrols to watch that military, political, or governmental personnel do not penetrate our positions. This suspension of our roadblocks will be continued as long as the dialogue moves in a good direction.

From the mountains of the Mexican Southeast
CCRI-CG of the EZLN
Mexico, January 1994

• 22 •
"'A POLITICAL FORCE IN FORMATION': IS THIS SOME KIND OF JOKE?"

To the national weekly *Proceso*
To the national newspaper *La Jornada*
To the national newspaper *El Financiero*
To the local newspaper *Tiempo*, SCLC, Chiapas

January 31, 1994

Gentlemen,

Attached are a series of communiqués from the CCRI-CG of the EZLN. I again ask that they be published in your papers.

The recognition by Monsieur Cordoba that the EZLN is a "political force in formation" must be some kind of joke. What does it mean? That the misery of the indigenous people does not exist, but rather is "in formation"? That January 1, 1994, did not exist, but rather is "in formation"? That thousands of indigenous people did not rise up in arms ("1,500" say the geniuses at the Pentagon), but rather they are "in formation"? Why this repeated denial of reality? Do they still believe they can fool society, or are they trying to calm themselves with this negation, "in formation"? What are they going to do? Repeat a million times, "The EZLN does not exist, it is in formation"? Why? Do they hope that repeating this lie will make it the truth.

Why is everybody silent? Is this the "democracy" that everyone wanted? Complicity with lies? Do you turn a deaf ear to Sr. Salinas de Gortari's cynical support for the PRI candidate, right after he praised to the four winds the democratic participation of eight political parties in national politics? Is this the democracy that we are offered in exchange for putting down our arms? A democracy in which the federal government is both a part of the electoral process and its final judge?

Why does the federal government take the question of national politics off the proposed agenda of the dialogue for peace? Are the indigenous people of Chiapas only Mexican enough to be exploited, but not Mexican enough to be allowed an opinion on national politics? Does the country want Chiapan oil, electrical energy, natural resources, labor, in short, the life blood of Chiapas, but not the opinions of the indigenous people of Chiapas about the future of the country? What kind of citizens are the indigenous people of Chiapas? "Citizens in formation"? According to the federal government, do the indigenous people of Chiapas continue to be children, that is to say, "adults in formation"?

When are they going to understand? How much more blood must fall before they understand that we want respect and not charity? Our every attempt to speak seems useless; the federal government wishes to speak only to itself. Why doesn't someone do us the favor of telling the federal government that what they are asking for is a monologue, not a dialogue? Or is a monologue just a "dialogue in formation"?

They want to make us out as intransigents, while placing more and more obstacles in the way of a mutually respectful dialogue. They are preparing to move us from a "political force in formation" to a "political-military force in the process of annihilation." It is not enough that they have us surrounded militarily. Now they begin to surround us politically and ideologically. Is Mexican civil society going to permit this?

The CCRI-CG will enter the dialogue with reservations, as we are worried about being betrayed by the federal government. They want to buy us with a mountain of promises, they want us to sell the only thing we have left: our dignity. The 1st of January was not enough for the government to learn to speak as equals with the governed. It seems that more 1sts of January are necessary.

Like Venustiano Carranza before them, they offer us the pittance of pardon. But Zapata is still here, alive and well. Go ahead, try to assassinate him again. Our blood falls as a pledge, let those with some pride left redeem it.

From the mountains of the Mexican Southeast
Subcomandante Insurgente Marcos

• 23 •
ALREADY TALKING ABOUT MEMORIES

To Sr. Gaspar Morquecho Escamilla, *Tiempo*
San Cristóbal de las Casas, Chiapas
From Subcomandante Insurgente Marcos, EZLN

February 14, 1994

Sir,

I just received your letter, undated of course. Today I also read in a newspaper that some accuse you and other noble people of being "spokesmen for the EZLN" or even "Zapatistas." Trouble. If you want to know where these denunciations and threats originate, look in the directories of the ranchers' associations and you will find enough leads to keep you busy for a while.

Well, let's move on to something else. Since we can already talk about memories, I hope that you have finally gotten over that mixture of drunkenness and hangover you had when you tried to interview us on that beautiful 1st of January. Perhaps you don't remember it well, but that day you were the interviewer and the interviewed; you asked me questions and then answered them yourself. I don't know how you could have gotten anything coherent for your newspaper out of that monologue of questions and answers with which you gallantly confronted the surprise and fear which seized the ancient capital of the state of Chiapas that first day of the year.

A lot of us burned our ships in the early dawn of the 1st of January and started down this hard road, ski-masks covering our faces. We took a one-way path that permits no return, knowing that at the end, death and not triumph probably awaits us. And what would triumph be? Seizing power? No, something even harder to win: a new world.

We have nothing; we left everything behind. And we are not repentant. Our step remains firm, even though tens of thousands of grotesque olive-green masks now follow our tracks in hopes of annihilating us. But, Señor Morquecho, we decided a long time ago, and not without pain, that we had to make ourselves strong in the face of the death of those at our side who were falling, dying with honor to be sure, but dying nonetheless. And we had to put blinders on our hearts, Señor Morquecho, when we saw our long-time compañeros from the mountains, their bodies riddled with bullets, their bones splintered by grenades, mortars, and rockets, their hands tied behind their backs and bullets in their heads, their blood, Señor Morquecho, staining the streets of Ocosingo and Las Margaritas red-brown, flowing on the earth of Rancho Nuevo and in the mountains of San Cristóbal, and falling in the pine hills of Altamirano. And we understand, Señor Morquecho, that in the middle of the blood, bullets, shrapnel, tanks, helicopter gunships, planes probing for places to launch their explosive rockets, there is a simple truth: we are invincible, we cannot lose . . . we do not deserve to lose.

But as we say here, our job is this: to fight and to die so that others may live, so that they may live better lives, much better lives, than the ones we now leave behind. That is our job, yes, but it is not yours. Please take care of yourself; the fascist beast lurks in hiding, directing its attacks against the most defenseless.

I want to say some things to you and your team of honest and noble people who give birth (and with the technical difficulties you face, producing a newspaper is a true act of creation) to this impartial and truthful press that goes by the name of *Tiempo*.

The true heroism of *Tiempo* is not so much making a newspaper with Fred Flintstone technology. Rather it comes from the fact that in this closed off-culture, as absurd as the *coleta*,* you give a voice to those who have none (now we have weapons). With four pages (sometimes six) filled with truths, you challenge the powerful men of commerce and the landowners who sit on their royal butts in their royal cities. You won't be blackmailed or intimidated into publishing a lie or leaving out a truth. In the middle of this suffocating cultural atmosphere of *ladino* mediocrity, you look for a fresh wind (a democratic one, perhaps?) that will clean the streets and minds of Jovel. When the Indians came down from the mountain (careful: I am talking about *before* the 1st of January), not to buy or to sell but rather to ask that someone listen to them, and they found only closed doors and ears, there was one door always open, the door under the *Tiempo* sign. And crossing that threshold, the Indians who today through their refusal to die quietly have put the world in a fury, found someone who listened to them, and who put their Indian voices in ink on a paper named *Tiempo*. That was, and is now even more, truly heroic. Because, Señor Morquecho, heroism and bravery are not only found behind a rifle and ski-mask, but also in front of a typewriter when the love of truth is what animates the hands that touch the keys.

I now hear that they accuse all of you of being "Zapatistas." If saying the truth and searching for justice make you a "Zapatista," then we are millions. Bring on the army!

But when the police come to intimidate you, tell them the truth, Señor Morquecho. Tell them that you have always spoken out to warn people that if the daily injustice of oppression does not change, the indigenous people would revolt. Tell them that you always recommended that people look for other ways to fight, legal and peaceful ones, against the desperation that surrounds the cities of Chiapas (and of Mexico—don't believe Salinas when he says the problem is a local one). Tell them that you, together with other honest professionals (a rare breed)—doctors, newspapermen, and lawyers—looked all over for help to start up economic, educational, and cultural projects that would ease the misery that is woven through the indigenous communities. Tell them the truth, Señor Morquecho. Tell them that you always sought a peaceful and just road, dignified and true. Tell them the truth, Señor Morquecho.

But please, Señor Morquecho, don't tell them what you and I know has happened to you, don't tell them what your heart whispers to your ear, what your lips want to tell when you talk, what your hands want to say when you write, don't tell them what began in your breast and slowly rose to your head as the year passed and you traveled to the mountains and canyons, don't tell them what you now want to shout: "I am not a Zapatista, but after the 1st of January . . . I wish to be one!"

Give my regards, if it is possible, to a reporter named Amado Avendaño. Tell him I have not forgotten how cool he was on the happy morning (at least for us) of Mexico's triumphant entry into the "first world," when I advised him not to come over and talk to me and he answered, "I am doing my job." And while you are at it, give my regards to Concepción Villafuerte, whose strong, brave writing we read with joy whenever all the unlikely connections are made and the newspaper actually arrives. And say hello to everyone at your newspaper; they not only deserve better machinery but the respect of all the honest journalists of the world. And pay my respects to the professionals at *Chiltak* who sacrifice money and material goods to work with and for people who have nothing. Tell all of them (the people at *Tiempo* and at *Chiltak*) that if those who govern today had half the moral stature of you people, there would have been neither guns, nor ski-masks, nor blood on the mountains south of San Cristóbal, or in Rancho Nuevo, or Ocosingo, or Las Margaritas, or Altamira. And maybe rather than being here writing with the cold numbing my hands (but not my heart), and under the constant threat of planes and helicopters, we would be talking together, you and I, with no greater barrier between us than two beers in the middle of the table. The world would not be the world, but something better, and better for everyone. Of course I don't drink alcoholic beverages, so if that day should arrive (God forbid, but it could happen), it would be better to say, "with no greater barrier between us than a beer (yours, no offense intended), and a soft drink (mine) in the middle of the table."

Health and a great, tender hug. And please, learn to put the date on your letters; history is moving so fast, it might even be good to put the time of day.

> From the mountains of the Mexican Southeast Chiapas
> Subcomandante Insurgente Marcos
> Mexico, February 2, 1994

P.S.: It's 10 p.m., it's cold, and the noise from the plane flying overhead almost seems like a lullaby.

• 24 •
"YOU CAN'T HAVE A GOOD CONSCIENCE AND A HEART"

EZLN, Mexico, February 6, 1994

To the University Student Council (CEU) of the National Autonomous University of Mexico (UNAM), Mexico City

Compañeros and compañeras,

We received your letter of January 29, 1994, on which appears the signature of "Argel Gómez C." We are grateful for the thoughts you send our way.

We are mostly indigenous people and mostly illiterates. We did not even have the opportunity to finish elementary school. We would have liked not only to finish elementary school and high school, but to have gone on to a university.

With great pleasure, we receive the greetings and support of men and women like you, who struggle on different turf and with different methods for the same liberties, democracy, and justice that we all desire. We know that at other times the brave voice of Mexican students has made the bad government tremble, and that if your voice and ours were united with the voices of all the dispossessed, nothing would be left standing of the gigantic lie that they make us swallow every day and every night, in death and in life, always. That is why, men and women students of Mexico, with all respect, we want to ask something of you:

Perhaps it would be possible for you to organize yourselves and, when things calm down a little, come to our mountains and visit us and talk to us and help us with all that you know about technical things and words and all that comes from books but doesn't come to us. We don't want you to come here to politicize us or convert us to one or another political tendency. (I believe it is more likely that you would learn from us what a true democratic and participatory organization is.) But you can help us harvest coffee, prepare the fields—help us do the communal jobs of our people. And you can help us learn to read and to write, to improve our health and diet, to use techniques with which we can work the earth more fruitfully. You can come and teach us to learn, you can come even if it is only for a few days so that you get to know this part of Mexico, which existed before the 1st of January . . .

If you accept this invitation, we need you to send some delegates so that, through an intermediary, we can arrange the details; we must organize everything well so that spies from their government don't slip through. And if you can't accept it, don't worry, just continue struggling on your own terrain so that there can be justice for all the Mexican people.

That's all, men and women students of Mexico. We will be expecting a written response from you.

Respectfully,
From the mountains of the Mexican Southeast
CCRI-CG of the EZLN
Mexico, February 1994

P.S.: The Sup's section: "The repeating postscript."

P.S. to the P.S. of the letter from CEU* which said, "To the Sup Marcos: Don't worry, we will take the Zócalo* for you." I, myself, had said to the CCRI-CG that the capital is on the other side of the world and we don't have enough ammunition, and, furthermore, as I-don't-remember-who told me, guerrilla fighters who seize zócalos sooner or later end up "ham-burgher-ing" themselves. (Taking advantage of your trip, however, send back two, hold the onions and ketchup. Thank you.)

P.S. to the previous P.S.: Given that we are into sending postscripts, which one of the CEU's is writing to us? Because when I was an elegant young man of twenty-five ('Orale! Inform the PGR computer so that it can start calculating!), there were at least three CEU's. Did they finally unite?

P.S. to the P.S. to the P.S.: In case that, whew, you do take the Zócalo, don't be greedy and save a little piece so that people can continue to sell crafts there; because I would rather become an underemployed "professional of violence" than an unemployed one (the effects of NAFTA, *"you know"*).

P.S. to the nth power: These postscripts are really a letter disguised as a postscript (to hide it from the PGR and all the rest of the strong men in dark glasses), and, *"but of course,"* it requires neither an answer, nor a sender, nor an addressee (obvious advantage of a letter disguised as a postscript).

Nostalgic P.S.: When I was young (Hello? PGR? Here comes more data), there used to be a lightly wooded place between the main library, the Faculty of Philosophy and Letters, the Humanities Tower, Insurgentes Avenue, and the interior circuit of CU.* We used to call that space, for reasons obvious to the initiates, the "Valley of Passions," and it was energetically visited by diverse elements of the fauna who populated the CU beginning at 7 p.m. (an hour when those of good conscience drink hot chocolate and the bad ones make themselves hot enough to melt); they came from the humanities, sciences, and other areas (are there others?). At that time, a Cuban (Are you ready, Ambassador Jones? Make a note of more proof of pro-Castroism) who used to give lectures seated in front of piano keys the color of his skin, and who called himself Snowball, would repeat over and over:

"You can't have a good conscience and a heart . . ."

Finale fortissimo P.S.: Did you notice the exquisite, cultured air of these postscripts? Aren't they worthy of our entry into the first world? Don't they call attention to the fact that we "transgressors" are also preparing ourselves to be competitive in NAFTA?

"Happy ending" P.S.: Okay, Okay, I'm going . . . this trip is coming to an end, and the guard, for a change, is still asleep and someone is tired of repeating, "Who lives?" and I answer to myself, "Our country" . . . and what is your answer?

• 25 •

EZLN IN SOLIDARITY WITH THE NATIONAL COORDINATING COMMITTEE OF THE PLAN DE AYALA

EZLN, Mexico, February 8, 1994

To the National Coordinating Committee of the Plan de Ayala

Brothers and sisters,

We received your letter of February 5, 1994, and we would like to give you our thoughts about it and tell you some other things.

We welcome the independent and honest fight of the National Coordinating Committee of the Plan de Ayala (CNPA).* We thank you for your brave and precise declaration of unconditional support for our righteous struggle. Once united, indigenous people, poor campesinos, and agricultural workers will have to completely change the agricultural system of exploitation and hate that exists in our country. From the unity of our forces will rise a new Mexican country-side, more just and egalitarian, where the severe gaze of General Emiliano Zapata will make sure that oppression, under some new name, will not be reborn.

Campesino brothers and sisters of the CNPA, it will be a great honor to talk to you and to listen to your words of truth and justice. With humble attention we will stand before you—you who for so long have fought for land and freedom. We, the small men of the land, will listen to the words of your great, independent organization.

Salud, brothers and sisters of CNPA!

Viva Emiliano Zapata and the organizations that do honor to his name!

Out with the Salinas' revisions of Article 27 of the Constitution!

Respectfully,
From the mountains of the Mexican Southeast
CCRI-CG of the EZLN
Mexico, February 1994
Subcomandante Insurgente Marcos

• 26 •
"THE BELT OF PEACE"

To the Association of Regional Liberation in Favor of Human
Economical, Social, and Political Rights
Lardizabal No. 7-A Col. Centro, Tel. (91-246) 2-35-57
Tlaxcala, Tlax. CP. 90000
From the CCRI-CG of the EZLN

C. Lucrecia Ortega Sánchez, Administrative Director,

The CCRI-CG of the EZLN respectfully thanks you for your letter
dated February 7, 1994, in which you tell us that you agree to form a
"Belt of Peace" around the dialogue table, in between our EZLN and
the federal government.

We know that your organization has remained neutral in the present conflict and that you have been concerned at all times to help
ease the grave conditions of the civilian population, as well as encourage the peace effort. We respectfully congratulate you for the
honesty that invariably accompanies your neutrality, and for your
enthusiasm for peace with justice. We thank you in advance for
extending our invitation to other nongovernmental organizations,
since, up until now, you are the only ones who have given us an
affirmative answer.

We are asking Sr. Samuel Ruiz García, Bishop of San Cristóbal de las
Casas and Nationally Appointed Mediator, to inform you promptly
when a date and place for the dialogue has been established.

Respectfully,
From the mountains of the Mexican Southeast
CCRI-CG of the EZLN
Mexico, February 1994
Subcomandante Insurgente Marcos

• 27 •
A LETTER TO SCHOOLCHILDREN

EZLN, Mexico, February 8, 1994

To the Solidarity Committee of Elementary Boarding School
#4, "Beatriz Hernández," Guadalajara, Jalisco

Boys and girls,

We received your letter of February 19, 1994, and the poem "Prayer for Peace" that came with it. It makes us very happy to know that boys and girls who live so far away from our mountains and our misery are concerned that peace should come to Chiapan lands. We thank you very much for your brief letter.

We would like you (and your noble teachers) to know that we did not take up arms for the pleasure of fighting and dying; it is not because we don't want peace that we look for war. We were living without peace already. Our boys and girls are like you, but infinitely poorer. For our children there are no schools or medicines, no clothes or food, not even a dignified roof under which we can store our poverty. For our boys and girls there is only work, ignorance, and death. The land that we have is worthless, and in order to get something for our children we have to leave home and look for work on land that belongs to others, powerful people, who pay us very little for our labor. Our children have to begin working at a very young age in order to be able to get food, clothing, and medicine. Our children's' toys are the machete, the ax, and the hoe; from the time they are barely able to walk, playing and suffering they go out looking for wood, cleaning brush, and planting. They eat the same as we do: corn, beans, and chile. They cannot go to school to learn Spanish because work kills the days and sickness kills the nights. This is how our children have lived and died for 501 years.

We, their fathers, mothers, sisters, and brothers, no longer want to carry the guilt of not doing anything to help our children. We look for peaceful roads to justice and we find only mockery, imprisonment, blows, and death; we always find pain and sorrow. We couldn't take it anymore, boys and girls of Jalisco, it was too much pain and sorrow. And then we were forced to take the road to war, because our voices had not been heard.

Boys and girls of Jalisco, we do not ask for handouts or charity, we ask for justice: a fair wage, a piece of good land, a decent house, an honest school, medicine that cures, bread on our tables, respect for what is ours, the liberty to say what is on our minds and to open our mouths so that our words can unite with others in peace and without death. This is what we have always asked for, boys and girls of Jalisco, and they didn't listen. And it was then that we took a weapon in our hands, it was then that we made our work tools into tools of struggle. We then turned the war that they had made on us, the war that was killing us—without you, boys and girls of Jalisco, knowing anything about it—we turned that war against them, the rich and the powerful, those who have everything and deserve nothing.

That is why, boys and girls of Jalisco, we began our war. That is why the peace that we want is not the peace that we had before, because that wasn't peace, it was death and contempt, it was pain and suffering, it was disgrace. That is why we are telling you, with respect and love, boys and girls of Jalisco, to raise high the dignified flag of peace, to write poems that are "Prayers for a Dignified Life," and to search, above all, for equal justice for everyone.

Salud, boys and girls of Jalisco.

From the mountains of the Mexican Southeast
CCRI-CG of the EZLN
Mexico, February 1994
Subcomandante Insurgente Marcos

• 28 •
SORRY ABOUT THE DELAY

To the national weekly *Proceso*
To the national newspaper *La Jornada*
To the national newspaper *El Financiero*
To the local newspaper of SCLC, Chiapas, *Tiempo*

February 8, 1994

Sirs,

I include here another series of letters that the CCRI-CG of the EZLN is sending to various places. I hope that you will have the time to see that they arrive at their destinations.

I understand your frustration (and that of your bosses because of the high hotel, restaurant, and gasoline bills) about the delay of the beginning of the dialogue for peace. It is not our fault, nor is it the fault of the Commission—we are not prima donnas who like to keep people waiting. Nor has the delay been caused by disagreements about the agenda or anything like that. It is because there are still some security details that have to be arranged for our delegates. We must take care of these details so as to avoid "surprises" or bitter misfortunes. In sum, "serenity and patience, lots of patience."

As a consolation, I will tell you that the dialogue will not be in the jungle. Among other things, because those who can communicate via satellite would have an advantage, and as for phone or fax, "*forget it.*" And, as the times favor the little ones,* we prefer democracy and equality of opportunity for the media too, and do not want the "exclusives" to be only for the powerful.

Health and patience.

From the mountains of the Mexican Southeast
Subcomandante Insurgente Marcos

• 29 •
AN END TO UNDEMOCRATICALLY IMPOSED MUNICIPAL GOVERNMENTS

EZLN, Mexico, February 8, 1994

To the Mapastepec Civic Front, Mapastepec, Chiapas

Brothers and sisters,

We want to say our word to you. We received your letter of February 6, 1994.

The vast majorities of the presidents of the municipalities of Chiapas hold their office because of electoral fraud. All of the municipal presidents of Chiapas must resign or be deposed. In their place, democratically elected municipal councils should be formed. Collective government is better than the government of a single person, but it must be democratic. There is no point in substituting an undemocratically chosen municipal council for a president imposed by the state government; the anti-democratic council must also fall. This process should continue until the just will of the majority is respected.

The EZLN unconditionally supports the just demands of the people of Mapastepec who are struggling for an authentic democracy, and also supports all popular forces that, now and in the future, struggle against arbitrary municipal presidents undemocratically imposed on their communities. Municipal democracy is, and has been, a part of the Zapatista list of demands.

Out with undemocratically imposed municipal presidents!

Viva democratic municipal councils!

Respectfully,
From the mountains of the Mexican Southeast
CCRI-CG, Mexico, February 1994

• 30 •
SOLIDARITY IN MICHOACÁN

EZLN, February 8, 1994

To Citizen Attorney Mario Robledo, Municipal President,
  Municipal J. Sixto Verduzco, Michoacán, Mexico

Brother,

We received your letter of February 5, 1994. We are very happy to know that your greetings come to us all the way from the lands of Michoacán. We are even happier to know that in some of the municipal presidencies of this country, there are brave and dignified people who walk with prudence and truth. It is good that you exist and are in the government, if your people have put you there. Because that which comes from the respect and will of the people creates a good path for us all.

We, little men and women, have given ourselves the task of becoming great, so that we might live even as we die. We see that to become great, we have to look at all those who are suffering in these lands and to throw in our lot with them. We see that we have not been able to do this in the past, and we see that they have not really let us be brothers and sisters in truth and justice. We see that it is the bad government that has kept our paths apart. And we see that good men and women must fight so that the government changes. We see that being only good and polite changes nothing. We see that we must take up arms. All this we see, and so have we done.

But we also see that it is not only the mouth of a gun that will achieve liberty. We see that many other mouths must open and shout so that the powerful tremble. We see that the struggles are many, and those who walk in struggle are of many colors and use many tongues. And we see that we are not alone. And we see that we do not die alone.

Salud, brothers and sisters of Michoacán! May the struggle never end! May hope never die!

Respectfully,
From the mountains of the Mexican Southeast
CCRI-CG of the EZLN
Mexico, February 1994

• 31 •
"WE, AS MAYANS AND AS MEXICANS . . ."

EZLN, Mexico, February 8, 1994

To the Supreme Council of the National Coordinating Committee of Indian Peoples, Tenochtitlán/Mexico, Mexico City

Brothers and sisters,

We wish to say our word to you. We received your letter of February 5. We bow our heads in honor of receiving the words of truth that you send us. We put our arms aside to listen to the word of our indigenous brothers and sisters and to Mexicans from all over the country. Great is the wisdom of your thoughts which remind everyone that "Mexico belongs to the Mexicans, our essence lies in community, in mutual aid, in justice, in freedom and dignity."

We, as Mayans and as Mexicans, unite our force and our knowledge to the great words of truth of the National Coordinating Committee of Indian Peoples. We will not let our dignity be offered for sale in the great marketplace of the powerful! If we lose our dignity, we lose everything. We hope that our struggle may bring happiness to all our brothers and sisters, and that we may unite our hands and our footsteps in the path to truth and justice.

Viva the Mexican eagle and the shield of Zapata, brothers and sisters of the CNPI!

May the unity of those who fight for justice live forever!

Freedom! Justice! Democracy!

Respectfully,
From the mountains of the Mexican Southeast
CCRI-CG of the EZLN
Mexico, February 1994

• 32 •
"REASONS AND NON-REASONS WHY SOME MEDIA WERE CHOSEN"

EZLN, February 11, 1994

To the newspaper *El Sur, XXI-Century Journalism*
  Attention: Jesus García, Claudia Martínez Sánchez, Pablo
  Gómez Santiago
From Subcomandante Insurgente Marcos, EZLN
  The Mountains of the Mexican Southeast, Chiapas, Mexico.
  Still without a fax machine . . . (sigh).

Sirs,

I received your letter, dated February 9, 1994. Wow! If you were to write newspaper articles with half the aggressiveness of the letter you sent me, when this country is truly free and just, you will win the National Prize for Journalism. I accept your friendly reminder (it is really a scolding, but this morning I woke up in a diplomatic mood). I hope that in the midst of your indignation, you might find the space to listen to me.

We are at war. We rose up in arms against the government. They are searching for us to kill us, not to interview us. We confess that we do not know of *El Sur, XXI-Century Journalism,* but you must confess that it is difficult to reproach us, surrounded as we are, without resources, and under the constant threat of armed, military planes. Good, we have mutually confessed.

Many honest journalists, some not so honest, and others not even journalists (but who present themselves as such) have come into the jungle. We have to be suspicious of everyone we don't directly know, because, I repeat, the government also wants to take a picture of us . . . but dead. I know that for "professionals of violence" death is a natural consequence of what we do, but there is a great gap between knowing this and helping your enemy. I am not trying to get your sympathy, I just want you to understand our situation. We have little margin for maneuver, but paradoxically, more than ever we need to make contact with those news media that tell the truth. The movement of journalists back and forth through our lines weakens our security system, and there is also a risk that people working for the news media may suffer an attempt on their lives and we would be blamed.

Personally, I do not think I have been interviewed enough; in fact, the interview published in *La Jornada* is the only one I have given in my life, and I believe the reporters left many empty spaces that could have been filled by questions that were not asked. I am not behaving like a prima donna who "chooses" to whom she will give her "honorable" presence; I am simply taking into account the extra risk for those who are here already and those who might come to interview me. Anyway, we are what we are, people persecuted by the government, not by journalists.

If you had started by mentioning that you are supported by the San Cristóbal newspaper *Tiempo,* you would have saved yourself from the righteous indignation that filled the pages that I received by fax. For me, the word of *Tiempo* is enough to accept someone's honesty, and so I'm sending a letter to the Nationally Appointed Mediator, Bishop Samuel Ruiz García, asking him to give you a safe-conduct pass allowing you through our lines to take the photographs you want and interview whoever you can (please remember we are at war). I solemnly promise that when possible I will have the honor of receiving you personally and answering your questions, if they can be answered.

As this improbable day has yet to arrive, I send you a letter. Here it is, without anesthesia, entitled,

reasons and nonreasons
why some media were chosen

When bombs were falling over the mountains of San Cristóbal de las Casas, when our combatants were fighting off the attacks of federal troops in Ocosingo, when our troops were regrouping after the attack on the army barracks at Rancho Nuevo, when we were fortifying ourselves in Altamirano and Las Margaritas, when the air smelled like gun powder and blood, the CCRI-CG of the EZLN called me and said: "We need to say our word and for others to listen. If we don't do it now, others will take our voices and unwanted lies will come out of our mouths. Find out how our truth can get to those who want to hear it."

This is how the CCRI-CG put me in charge of finding media that could report what was really happening and what we were thinking. As I have said on other occasions, newspapers are not delivered in the mountains. We do get signals from some radio stations (mostly government ones). Given what we knew, we had to decide which media to address. We had to consider various things: First of all, our communications would provoke a logical question in the media that received them: are the communiqués authentic, that is, were they really from those who had risen up in arms or were they fakes? Supposing their authenticity was accepted (they would have no way to know for sure), then comes the key question: should we publish them? Certifying the authenticity of the communiqués was already a risk for the editorial committees of these media; the responsibility of publishing them was an even greater one. Perhaps only the editors themselves can tell us the story of their decision to create an opening for a movement that no one except us knew well—a movement whose origin, at the very best, was an enigma, and, at the very worst, a provocation.

The EZLN had risen up against the almighty government, had taken seven municipal seats, was fighting against the Federal Army, and was formed by indigenous people—all this was a fact. But who was behind the EZLN? What did they really want? Why do it this way (with arms)? Who financed them? In sum, what was really happening? There must have been more than a million questions. Some day the media will tell us their version of this story (surely an important one). We were thinking about all this, and we asked ourselves: Who is going to accept all these risks? Our answer was: those media whose eagerness to know the truth of what is happening will be greater than their fear of finding it.

Well, the answer was right (I think) but didn't solve anything. The most important thing had not been done: to decide the destination of these first letters and communiqués. I will briefly tell how and why we chose those particular media; it is clear why we had to list them at the beginning of our letters and communiqués.

Tiempo. The decision to address this magazine was unanimous in the CCRI-CG of the EZLN, and was made by acclamation. Remember that our compañeros don't come to armed struggle just like that, eager for adventure. They have traveled a long road of political, legal, peaceful, and economic struggle. They know many local and state jails and torture centers. They also know who listened to them in the past and who closed their doors and ears. I already explained in a letter to a journalist what *Tiempo* means for indigenous Chiapans, so I will not push the point.

Nevertheless, it wasn't easy to decide to put the name *Tiempo* at the top of our letters. We were sure of the honesty and impartiality of these people, but there was a war going on, and in a war it is easy to confuse the lines that separate one force from another. I'm not referring only to lines of fire, but also to political and ideological lines that separate groups. What do I mean? Simply that the fact of publishing one of our communiqués could win for *Tiempo* the accusation, gratuitous of course, of being "spokesmen" for those "who break the law." For a large newspaper this could mean problems, for a small one it could mean its complete disappearance. Anyway, our compañeros said: "Send it to *Tiempo*, if they don't publish it, at least they deserve to know the truth of what is happening." This was part of the story of why we chose *Tiempo*. Of course, we are still missing the part of the story of how the noble people at *Tiempo* decided to run such risks, up to the point of jeopardizing their very existence, by publishing what we sent them. Whatever that story may be, we can only salute the courage of this media which, among all others, had the most to lose, if not everything. That's why the CCRI-CG of the

EZLN has always insisted on sending a copy of everything we write to *Tiempo.*

After deciding what local media we were going to address, we had to decide about the national media. For obvious reasons, television was out of the question. Radio presented the problem of how to deliver the material without extra risk. That left the national press. Remember that we did not know what was being said in the press about what was going on here, as we were fighting in the mountains, in the cities, everywhere. And so, as I said before, we had to decide on the basis of previous experiences.

La Jornada. At that time, we valued what *La Jornada* had done. Their editorial politics were, as we say now, pluralistic. They made space in their newspaper for diverse ideological and political currents. We appreciated, and still do, their broad range of interpretations of national and international reality. That is, this newspaper presents an ideological mosaic that represents most of what we call Mexican civil society. I believe this was shown in the slow change from their early sentencing of the EZLN to stoning (remember the editorial of January 2, 1994) to a critical analysis of what was happening. I believe, *mutatis mutando,* that that is what happened with so-called civil society: it went from condemning us to trying to understand us.

In *La Jornada* they have what we used to call a left, a center, and a right—multiple subdivisions first created, and now dissolved, by history. There are sane and level-headed polemics. Well, I think it's a good newspaper. It's difficult to brand it as leftist, rightist, or centrist (although the Mexican Anti-Communist Front puts it in the first category). I think the mosaic of editorial currents is an important part of the paper's success (when I was a journalist, a newspaper's "editorial success" meant being able to publish the next edition). Nevertheless, it wasn't the existence of this ideological mosaic that made us decide to include *La Jornada* among the media receiving our communiqués; it was the courage and honesty of its correspondents. We've seen brilliant pages of journalism ("field reports," they used to call them) in this paper's articles and reports. For some reason, the journalists who make these field reports (and many others as well, but I'm only talking about *La Jornada* now) are not satisfied with official bulletins. They are so eager to find out what is happening that they annoy the people they are reporting about. Moreover, when something important happens (at least in their opinion), *La Jornada* is not satisfied with sending one reporter; instead they send a veritable assault team, which immediately begins to unveil the various aspects of the event they are covering. They have what in my time we used to call "total journalism," just like a movie that films the same act with many cameras from different angles and with different focuses. But what hypnotizes in the movies, in the press leads to reflection and analysis. Still fighting with fire and lead, we thought maybe *La Jornada* would like to see the face behind the ski-masks. I'm not saying others wouldn't like to see us as well (including the federal government), but now I'm talking about this newspaper. What made us decide to add *La Jornada's* name to the list of media receiving our communiqués was, above all, its team of correspondents. There are other less important reasons, such as the occasional sections (or are they regular?) of "Doble Jornada," "Perfil," and, "*last but not least*," "Histerietas."

El Financiero. Someone asked me why we chose a newspaper that specializes in economic problems. To say that *El Financiero* is a financial paper would be, at best, short of the truth; at worst, it means that the speaker hasn't read it. We think *El Financiero* has a team of responsible columnists who take their jobs seriously. Their analyses are objective, and above all very critical. The ideological pluralism of their columns is a treasure that is difficult to find in other dailies. That is to say, the paper has balanced coverage. Its editorial writers are not content to throw in a few critical pens amidst all the others that are aligned with power. Rather, it opens real space for incisive analysis from one side and the other (I doubt if there are only two sides, but the figure of speech helps, I think). Its team of correspondents has an instinct for "dissecting" reality, which is what ultimately distinguishes a correspondent from an observer. *El Financiero* reflects in itself ("reflects in itself?" I think I'd better say, "conditions and is conditioned by") different economic, political, cultural influences.

It's like reading a history book, but one of current and daily history, which is certainly the most difficult history to read. When I was young and beautiful, intellectuals tended to group themselves around a single publication, entrench themselves, and from there tell the truth to the ignorant world of mortals. In those days they were called "elite intellectuals" and there were many of them, since magazines and ideological tendencies were all the fashion. They were publications to be read by those who published them. "Editorial masturbation," says Lucha. If you, innocent earthling, wanted to touch their ivory towers, you had to go through a field of thorns.

If one newspaper seems to have distanced itself from this "journalism of the elite," which exaggerates, selects, and eliminates, it is *El Financiero*. It didn't immediately condemn a movement that nobody understood, it didn't rush in with the intellectual lubricants that affected and were affected by other media. It waited (which in the art of war is the most difficult virtue to learn), investigated, reported, and, with a firm base, began to weave the interdisciplinary analysis that its readers now enjoy.

We didn't know anything about this until some time later, when we received a copy of their newspaper. We congratulated ourselves for having chosen well, although we must admit that we didn't have anything to lose. If *La Jornada's* team of correspondents made us decide to choose them, for *El Financiero* it was its team of editors (notwithstanding Sr. Pazos).

Proceso. It's worth reiterating our apologies for the late appearance of this weekly magazine among the chosen media. I already explained this somewhere else. Let me tell you a story from January 1, 1994, one of the many floating around in our minds and conversations. At nightfall, most of the civilians who had been with us in the Municipal Palace in San Cristóbal—half curious and half shocked by what they had seen—had returned frightened to their homes and hotels, because of the insistent rumors that the Federal Army would try to assault our positions in the dark of night. Nevertheless, we ran into one or two drunks who had been celebrating New Year's for more than twenty-four hours. Barely able to stand up, these drunkards asked us what kind of religious procession was taking place because they saw a lot of "indios" in the central plaza. After we told them what was happening, they offered us a useless drink from an empty bottle, and left, tottering and arguing about whether the procession was for La Virgen de Guadalupe or because of the Santa Lucía festival. But some people approached us who weren't drunk, or so it appeared. And then happened what happened: war strategists and spontaneous military advisors emerged, giving us fully developed directions on how to run the war and avoid casualties from government attacks. They all unanimously agreed that we were about to be completely crushed.

As night continued to fall and our troops were getting ready to be transferred to their new positions before the assault on Rancho Nuevo, someone approached me, and, in a manner more like a father than a doctor, said: "Marcos, you made a strategic mistake starting the war on a Saturday." I adjusted the ski-mask that, along with my eyelids, was starting to fall over my eyes, and dared a fearful, "Why?"

"Look," said my impromptu strategic military advisor, "the error is that *Proceso* closes its edition on Saturdays, so honest coverage and analyses of your struggle will not come out until next week." I continued to adjust the ski-mask, more to give me time than because it was out of place. My *ladino* military advisor added relentlessly, "You should have attacked on Friday." I timidly tried to argue in my defense about New Year's dinner, the fireworks, the parties, and all the etceteras that now I can't remember but I'm sure I said. But the person in front of me wouldn't let me continue, and interrupted me with, "And now who knows if you will last 'till next week." There wasn't sorrow in his tone, it was just a dismal death sentence. He left, giving me an understanding slap on the back for the strategic stupidity of attacking on Saturday.

I haven't read *Proceso* of the week after January 1, but the late-night strategist was right when he said that *Proceso* has accurate coverage and analyses. I can add very little to what everyone has said about the virtues of this weekly magazine, which has received international recognition. It is enough to call your attention to the deep analyses always present in the articles in *Proceso*, and its different approaches to problems, national and international.

Other publications. I agree with you that there are other news media of equal or greater value than the ones mentioned above. We look forward to augmenting the list of media, or just addressing the press in general. I think this would be the most prudent because there really are a lot of good news agencies that do the job they are supposed to do: report the news.

El Sur (Oaxaca). I repeat that we didn't know about this news agency, and I repeat again that we cannot give interviews and press conferences like the Federal Army can, and I repeat once again that we are surrounded and at war. But let's make a deal: until a personal interview becomes possible, let's start by mail. I know that an interview by mail is not a reporter's first choice, but we could accomplish something. Moreover, I promise to "hunt down" other officials of the EZLN for you to interview, with the one condition that when you come to Chiapas, you pick up your credentials as war correspondents, issued by the EZLN, at the National Mediation Commission.

As you might know, the dialogue hasn't started yet. Maybe we can't start without you. Okay, good journalists of *El Sur de Oaxaca*, I believe that I have bored you enough. However, the advantage of this long letter is that no news agency will dare publish it. *Vale.*

Salud and a hug without resentments . . .

From the mountains of the Mexican Southeast

P.S.: Could you send us a copy of your newspaper? We solemnly promise to pay you if someday we have money. (Would you accept letters instead of cash?)

Another P.S.: The trip isn't over yet and the water from the pot has already evaporated. How about bringing some of that delicious oaxaqueño cheese when you come by? We will provide the tortillas and the appetite. You're welcome.

cc *Tiempo*, San Cristóbal de las Casas, Chiapas
cc *La Jornada,* Mexico City
cc *El Financiero*, Mexico City
cc *Proceso*, Mexico City

• 33 •
GENERAL CASTELLANOS DOMÍNGUEZ SET FREE

Communiqué from the CCRI-CG of the EZLN
February 15, 1994

To the national and international press
To Samuel Ruiz García, Nationally Appointed Mediator
To Manuel Camacho Solís, Envoy for Peace and Reconciliation
    in Chiapas

Sirs,

We, the CCRI-CG of the EZLN, write once again to convey the following:

(1) With the purpose of helping to bring about the earliest possible beginning to the dialogue for the peace with dignity that all Mexicans desire, and as a sign of the sincere disposition of our EZLN, we wish to inform you that Wednesday, February 16, 1994, General Absalón Castellanos Domínguez will be set free.

(2) General Absalón Castellanos Domínguez will be delivered to the Envoy for Peace, Manuel Camacho Solís and the Nationally Appointed Mediator, Samuel Ruiz García, in the town of Guadalupe Tepeyac, municipality of Las Margaritas, Chiapas. The state of health of General Absalón Castellanos Domínguez in the moment of his liberation shall be determined by staff doctors from the International Committee of the Red Cross.

(3) With the purpose of easing the tension in the conflict zone during the course of the dialogue for peace with dignity, the CCRI-CG of the EZLN announces its decision to suspend the collection of war taxes in the territories under the control of our troops, beginning on February 17, 1994.

Respectfully,
From the mountains of the Mexican Southeast
CCRI-CG of the EZLN, Mexico, February 1994

• 34 •
INVITATION TO THE PEACE TALKS

National Zapatista Liberation Army
February 13, 1994

To the national and international press
To the nationally registered political parties
To the candidates aspiring to the presidency of the Mexican
    Republic
To the National Action Party (PAN)
To the Institutional Revolutionary Party (PRI)
To the Democratic Revolutionary Party (PRD)
To the Cardenista Front for National Reconstruction (PFCRN)
To the Workers' Party
To the Authentic Party of the Mexican Revolution (PARM)
To the Green Ecologist Party of Mexico (PVEM)
To the Popular Socialist Party (PPS)

Sirs,

By means of this letter, we, the CCRI-CG of the EZLN, speak to you
to tell you the following:

First. Everyone knows that in only a few days the Meetings for Peace
and Reconciliation in Chiapas, between the federal government and
the EZLN, mediated by the Bishop Samuel Ruiz García, will begin.

Second. The beginning of the dialogue can be an important part
of the peace process if, at the very outset, it moves in the direction
of peace with dignity, justice, freedom, and democracy. We think,
however, that any agreements that are made with the representative
of the federal government may prove difficult to implement because
of the upcoming election and the change of federal power that goes
with it.

Third. For these reasons we thought we should invite you to send
delegates from the national offices of your political parties so that
you may stay informed about the peace dialogue and so that you can
give us your opinion about how the agreements can be implemented,

if in fact that is possible. We are sure that the next federal executive of our country will emerge from among your presidential candidates, and that it will be the responsibility of the next president of the republic to fulfill the agreements.

Fourth. We hope that our invitation to participate in the dialogue will be accepted by the leadership of your political parties and by the campaign teams of the various presidential candidates. It will be a great honor for us to speak, when the opportunity arises, with the delegates that you send.

Respectfully,
From the mountains of the Mexican Southeast
CCRI-CG of the EZLN
Mexico, February 1994

• 35 •
"WE ARE NOTHING
IF WE WALK ALONE"

EZLN, February 14, 1994

To the organizations that make up the National Coordination
of Civic Action for National Liberation (Conac-LN)
From CCRI-CG of the EZLN, Mountains of the Mexican
Southeast, Chiapas, Mexico

Brothers and sisters,

We received your letter of February 9, 1994. Our honor is great and
we bow our heads in recognition of the words of our General Emiliano
Zapata in the mouths of the workers, campesinos, students, teachers,
and intellectuals, honest men and women who make up the National
Coordination of Civic Action for National Liberation (Conac-LN).

Following the words of our leader Zapata, we call for the people
of Mexico to support the just cause that is the spirit in the song of
our guns. We respectfully welcome any response that might come
from other parts of the country to this, our call for unity:

Brothers and sisters,

For years and years we harvested the death of our people in the
Chiapan countryside; our sons and daughters died from a force that
we didn't understand; our men and women walked in the long night
of ignorance that a shadow threw over our paths; our peoples walked
without truth or understanding. Our feet moved without destination; alone, we lived and we died.

The oldest of the old of our peoples spoke words to us, words that
came from very far away, about when our lives were not, about when
our voice was silenced. And the truth journeyed in the words of the oldest
of the old of our peoples. And we learned through the words of the
oldest of the old that the long night of pain of our people came from
the hands and words of the powerful, that our misery was wealth for a
few, that on the bones and the dust of our ancestors and our children,

the powerful built themselves a house, and that in that house our feet could not enter, and that the light that lit it fed itself on the darkness of our houses, and that its abundant table filled itself on the emptiness of our stomachs, and that their luxuries were born of our misery, and that the strength of their roofs and walls lifted itself over the fragility of our bodies, and that their health came from our death, and that the wisdom that lived among them nourished itself with our ignorance, that the peace that covered them was war for our people, that foreign preferences carried them far from our land and our history.

But the truth that traveled on the paths of the word of the oldest of the old of our peoples was not just of pain and death. In the word of the oldest of the old also came hope for our history. And in their word appeared the image of one like us: Emiliano Zapata. And in it we saw the place toward which our feet should walk in order to be true, and our history of struggle returned to our blood, and our hands were filled with the cries of our people, and dignity returned once again to our mouths, and in our eyes we saw a new world.

And then we made ourselves soldiers; our soil was covered with war, our feet began to walk armed with lead and fire; our fear was buried along with our dead, and we saw that our voice was carried to the land of the powerful, and we carried our truth to plant it in the middle of the land where the lie governs; we arrived in the city carrying our dead to show them to the blind eyes of our compatriots, of the good ones and the bad, of the wise and of the ignorant ones, of the powerful and the humble, of the governments and the governed. Our war cries opened the deaf ears of the almighty government and its accomplices. Before, for years and years, our voice of dignified peace could not come down from the mountains; the governments built tall strong walls to hide themselves from our death and our misery. Our strength had to break down those walls in order to enter our history again, the history they had snatched away from us, along with the dignity and reason of our peoples.

In that first blow to the deaf walls of those who have everything, the blood of our people, our blood, ran generously to wash away injustice. To live, we die. Our dead once again walked the way of truth. Our hope was fertilized with mud and blood.

But the word of the oldest of the old of our peoples didn't stop. It spoke the truth, saying that our feet couldn't walk alone, that our history of pain and shame was repeated and multiplied in the flesh and blood of the brothers and sisters of other lands and skies.

"Take your voice to other dispossessed ears, take your struggle to other struggles. There is another roof of injustice over the one that covers our pain." So said the oldest of the old of our peoples. We saw in these words that if our struggle was alone again, once again it would be useless. So we directed our blood and the path of our dead to the road that other feet walked in truth. We are nothing if we walk alone; we are everything when we walk together in step with other dignified feet.

Brothers and sisters, this is how our thoughts reached our hands and our lips. And this is how we began to move forward. May your steps walk toward us, brothers and sisters of the National Coordination of Civic Action for National Liberation, our heart is already open to your word and your truth. We have little to offer you since the poverty of our lands is still very great and our place in the history of Mexico is still very small. But walking in step with you and with all the good people of this world, we will have to grow and finally find the place that our dignity and our history deserve.

Salud, brothers and sisters of the Conac-LN.

Freedom! Justice! Democracy!

Respectfully,
From the mountains of the Mexican Southeast
CCRI-CG of the EZLN
Mexico, February 1994

• 36 •
OOPS, WE LEFT OUT TWO PARTIES

EZLN, February 15, 1994

To the national and international press
To the registered national political parties, Democratic
    Mexican Party (PDM) and National Opposition Union (UNO)
To the candidates aspiring to the presidency of the Republic
    of Mexico from PDM and UNO

Sirs,

With this letter we, the CCRI-CG of the EZLN, speak to you in order
to inform you of the following:

First. By unfortunate error, due to haste and lack of attention, the
names of your political organizations were omitted among those
invited to send delegates to the Meetings for Peace and Reconciliation in Chiapas. We are really quite embarrassed and we sincerely
hope that you forgive us and will honor us with the presence of your
delegates at this important event.

Second. The beginning of the dialogue can be an important part
of the peace process if, at the very outset, it moves in the direction
of peace with dignity, justice, freedom, and democracy. We think,
however, that any agreements that are made with the representative
of the federal government might prove difficult to implement because of the upcoming election and the change of federal power that
goes with it.

Third. For these reasons we thought we should invite you to send
delegates from the national offices of your political parties so that
you may stay informed about the peace dialogue and so that you can
give us your opinion about how the agreements might be implemented, if, in fact, that is possible. We are sure that the next
federal executive of our country will emerge from among your presidential candidates, and it will be the responsibility of the next
president of the republic to fulfill the agreements.

Fourth. We hope that our invitation to participate in the dialogue will be accepted by the leadership of your political parties, and by the campaign teams of the various presidential candidates. It will be a great honor for us to speak, when the opportunity arises, with the delegates you send.

Respectfully,
From the mountains of the Mexican Southeast
CCRI-CG of the EZLN
Mexico, February 1994

• 37 •
CYNICAL AGONY: THE SUP PREPARES TO EXPLOIT HIMSELF

To the national weekly *Proceso*
To the national newspaper *La Jornada*
To the national newspaper *El Financiero*
To the local newspaper of San Cristóbal de las Casas, Chiapas, *Tiempo*
To the national and international press

February 16, 1994

Sirs,

Okay, here I'm sending you the communiqué of the CCRI-CG of the EZLN which defines, more or less, the position it will bring to the dialogue with the Peace Envoy this February 21.

Our job here is to see that the delegates arrive on time to the places where they'll be picked up.

I don't know if the noble city of *coletos** will welcome them, but, in short, it's a risk we have to run.

The CCRI-CG of the EZLN is in the process of deciding whether or not it will send me to the dialogue; meanwhile, I am quite frantic, trying to decide what clothes to wear (if I do end up going). I look

141

critically through the giant wardrobe I carry in my pack and I wonder anxiously whether winter clothes are still in style or if I should wear something a little more flirty for spring. Finally I decide on a brown shirt (the only one), a pair of black pants (the only ones), a festive red bandanna (the only one), a pair of dirty boots (the only ones), and the ski-mask, a discreet black (the only one).

But whether or not I go, the CCRI-CG has ordered me to maintain a written silence, so I'll put away my powerful "communiqué-making machine" (a pen) as soon as I finish this.

Good health and good luck in your journalistic cannibalism. (Hey: leave something for the littlest guys. Take the political initiative and start up the PRONASOL of communications, you know, a *"pool."*)

From the mountains of the Mexican Southeast
Subcomandante Insurgente Marcos

The *"Mercantilist Postscript"* Section

P.S.: What's the going price, in dollars, for a dirty, smelly ski-mask? How much more could we get from the PGR?

P.S. to the P.S.: How much can we get if a particular brand of bottled sodas appears on the dialogue table?

P.S. with rising interest rates: How about a ski-mask *"streap tease"* (is that how it's spelled?)? *"How much for this show?"* You know, how much dough for that?

P.S. going down in the stock exchange: How much for a minute of saying silly things? How much for half a minute saying truths? (Remember that truths are always less ornate than lies, and therefore don't sell as well.)

Machista, but quoted in the stockmarket P.S.: How much for a mug shot of me from the waist down?

Stockmarket crash P.S.: How much for an exclusive *"close-up"* of the prominent nose?

Devalued by "foreign pressures" P.S.: And the "communiqué-making machine": How much if it keeps going? How much if it shuts up?

P.S. without monetary value: And for our dead, how much pain will it take to pay for them? How much money will it take to fill their pockets? How much more blood so that their silence won't have been in vain? Who wants the exclusive on their grief? Nobody? So be it . . .

P.S. that pulls us out of the stockmarket: Good-bye . . . Thanks to those who told the truth. My most heartfelt condolences to those who followed the path of lies.

Vale. The ostracized Sup.
(Yours truly)

• 38 •
"THOSE WHO FIGHT WITH HONOR, SPEAK WITH HONOR"

Communiqué from the CCRI-CG of the EZLN, Mexico
February 16, 1994

"Those who fight with honor, speak with honor."

To the people of Mexico
To the peoples and governments of the world
To the national and international press

Brothers and sisters,

The CCRI-CG of the EZLN addresses you respectfully and honorably, to say its word, to say what is in its heart and its thoughts:

On February 21, 1994, the dialogue between the federal government and the EZLN will begin, in an attempt to find a fair and dignified political solution to the current conflict. Honoring its commitment, the CCRI-CG of the EZLN has freed General Absalón Castellanos Domínguez and has already named the delegates who will represent it at the dialogue table with the Nationally Appointed Mediator, Sr. Samuel Ruiz García, and the Envoy for Peace and Reconciliation in Chiapas, Sr. Manuel Camacho Solís. Our delegates, regardless of the risk to their lives, will be at the designated place and will represent, honorably and truthfully, the thought and heart of the men and women who walk with truth.

The words of truth that come from the deepest depths of our history, of our pain, of the dead who live with us, will do dignified battle on the lips of our chiefs. The mouths of our guns will be silent so that our truth may speak with words for all those who fight with honor and talk with honor. There will be no lies in our heart, the heart of true men and women.

In our voice will travel the voice of the rest, of those who have nothing, of those condemned to silence and ignorance, of those cast from their land and their history by the sovereignty of the powerful, of all the good men and women who walk through these worlds of pain and rage, of the children and elders dead from loneliness and abandonment, of the humiliated women, of the humble men. Through our voice the dead will speak, our dead, so alone and forgotten, so dead and yet so alive in our voice and our step.

We will not go to ask forgiveness nor to petition; we will not go to beg for handouts or to pick up the crumbs that fall from the tables where the powerful sit. We will go to demand what is the right and reason of all people: freedom, justice, democracy—everything for everyone, nothing for ourselves.

For all the indigenous peoples, for all the campesinos, for all the workers, for all the teachers and students, for all the children, for all the elderly, for all the women, for all the men, everything for everyone: freedom, justice, democracy.

For us, the smallest people of these lands, those without face and without history, those armed with truth and fire, those of us who come from the night and the mountain, the true men and women, the dead of yesterday, today and forever ... for ourselves nothing. For everyone, everything.

If the mouth of the powerful lies once again, our voice of fire will speak once again: for everyone, everything.

Receive our blood, brothers and sisters, so that so much death won't be wasted, so that truth will return to our lands. For everyone, everything.

Freedom! Justice! Democracy!

Respectfully,
From the mountains of the Mexican Southeast
CCRI-CG of the EZLN
Mexico, February 1994

• 39 •
IN SOLIDARITY WITH DISPLACED PEOPLES

EZLN, Mexico, February 17, 1994

To the displaced people of San Juan Chamula
To all the indigenous peoples cast out of their lands
  and their history
San Cristóbal de las Casas, Chiapas

Brothers and sisters,

We received your letter of February 15, 1994. It is with great honor that we receive your word. Receive now our humble word that speaks with truth.

Several days ago the CCRI-CG of the EZLN began to meet to draft the list of demands it will make to the federal government. Through the analysis that we developed in those meetings, the compañeros of the CCRI-CG of the EZLN have come to believe that the injustice that lives in the heart of the *caciques** is great, and that all men and women deserve liberty and respect for their thinking and beliefs.

Therefore we demand the unconditional return of *all* displaced peoples to their legitimate lands and the punishment of those who oppress their own race and bleed their own brothers. This demand has an important place on the path to a world of justice and truth that will have to be born out of our death.

Your voice, brothers and sisters, *and that of all displaced peoples*, will speak through our voice. All men and women have the right to freedom, justice, and democracy. When we achieve this, the world will be a world and not this long chain of injustices that binds and oppresses our history.

Salud, outcast brothers and sisters!

Your demand for justice and respect is our demand!

Respectfully,
From the mountains of the Mexican Southeast
CCRI-CG of the EZLN
Mexico, February 1994

• 40 •
TO THE NGOS:
YOU GAVE ALL YOU HAD

EZLN, Mexico, February 20, 1994

To all the Non-Governmental Organizations in Mexico
From CCRI-CG of the EZLN, Mexico

Brothers and sisters,

The CCRI-CG of the EZLN addresses you respectfully so that we may send you our word that speaks truthfully.

As everyone knows, the EZLN is fully willing to enter into a fair and honest dialogue. This dialogue is taking place inside a conflict zone, which means that there is a risk that it might be disrupted by provocations. It is also possible that there might be attempts on the lives and liberties of the delegates from one side or the other. In order to reduce the chances that this should occur, it was necessary to seek out honest people to ask them to help us in forming a "safety belt" or "belt of peace" around the place of dialogue.

We realize that what are known as Non-Governmental Organizations (NGOs) have become a fundamental part of the movement toward a decent peace for those of us who have nothing and for those of us who consider ourselves obligated to take up arms to make ourselves count as human beings. The NGOs have remained neutral at all times, including those occasions when members of our EZLN have committed violations, and the efforts of the NGOs to preserve everyone's human rights are obvious to all. Moreover, they have always tried to alleviate the grave conditions of the civilian population.

We have decided to entrust our lives and liberties—our arrival and departure routes, as well as the lodging accommodations during the dialogue—to the Non-Governmental Organizations, because we have seen in them the future to which we aspire: a future in which civil society, with its force for true justice, makes not only wars but armies unnecessary; and a future in which governments, whatever their political tendency, work under the constant and strict vigilance of a free and democratic civil society.

Our safe and healthy arrival to this place of dialogue we owe to the vigilant and protective cloak of all of these good people who, without pay, offer their time, their efforts, and their work, and *at risk to their own lives, liberties, and well being,* protect us, the smallest of all Mexicans.

Therefore, we want to ask respectfully that you accept this grateful acknowledgment that our EZLN gives your work. Whatever might be the result of this process, our country's history will record, not so much the voices of our guns and our deaths, but rather the bravery of the women and men, all of you, who, asking nothing in return but the satisfaction of fulfilling your duty, gave all you had.

Salud, brothers and sisters of the NGOs.

Respectfully,
From the mountains of the Mexican Southeast
CCRI-CG of the EZLN
Mexico, February 1994

• 41 •
IN TRUTH, ANYTHING CAN HAPPEN

**Communiqué from the CCRI-CG of the EZLN, Mexico
February 26, 1994**

To the people of Mexico
To the peoples and governments of the world
To the national and international press

Brothers and sisters,

The CCRI-CG of the EZLN addresses you with respect and honor in order to say what is in our hearts and in our thoughts.

When the EZLN was only a shadow creeping between the fog and the darkness in the mountains; when the words justice, freedom, and democracy were only that—words; in that hour when day finally yields to night, when the old people of our communities, the true guardians of the words of our dead, had for the first time recounted their dream; when hatred and death were beginning to grow in our breasts; when there was nothing but hopelessness; when time seemed to repeat itself, and there was no way out, no open door, no tomorrow . . . when everything unjust, just was . . . then it was that the true men and women spoke, those without faces, those who walk in the night, those who are mountain, and they said:

"It is both the opinion and the will of all good men and women that they must look for and find the best way to govern and to be governed; and the main truth of that best way is that what is good for the many is good for everyone. But the voices of the few must not be silenced; they should continue to speak, waiting for heart and thought to become one in the will of the many and in the point of view of the few. Thus the communities of true men and women will grow internally strong and become great, and no outside force will be able to break them or pull them from their true paths.

"It has always been our way that the will of the majority is in the hearts of the men and women who command. It was this majority will that determined the road that the leaders had to follow. If they strayed from this road, and didn't follow the word of the people, then the heart of command had to be replaced by another who would obey. That is how our force was born in the mountains; those who command, obey if they are true leaders, and those who obey, command through the common heart of true men and women. A far-away word names this form of government, and this word that names the road we have traveled since the time before words is 'democracy.'"

Those who traveled by night also spoke: "And we see that the road of the government is not the road of the many, we see that it is the few who now command, and command without obeying, they command by commanding. And the power of command is passed around among the few, who don't listen to the many, the few who command by commanding, without obeying the command of the many. The few command without reason—the word that comes from afar says that they command without democracy, without following the command of the people. We see that the lack of reason among those who command by commanding is what causes our pain and deepens the sorrow of our dead, and we see that those who command by commanding should go far from here so that there might be another form of reason and another truth on our soil. And we see that there must be change, and that those who command should obey, and we see that this far-away word, 'democracy,' which names government with reason, is good for the many and the few."

The faceless men kept talking: "The world is another world where the reason and will of true men does not govern any longer; we are few and forgotten, death and scorn walk with us, we are small, our word is ignored. Silence has lived with us in our houses for a long time, but now the time has come for our hearts and the hearts of others to speak. Our dead will come forth, out of the night and out of the earth, and those without faces, those that are mountain, will come forth, and they shall all dress for war so that their voice will be heard, and afterward fall silent and return again to the night and the earth. Then other men and women, who walk on other lands, must speak, and they too should speak the truth and not get lost in lies.

"Look for men and women who command by obeying, those whose strength is in words and not in fire, and when you find them, talk to them and give them the staff of command, so that those without faces, those who are mountain, may return to the earth and the night; and if reason returns to these lands, the fury of fire shall fall silent, and those that are mountain, those without faces, those who walk in the night will finally rest beside the earth."

Thus spoke the faceless men. There was no fire in their hands, and their word was clear and straight. And before the day was again overcome by the night, they left, and on the earth remained only their word:

"Enough!"

The men and women of the EZLN, those without faces, those who walk in the night, those who are mountain, have looked for words that others might understand, and now we say the following:

First. We demand a truly free and democratic election, with equal rights and obligations for all political organizations struggling for power, in which people will have real liberty to choose between different proposals and the will of the majority is respected. Democracy is the fundamental right of all peoples, indigenous and non-indigenous, and without democracy there can be neither freedom, nor justice, nor dignity, and without dignity there is nothing.

Second. So that there can be truly free and democratic elections, the incumbent federal executive and the incumbent state executives, which got their power through electoral fraud and whose legitimacy does not come from the will of the majority but rather through the usurpation of that will, must resign. Consequently, a transitional government is necessary so that there can be equal respect for all political currents.

Legislative powers, at the federal and state levels, elected freely and democratically, must assume their true function of making just laws for everyone and making sure that the laws are followed.

Third. Another way of guaranteeing free and democratic elections is to recognize in national, state, and local law the legitimacy of citizens and groups of citizens, who without party affiliation would watch over the elections, sanction the legality of its results, and have the maximum authority to guarantee the legitimacy of the whole electoral process.

This is the word of the EZLN. With democracy, freedom, and justice are possible. In an atmosphere of deceit, nothing flowers; in truth, anything can happen.

Liberty! Justice! Democracy!

Respectfully,
From the mountains of the Mexican Southeast
CCRI-CG of the EZLN
Mexico, February 1994

• 42 •
CALM DOWN, IT WASN'T YOU

EZLN, Mexico

To Srs. Samuel del Villar, Alejandro Encínas, representatives
of the CEN of the PRD
From Subcomandante Insurgente Marcos
Mountains of the Mexican Southeast, Chiapas, Mexico

February 25, 1994

Sirs,

I just received your righteously indignant letter. Imagine my joy at being able, for the first time in a long time, to respond immediately without a long wait for your letter to arrive here and for my answer to return there.

I understand your consternation. But look, you (or some of you) were present when we were visited by representatives of the political parties. You heard how at least two of them launched into a political oratory competition, with the approval of their fellow party members, and you saw how surprised we were, as we had naively thought that people had come to listen to us and not to *"speechalize"* us (oops, sorry for such a stupid word . . .)

When we finally managed to extract ourselves from the smooth "magic" of the words of these men, we withdrew with the following words: "Just don't abandon us. Hope to God you learn to listen." Anyone who was there knows who the political party representatives were who grabbed the "pulpit" in the Cathedral. The CCRI-CG has explicitly prohibited me from speaking for or against ANY of the political parties, which is why, when I commented on the incident in an interview, I referred only to "political parties."

You know who did this, and you also know that it wasn't you, so why get so worked up about it? I accept the legitimate anger of your letter, but you must understand that I cannot disobey my superiors, and so I cannot say publicly who the political parties were who blathered on without rhyme or reason. Nevertheless, I believe I am free to say who didn't do that: you.

Salud, and no postscripts this time because they might provoke something big, and we are slightly worn out here, *c'est à dire,* absolutely wasted.

Respectfully,
From the Mountains of the Mexican Southeast
Subcomandante Insurgente Marcos

• 43 •
EZLN DEMANDS AT THE DIALOGUE TABLE

**Communiqué from the CCRI-CG of the EZLN, Mexico
March 1, 1994**

To the people of Mexico
To the peoples and governments of the world
To the national and international press

Brothers and sisters,

The CCRI-CG of the EZLN addresses you with respect and honor in order to inform you of the list of demands presented at the dialogue table in the Meetings for Peace and Reconciliation in Chiapas.

"We are not begging for change or gifts; we ask for the right to live with the dignity of human beings, with equality and justice like our parents and grandparents of old."

To the people of Mexico:

The indigenous peoples of the state of Chiapas, having risen up in arms in the EZLN against misery and the bad government, hereby present the reasons for their struggle and their principal demands:

The reason and causes of our armed movement are the following, problems to which the government has never offered any real solution:

(1) The hunger, misery, and marginalization that we have always suffered.

(2) The total lack of land on which to work in order to survive.

(3) The repression, eviction, imprisonment, torture, and murder with which the government responds to our fair demands.

(4) The unbearable injustices and violations of our human rights as indigenous people and impoverished campesinos.

(5) The brutal exploitation we suffer in the sale of our products, in the work day, and in the purchase of basic necessities.

(6) The lack of all basic services for the great majority of the indigenous population.

(7) More than sixty years of lies, deceptions, promises, and imposed governments. The lack of freedom and democracy in deciding our destinies.

(8) The constitutional laws have not been obeyed by those who govern the country; on the other hand, we the indigenous people and campesinos are made to pay for the smallest error. They heap upon us the weight of a law we did not make, and those who did make it are the first to violate it.

The EZLN came to dialogue with honest words. The EZLN came to say its word about the conditions that were the origin of its righteous war and to ask all the people of Mexico to help find a solution to these political, economic, and social conditions that forced us to take up arms to defend our existence and our rights.

Therefore we demand . . .

First. We demand truly free and democratic elections, with equal rights and obligations for all the political organizations struggling for power, with real freedom to choose between one proposal and another and with respect for the will of the majority. Democracy is the fundamental right of all peoples, indigenous and not indigenous. Without democracy there cannot be liberty or justice or dignity. And without dignity there is nothing.

Second. In order for there to be truly free and democratic elections, the incumbent federal executive and the incumbent state executives, which came to power via electoral fraud, must resign.

Their legitimacy does not come from respect for the will of the majority but rather from usurping it. Consequently, a transitional government must be formed to ensure equality and respect for all political currents. The federal and state legislative powers, elected freely and democratically, must assume their true functions of making just laws for everyone and ensuring that the laws are followed.

Another way to guarantee free and democratic elections is to recognize in national, state, and local law, the legitimacy of citizens and groups of citizens who, without party affiliation, would watch over the elections, sanction the legality of its results, and have maximum authority to guarantee the legitimacy of the whole electoral process.

Third. Recognition of the EZLN as a belligerent force, and of its troops as authentic combatants, and application of all international treaties that regulate military conflict.

Fourth. A new pact among the elements of the federation, which puts an end to centralism and permits regions, indigenous communities, and municipalities to govern themselves with political, economic, and cultural autonomy.

Fifth. General elections for the whole state of Chiapas and legal recognition of all the political forces in the state.

Sixth. As a producer of electricity and oil, the state of Chiapas pays tribute to the federation without receiving anything in exchange. Our communities do not have electric power; the export and domestic sale of our oil doesn't produce any benefit whatsoever for the Chiapan people. In view of this, it is vital that all Chiapan communities receive the benefit of electric power and that a percentage of the income from the commercialization of Chiapan oil be applied to the agricultural, commercial, and social-industrial infrastructure, for the benefit of all Chiapans.

Seventh. Revision of the North American Free Trade Agreement signed with Canada and the United States, given that in its current state it does not take into consideration the indigenous populations and sentences them to death for the crime of having no job qualifications whatsoever.

Eighth. Article 27 of the Magna Carta must respect the original spirit of Emiliano Zapata: the land is for the indigenous people and campesinos who work it. Not for the latifundistas.* We want, as is established in our revolutionary agricultural law, the great quantity of land that is currently in the hands of big ranchers and national and foreign landowners to pass into the hands of our peoples, who suffer from a total lack of land. The land grants shall include farm machinery, fertilizers, pesticides, credits, technical advice, improved seeds, livestock, and fair prices for products like coffee, corn, and beans. The land that is distributed must be of good quality and include roads, transportation, and irrigation systems.

The campesinos who already have land also have the right to all the above-mentioned supports in order to facilitate their work in the fields and improve production. New *ejidos* and communities must be formed. The Salinas revision of Article 27 must be annulled and the right to land must be recognized as per the terms of our Magna Carta.

Ninth. We want hospitals to be built in the municipal seats, with specialized doctors and enough medicine to be able to attend to the patients; we want rural clinics in the *ejidos,* communities, and surrounding areas, as well as training and a fair salary for health workers. Where there are already hospitals, they must be rehabilitated as soon as possible and include complete surgical services. In the larger communities, clinics must be built and they too must have doctors and medicine in order to treat people more quickly.

Tenth. The right to true information about what happens at the local, regional, state, national, and international levels must be guaranteed to the indigenous peoples by way of an indigenous radio station independent of the government, directed by indigenous people and run by indigenous people.

Eleventh. We want housing to be built in all the rural communities of Mexico, including basic services like: electricity, potable water, roads, sewer systems, telephone, transportation, etc. And these houses should also have the advantages of the city, like television, stove, refrigerator, washing machine, etc. The communities shall be equipped with recreation centers for the healthy entertainment of their populations: sports and culture that dignify the human condition of the indigenous people.

Twelfth. We want the illiteracy of the indigenous peoples to come to an end. For this to happen we need better elementary and secondary schools in our communities, including free teaching materials, and teachers with university education who are at the service of the people and not just in defense of the interests of the rich. In the municipal seats there must be free elementary, junior high, and high schools; the government must give the students uniforms, shoes, food, and all study materials free of charge. The larger, central communities that are very far from the municipal seats must provide boarding schools at the secondary level. Education must be totally free, from preschool to university, and must be granted to all Mexicans regardless of race, creed, age, sex, or political affiliation.

Thirteenth. The languages of all ethnicities must be official and their instruction shall be mandatory in elementary, junior high, and high school, and at the university level.

Fourteenth. Our rights and dignity as indigenous peoples shall be respected, taking into account our cultures and traditions.

Fifteenth. We indigenous people no longer want to be the object of discrimination and contempt.

Sixteenth. We indigenous people must be permitted to organize and govern ourselves autonomously; we no longer want to submit to the will of the powerful, either national or foreign.

Seventeenth. Justice shall be administered by the same indigenous peoples, according to their customs and traditions, without intervention by illegitimate and corrupt governments.

Eighteenth. We want to have decent jobs with fair salaries for all rural and urban workers throughout the Mexican republic, so that our brothers and sisters don't have to work at bad things, like drug trafficking, delinquency, and prostitution, to be able to survive. The federal Labor Law shall be applied to rural and urban workers, complete with bonuses, benefits, vacations, and the real right to strike.

Nineteenth. We want a fair price for our products from the countryside. Thus we need the liberty to find a market where we can buy and sell and not be subject to exploiting *coyotes.**

Twentieth. The plunder of the riches of our Mexico and above all of Chiapas, one of the richest states of the republic but where hunger and misery most abound, must come to an end.

Twenty-first. We want all debt from credits, loans, and taxes with high interest rates to be annulled; these cannot be paid due to the great poverty of the Mexican people.

Twenty-second. We want hunger and malnutrition to end; it alone has caused the death of thousands of our brothers and sisters in the country and the city. Every rural community must have cooperative stores supported economically by the federal, state, or municipal governments, and the prices must be fair. Moreover, there must be vehicles, property of the co-ops, for the transportation of merchandise. The government must send free food for all children under fourteen.

Twenty-third. We ask for the immediate and unconditional liberty of all political prisoners and of all the poor people unfairly imprisoned in all the jails of Chiapas and Mexico.

Twenty-fourth. We ask that the Federal Army and the public security and judicial police no longer come into rural zones because they only come to intimidate, evict, rob, repress, and bomb campesinos who are organizing to defend their rights. Our peoples are tired of the abusive and repressive presence of the soldiers and public security and judicial police. The federal government must return to the Swiss government the Pilatus planes used to bomb our people, and the money resulting from the return of that merchandise shall be applied toward programs to improve the lives of the workers of the country and the city. We also ask that the government of the United States of North America recall its helicopters, as they are used to repress the people of Mexico.

Twenty-fifth. When the indigenous campesino people rose up in arms, they had nothing but poor huts, but now that the Federal Army is bombing the civilian population it is destroying even these humble homes and our few belongings. Therefore we ask and demand of the federal government that it compensate the families that have sustained material losses caused by the bombings and the actions of the federal troops. We also ask for compensation for those widowed and orphaned by the war, for civilians as well as Zapatistas.

Twenty-sixth. We as indigenous campesinos want to live in peace and quiet, and to be permitted to live according to our rights to liberty and a decent life.

Twenty-seventh. The Penal Code of the state of Chiapas must be revoked; it doesn't permit us to organize in any way other than with arms, since any legal and peaceful struggle is punished and repressed.

Twenty-eighth. We ask for and demand an immediate halt to the displacement of indigenous peoples from their communities by the state-backed *caciques*. We demand the guaranteed free and voluntary return of all displaced peoples to their lands of origin, and compensation for their losses.

Twenty-ninth. Indigenous women's petition:

We the indigenous campesina women ask for the immediate solution to our urgent needs, which the government has never met:

(1) Child-birth clinics with gynecologists so that campesina women can receive necessary medical attention.

(2) Day-care centers must be built in the communities.

(3) We ask the government to send enough food for the children in all the communities such as: milk, corn starch, rice, corn, soy, oil, beans, cheese, eggs, sugar, soup, oatmeal, etc.

(4) Kitchens and dining halls, with all the necessary equipment, must be built for the children in the communities.

(5) Corn mills and tortilla-makers must be placed in the communities according to the number of families in each area.

(6) We should be given the materials necessary to raise chickens, rabbits, sheep, pigs, etc., including technical advice and veterinary services.

(7) We ask for the ovens and materials necessary to build bakeries.

(8) We want craft workshops to be built, including machinery and materials.

(9) There must be a market where crafts can be sold at a fair price.

(10) Schools must be built where women can receive technical training.

(11) There must be preschools and day-care centers in the rural communities where the children can have fun and grow up strong, morally and physically.

(12) As women we must have sufficient transportation to move from one place to another and to transport the products of the various projects we will have.

Thirtieth. We demand political justice for Patrocinio Gonzáles Garrido, Absalón Castellanos Domínguez, and Elmar Setzer M.

Thirty-first. We demand respect for the lives of all members of the EZLN and a guarantee that there will be no penal process or repressive action taken against any of the members of the EZLN, combatants, sympathizers, or collaborators.

Thirty-second. All groups and commissions defending human rights must be independent, that is, non-governmental, because those that are governmental only hide the arbitrary actions of the government.

Thirty-third. A National Commission of Peace with Justice and Dignity should be formed, the majority of constituents being people with no government or party affiliation. This National Commission of Peace with Justice and Dignity should be the agency that ensures the implementation of the agreements reached between the EZLN and the federal government.

Thirty-fourth. The humanitarian aid for the victims of the conflict should be channeled through authentic representatives of the indigenous communities.

As long as there is no answer to these fair demands of our peoples, we are willing and determined to continue our struggle until we reach our objective.

For us, the least of these lands, those without face and without history, those armed with truth and fire, those who came from the night and the mountain, the true men and women, the dead of yesterday, today and forever . . . for ourselves nothing. For everyone everything.

Freedom! Justice! Democracy!

Respectfully,
From the Mexican Southeast
CCRI-CG of the EZLN
Mexico, March 1994

• 44 •
THANKS TO THE NGOS
FOR THEIR PROTECTION

March 1, 1994

To the Mexican people
To the people and governments of the world
To the Non-Governmental Organizations
To the national and international press

Brothers and sisters,

The CCRI-CG of the EZLN addresses you with respect and honor in order to say our word.

We have often expressed our admiration for the disinterested and honest work of the so-called Non-Governmental Organizations. Now we want to say thank you again to the good and upright people who came from various parts of Mexico and the world to surround us in a "belt of peace" these last few days, sacrificing their time, work, and comfort in order to accompany us in this first step on the road to a just and dignified peace.

In our dreams we have seen another world. A true world, a world more just than the one we now walk in. We saw that in this new world armies were not necessary, and that peace, justice, and freedom were not spoken of as distant ideals but as common, everyday things, named as easily as the other good things of this world: bread, bird, air, water, and even, for some, book and voice. And in this world, government by the many was the will and the reality of the people, and those that commanded were thoughtful people who commanded by obeying. And this new, true world was not a dream from the past; it was not something that came from our ancestors. It came to us from the future; it was the next step that we had to take.

And so it was that we began our journey to have this dream sit at our table, light up our house, grow among our corn, fill the hearts of our children, wipe the sweat from our brow, heal our history—and to win this dream for everyone.

That's what we want. Nothing more, nothing less.

Now we move on toward our own heart, to ask it what we should do. We will return to our mountains to talk with our own tongue at our own pace with our own people.

Thanks to the brothers and sisters who took care of us every day we were here; thank you for joining your path with ours. Adios.

Freedom! Justice! Democracy!

Respectfully,
Subcomandante Marcos
From the Mexican Southeast
CCRI-CG of the EZLN, March 1994

• 45 •
THE DIALOGUE WAS REAL

**Communiqué from the CCRI-CG of the EZLN, Mexico
March 1, 1994**

To the people of Mexico
To the peoples and governments of the world
To the national and international press

Brothers and sisters,

The CCRI-CG of the EZLN addresses all of you with respect and honor in order to say its word.

First. The EZLN came to this dialogue table in the true spirit of being heard and explaining all the reasons that obligated us to take up arms so as not to die an undignified death. We came to dialogue, which is to say we came to speak and to listen. We said our word to the federal government and to all the good and honest people that there are in the world. We also spoke to the bad people, that they might hear the truth. Some received our word, and others continued down the path of contempt for our voice and our race.

Second. We encountered attentive ears that were willing to hear the truth that came from our lips. The dialogue of San Cristóbal was real. There were no tricks or lies; nothing was hidden from our hearts or from the people of reason and goodness. There was no buying and selling of dignities. There was a balance in the speaking and the listening. There was good and honest dialogue.

Third. Now that we have a response that reflects the sincere interest of the gentleman commissioned as Peace Envoy, it is our obligation to reflect well on what his words say. We must now speak to the collective heart that commands us. We must listen to its voice in order to start again; from them, from our people, from the indigenous peoples in the mountains and canyons, will come the decision on the next step to take along this road whose destiny will, or will not, be peace with justice and dignity.

Fourth. We have found in the Envoy for Peace and Reconciliation in

Chiapas a man willing to listen to our reasons and our demands. He was not content just to listen to and understand us; he also sought possible solutions to the problems. We salute the attitude of the Peace Envoy Manuel Camacho Solís.

Fifth. We have seen in the Nationally Appointed Mediator, Bishop Samuel Ruiz García, a real and permanent concern to overcome all the obstacles that could block the road to peace. Along with him, good men and women worked day and night so that nothing would interrupt the dialogue process. Sacrificing their personal security, their well being and their health, the mediators did their job not in the middle of war and peace, but in the middle of two voices who are trying, still, to find each other. In the interest of peace, these men and women received us; if some tranquillity blossoms in these lands it will be due, above all, to their peace-making work. We salute the sacrifice and the dedication of the group of the National Mediation Commission, and especially Bishop Samuel Ruiz García.

Sixth. Now this stage of the dialogue has come to an end and it is going in a good direction. Let us move aside all obstacles so that we can keep going.

Freedom! Justice! Democracy!

Respectfully,
Subcomandante Marcos
From the Mexican Southeast
CCRI-CG of the EZLN
Mexico, March 1994

• 46 •
A LETTER TO A
THIRTEEN-YEAR-OLD BOY
IN BAJA CALIFORNIA

EZLN, Mexico

To Miguel Vázquez Valtierra, La Paz, Baja California
From Subcomandante Insurgente Marcos
Mountains of the Mexican Southeast, Chiapas

Miguel,

Your mother gave me your letter and the photo of you and your dog. I am taking advantage of your mother's return home to write you these hurried lines, that perhaps you are not yet ready to understand. Nevertheless, I am sure that some day, just like he who wrote what appears here, you will understand that it is possible for men and women like us to exist, without faces and without names, who have left everything behind, even life itself, so that others (children like you and those not like you) are able to get up in the morning without being told to shut up, and with no need for masks to confront the world. When this day arrives, we, those without faces and without names, will be able to rest, at last, under the ground, very dead indeed, but happy.

Our profession: hope.

The day is almost dead, dark now as it dresses as night, getting ready for the next day that is coming to be born, first with its black veil, and later with one of gray or blue, depending on how much the sun feels like shining on the dust and mud of our path. The day is dying in the night-time arms of the crickets, and suddenly I have the urge to write you and tell you something about being the "professionals of violence," as we have so often been called.

Yes, we are professionals. But our profession is hope. We decided one good day to become soldiers so that a day would come when there would be no need for soldiers. That is to say, we chose a suicidal profession, because it is a profession whose goal is to disappear: soldiers who are soldiers so that one day no one will have to be a soldier. That's clear, isn't it?

And it so happens that we soldiers who wish to stop being soldiers have something that books and speeches call "patriotism." Because that which we call "our country" is not a vague bookish idea, but rather a huge body of flesh and blood, of pain and suffering and sorrow, and of hope that some fine day everything might finally change. And the country that we want will also have to be born out of our errors and our blunders. Out of our spent and broken bodies must rise up a new world.

Will we see it? Does it matter? I believe that it doesn't matter as much as knowing with undeniable certainty that it will be born, and that we have put our all—our lives, bodies, and souls—into this long and painful but historic birth. *Amor y dolor*—love and pain: two words that not only rhyme, but join up and march together.

This is why we are soldiers who wish to stop being soldiers. But then it turns out that to end the need for soldiers it is necessary to become one, and to prescribe a certain small amount of lead, hot lead with which to write liberty and justice for all, not for one or for a few, but for all, for the dead from long ago and the dead of tomorrow, for the living of today and forever, for those who speak of community and nation, for those with nothing, for the eternal losers, those without names, without faces.

And to be a soldier who wishes that soldiers were no longer necessary is very simple; it is enough to respond decisively to that little piece of hope inside us, deposited there by the many, those who now have nothing and will have everything. And we must do it, for them and for those who have been left behind by the side of the road, for one or another unjust reason; for them we must truly try to change and better ourselves every day, every afternoon, every rain- and cricket-filled night. We must patiently store up hate and love. We must tend the wild tree of hatred of the oppressor with the love that fights and liberates. We must cultivate the powerful tree of a love that is a cleansing and healing wind, not a small egoistic love, but the grand one, the one that improves us and makes us grow. We must cultivate among us the tree of love and hate, and the tree of obligation. And we must water these trees with our whole lives—our bodies and souls, our breath and hope. We must grow, little by little, step by step.

And we must not be afraid during the rise and fall of red stars, not be afraid of anything but surrender, of remaining in our seats and resting while others continue on, of taking a break while others struggle, sleeping while others are on watch.

Abandon, if you have it, the love of death and fascination with martyrdom. The revolutionary loves life without fearing death, and seeks a dignified life for everyone; if that requires that he pay with his death, he will do it without hesitation and without histrionics.

I send you my best hug; receive this tender pain that will forever be hope.

Salud, Miguel.

> From the mountains of the Mexican Southeast
> Subcomandante Insurgente Marcos

P.S.: Here we live worse than dogs. We had to choose: to live like animals or die like dignified men. Dignity, Miguel, is the only thing that must never be lost . . . ever.

• 47 •
POSTSCRIPTS:
NOSTALGIC AND POETIC

To the national and international press

March 15, 1994

Sirs,

Did you miss me? Well, here I am anew and not so new. It's difficult to talk about peace with the other shadows that reach us from San Cristóbal. We are attentive more to the voice of those who share our longings than to the voice of those who defend never-ending privileges and injustices. It hurts to see that even the "authentic ones" are corrupted. Do they want more war so that they can come to understand peace? Face it, *coletos*, you were happier with our troops inside the walls of your proud colonial city than you are now as you arm yourselves with fear. Learn now about this struggle that arms itself with honor . . .

Good health and good luck in the Ides of March.

From the mountains of the Mexican Southeast
Subcomandante Insurgente Marcos

P.S. OF IMMEDIATE NOSTALGIA (?):
Section: "Yesterday's (?) images of the guerrilla life."
(1) My work already had glimmers of "historic transcendence": I was taking care of a small monkey who, as ALL little ones should, had absolutely no respect for authority. Ignoring my gallant military bearing and the already somewhat faded red star on my chest (which said to the rest of the already powerful EZLN of that time, which is to say the other six, that there was an infantry lieutenant among us), the little monkey (we always suspected that it was a "she" and not a "he") was at pains always to climb up my chest onto my right shoulder and go along for the ride whenever it felt like it. Raúl, the greatest of all of us in every sense, was our teacher. Lucha sang tangos over and

over during the afternoons, hours of tangos and *grillos.*[*] The food was running out. We went on, knowing what was coming. We were already invincible and small. January was still a long way off. The year? 1984 (does that remind you of anything?). The Mad Hatter and the March Hare were singing:

"A happy happy un-birthday to you, I give to you (repeat).
If today is not your birthday
Well, we'll just have to celebraaate
etcetera (repeat)."

Alice managed to get out. We are still here ... And we're singing ... still ...

(2) And it was in 1987 and I was second captain of infantry and it was the country in our thoughts and it was, for example, a poem:

PROBLEMS

This thing about country
is a little difficult to explain.
But more difficult is understanding
that love of country thing.
For example,
They taught us that love of country is,
for example,
to salute the flag,
to stand up on hearing the national anthem.
To get as drunk as we want when
the national soccer team loses.
When the national soccer team wins,
to get as drunk as we want.
A few etceteras that don't change much from one
presidency to the next ...
And, for example,
they did not teach us that love of country
can be,
for example,
to whistle like someone getting ever further away,
but
behind that hill is our country too and no one is watching,

and we open our hearts
(because one always opens one's heart
when no one is watching)
and we say
(to our country),
for example,
how much we hate it
and how much we love it
and this is always better to say,
for example,
amidst gunfire
and smiling.

And, for example,
they taught us that love of country is,
for example,
to wear a big sombrero,
to know all the names of the Boy Heroes of Chapultepec*
to yell "Long live and up with Mexico!"
even though Mexico might be dead and down under.
Other etceteras that change little from one
presidency to the next.
And, for example,
they did not teach us that
love of country can be,
for example,
to fall silent like a dying person,
but no,
beneath this land there is country too
and no one hears us,
and we open our hearts
(because one always opens one's heart
when no one is listening)
and we tell
(our country)
the small hard story
of those who went on dying
to love her,

and who are no longer here to agree with me,
but they agree even without being here,
those who taught us
that one loves one's country,
for example,
amidst gunfire
and smiling.

P.S. THAT BIDS FAREWELL IN A FRIENDLY WINDSTORM: This March, like
everything else, is confusing. Take care of yourselves if you can. Carry on.

• 48 •
WE ARE SHADOWS OF TENDER FURY

Communiqué from the CCRI-CG of the EZLN, Mexico
March 15, 1994

"Shadows of tender fury, our path will clothe those who have nothing."

To the State Council of Indigenous Peoples and Campesinos (CEOIC)
To the people of Mexico
To the peoples and governments of the world
To the national and international press

Brothers and sisters,

The CCRI-CG of the EZLN addresses you to say its word:

The federal government, yesterday the usurper of popular will, has lied once again about what happened in the dialogue in San Cristóbal de las Casas, Chiapas. The bad government says there are "agreements" where there was only dialogue. The powerful now violate the truth and try to deceive the people by saying that peace is only a matter of a signature.

How can there be peace when the people who cause war still clamor for the perpetuation of our misery? The arrogance that lives in the government palaces and the houses of the lords of land and big business is still screaming for war and death for our race; they won't tolerate the idea that indigenous blood is equal to white. We seek an entrance into the nation and they refuse us. Now they mock the march of our dead by flinging contemptuous coins at their feet.

As long as they speak with contempt, how can there be peace in these lands? As long as they silence and murder our brothers, how can we ask our collective heart if it is time for peace to enter, hand in hand with dignity, through the doors of our impoverished lands? They want to shove us back in the corner, to wrench a surrender from us; over a road paved with the death of our dignity, they want to take us back to the peace that is war for our peoples.

We will not do it; we will not surrender. If they refuse a just and dignified peace, then we, men and women of the shadows, will dress ourselves once again for war, and this time our rage will be a product of deceit. The machetes of justice are being sharpened again; once again, our lands smell of gunpowder.

We are shadows of tender fury; our dark wings will cover the sky again, and their protective cloak will shelter the dispossessed and the good men and women who understand that justice and peace go hand in hand. If they deny us our rights, then our tender fury will enter those fine mansions. There will be no fence our shadows will not jump over; no door will be left unopened, no window left unbroken, no wall left standing. Our shadow will bring pain to those who call for war and death for our race; more tears and blood will flow before peace can sit down at our table with good will.

We, the shadows of tender fury, will come forth once again so that our voice can be heard and finally drown out the lie. The "Enough!" of our first call was not enough. It was not enough to make the earth bloom with the blood of our dead.

The men and women of tender fury will have to walk once again; again our dead will have to rise, and the history of our wounded heart will speak again, so that the deceit and lies will end, so that the arrogance in these Mexican lands will finally perish. May the men and women of the night come forth once again and, dressed in the dark clothing of tender fury, speak with a voice filled with the voices of everyone, to silence all these lies.

May the mouth of the powerful cease to speak; only poison and poverty come from its lips. May their lies and their duplicities finally be silent.

May our brothers speak now, they who walk different paths to bring our pain to new suns. May the voice of our brothers of the CEIOC speak, may all the indigenous peoples of these lands say their word. May the poor campesino not be silent; may the worker shout in the cities, may this warrior song not forget the voice of teachers and students, of the employees and of the small ones in all senses.

Do not leave this heavy flag in our hands alone; may everyone raise it. Let us all change the land that it envelops; Mexican brothers and sisters, do not forget this voice of the mountains. The light of our dead is still very small. Let us all join our lights; let us shatter this shameful night once and for all. It is time for dawn to break.

May the truth speak, may its voice now speak, may its step be firm; we, without face and without past, are listening with open heart and word. So that the many voices of the people might speak, our men and women stay silent, the shadows of tender fury stay quiet.

May our dream keep vigil over your step, to protect you from evil, so that black shadows do not threaten you; for you, brothers, we keep our heart and our fire burning—so that you may walk in well being, so that, finally, this furious tenderness may reign in these lands.

Peace is not possible in an atmosphere of deceit. Peace is born in freedom, it grows in justice, and is a dignified democracy for all.

Salud, brothers and sisters of the CEOIC!

Salud, indigenous brothers and sisters!

Salud, Mexican brothers and sisters; walk without fear, lift up your face and your steps; our arms are already protecting your path.

Freedom! Democracy! Justice!

Respectfully,
From the mountains of the Mexican Southeast
CCRI-CG of the EZLN
Mexico, March 1994

• 49 •
EZLN GRANTS POWER OF ATTORNEY

Communiqué from the CCRI-CG of the EZLN, Mexico March 15, 1994

To the people of Mexico
To the peoples and governments of the world
To the national and international press

Brothers and sisters,

Since the previous stage of the San Cristóbal dialogue, the CCRI-CG of the EZLN has asked for legal support to consider various problems that the process of war and the process of peace presented to our army. We did not receive immediate answers; the righteousness of our struggle was getting lost among all the slander and mistrust. Only one response reached us during those hours: that of the brothers and sisters of the National Coordination of Civic Action for National Liberation (Conac-LN), who offered the support of their Legal Commission.

We are thankful for this gesture and grant these people our trust. They will do everything within their capacities to support us in legal matters—and our needs are great. We welcome the selflessness and impartiality of the brothers and sisters of the Conac-LN and we address the Mexican people in order to ratify what we have written before: all legal matters of our EZLN will be entrusted to the Legal Commission of the National Coordination of Civic Action for National Liberation.

Freedom! Justice! Democracy!

Respectfully,
From the Mexican Southeast
CCRI-CG of the EZLN
Mexico, March 1994

• 50 •
THE GOVERNMENT IS LYING, THERE HAVE BEEN NO AGREEMENTS

**Communiqué from the CCRI-CG of the EZLN, Mexico
March 15, 1994**

To the people of Mexico
To the peoples and governments of the world
To the national and international press

Brothers and sisters,

The CCRI-CG of the EZLN addresses you with respect and honor to say its word:

First. The federal government, yesterday the usurper of the popular will, has lied once again about what happened during the dialogue in San Cristóbal de las Casas, Chiapas. The bad government says that there are "agreements" where there was only dialogue. The powerful now violate the truth and try to deceive the people by saying that peace is only a matter of a signature.

Second. They are trying to make people forget the fundamental causes of our uprising by replacing the truth of a dialogue with the lie of an "agreement." The CCRI-CG of the EZLN has made no treaty with the federal government. It has negotiated nothing other than the way the dialogue is to be carried out, and it has made no agreement whatsoever with the bad government which has been lying for so long.

Third. The CCRI-CG of the EZLN points out that ending the first phase of the dialogue with lies is the best way to ensure that peace will fail. We will not trust a government that, even when making propositions, lies. If the almighty government wants to present documents from San Cristóbal as "agreements," then let the EZLN's list of demands be the "agreement," and with the resignation of the federal executive as per those demands, let democracy be guaranteed in the upcoming elections.

Fourth. The CCRI-CG of the EZLN respectfully asks the honest press, national and international, that it not participate in the deceptions of the usurper and that it publicize, with truth and objectivity, what is really happening in the current stage of the dialogue.

Freedom! Justice! Democracy!

Respectfully,
From the Mexican Southeast
CCRI-CG of the EZLN
Mexico, March 1994

• 51 •
THE ZAPATISTAS
WILL NOT SURRENDER

Communiqué from the CCRI-CG of the EZLN, Mexico
March 19, 1994

To the State Council of Campesino and Indigenous Peoples' Organizations (CEOIC)
To all the honest organizations of indigenous people and campesinos in Mexico
To the people of Mexico

Brothers and sisters,

The CCRI-CG of the EZLN respectfully asks you to accept this humble greeting of our soldiers from the mountains of the Mexican Southeast.

We raise our arms and our heads high to say to the usurping government that we are tired of so many lies. They have sold us a grand farce for all these years and now they want to top it off with an insulting mask of peace. We do not want it. We have known this type of peace for five hundred years, and we know the cost and the scant benefits for our earth and our people. Someone who has never been to our mountains before wants to come now, and for a handful of spare change wants us to abandon our brothers and sisters of other lands and colors. They want to buy our fight with parodies of justice, with crumbs of freedom and promises of democracy.

We, the smallest and faceless ones, want to salute the good paths

180

of all of you. We want to ask you who are already there in front of the proud palace of the usurper and the bad government, to tell them, please, that the Zapatistas are not for sale, that the Zapatistas are not traitors, that the Zapatistas will not surrender. Explain to the bad government what it is to be a Zapatista, clear up their doubts, shout out our truths, take our voice, brothers and sisters, to speak to all the Mexican people.

Tell them that the federal government responded to our willingness for peace with signs of war, that they oppose our truth with lies, that they continue arresting us unjustly, that they continue filling their jails with indigenous flesh, and our blood continues to flow through these lands. The government lies, brothers and sisters! They continue their war against our cause; the whiteness of their hands is false; they are still covered with our people's blood.

Indigenous brothers and sisters of our Mexican lands, campesinos—poor in flesh and rich in honor and dignity—accept the way of our path so far from cities and the cheap flash of tinsel. Receive our greetings; fill your hearts with our song; listen to the speech of the mountain; raise your voice for those that do not have a voice. Rise up, all of Mexico!

Salud, brothers and sisters of the CEOIC!
Salud, indigenous brothers and sisters!
Salud, Mexican brothers and sisters!
Freedom! Justice! Democracy!

Respectfully,
From the mountains of the Mexican Southeast
CCRI-CG of the EZLN
Mexico, March 1994
Subcomandante Insurgent Marcos

• 52 •
EZLN CONDEMNS COLOSIO ASSASSINATION

**Communiqué from the CCRI-CG of the EZLN, Mexico
March 24, 1994**

To the people of Mexico
To the people and governments of the world
To the national and international press

Brothers and sisters,

The CCRI-CG of the EZLN addresses you to denounce the following:

First. During the night, via a radio transmission on March 23, 1994, we learned of the cowardly assassination of Sr. Luis Donaldo Colosio Murrieta, presidential candidate of the Revolutionary Institutional Party [PRI].

Second. The CCRI-CG of the EZLN explicitly condemns using terrorism as a means to acquire any goal.

Third. The CCRI-CG of the EZLN is deeply sorry that the governing class is not able to resolve its own internal conflicts without staining the country with blood. The hard line and the military wing within the federal government planned and executed this act as a provocation in order to demolish any and all peaceful attempts to democratize national political life.

Fourth. The CCRI-CG of the EZLN declares that Sr. Colosio always referred to our movement with prudence and respect. His last declarations demonstrated a clear commitment to compete on equal terms with all other political forces. He admitted that the country was weighed down by a great number of injustices and he established a clear distance from the Salinista regime and its economic and social policies. The forces opposed to the hope of peace with justice and dignity that was born in the San Cristóbal dialogue have sacrificed Sr. Colosio Murrieta in order to avoid the peaceful transition to freedom, democracy, and justice.

Fifth. The EZLN knows that the carefully calculated crime that is now shaking the nation is only a prelude to a big military offensive by the federal government against our positions and our forces, and the beginning of a dirty war against all those people who, by a number of different paths, are searching for the same flag that we are. Under the pretext that it is necessary to consolidate and toughen the regime to prevent occurrences like the assassination of Sr. Colosio, they will try to drum up political and ideological support for indiscriminate repression and the unjustified rupture of the cease-fire, and hence the peace dialogue.

Sixth. There are earlier and very clear signs that the federal government intends to use military force to resolve the present conflict: early in the morning on March 19, 1994, airplanes of the bad government began to bomb the road between Comitán and Altamirano, in the vicinity of the *ejido* La Mendoza. Four objects were dropped from these airplanes, lighting fires, as well as emitting strange gases, which suggests chemical warfare.

Without prior evidence and with the support of a list of names supplied by informers, the federal police in the municipal seats of Ocosingo and Altamirano are arresting and disappearing civilians suspected of sympathizing with our just cause.

Since March 20, the number of government troops and armaments in the conflict zone has increased to a level now twice what it was in January. The federal officials say that they are sending in relief personnel to replace the first deployment, but no troops have left.

The officials are taking advantage of this opportunity for personal profit, and take bribes from big ranch owners to keep special watch over their properties. The federal troops do not stay at their garrisons outside city limits but move freely within the urban zones under their control, with an openly belligerent attitude. The deployment of troops surrounding our territory in the municipalities of Las Margaritas, Altamirano, and Ocosingo is almost complete.

Next will come the hard-liners' long-cherished offensive. They are the same hard-liners who subterraneously encourage sabotage of the peace process by the big land owners and businessmen; the same people who obstruct peaceful efforts in this zone; the same group that has threatened the media and Bishop Samuel Ruiz García; the same ones who are against radical and democratic political reform. This is the same line that ordered the assassination of the PRI candidate, and the one that now wants to crown its infamy by breaking the cease-fire and restarting the war.

Seventh. The EZLN has demonstrated a sincere willingness for a just and dignified peace. The federal government has responded with lies, kidnappings, disappearances, threats, bombings, and now this reprehensible sacrifice of a public figure. Its troops are preparing to break the cease-fire. Our forces were in the process of consulting the communities to decide the next step in the peace and reconciliation dialogue, but we are now forced to suspend our consultations and prepare ourselves to defend our cause and our flag, the flag of democracy, freedom, and justice.

Eighth. The EZLN is now on red alert. Our troops are ready to defend Zapatista territory to the last man. We have mined the access points and our combatants await the bad government's attack. Indiscriminate press access, as part of our policy of not hiding anything from the eyes of our people, is, as of now, canceled. Given the imminent government aggression, we will only admit "war reporters" duly approved by the General Command [CG] of the EZLN. Any unknown people found within our territory will be arrested and investigated. Our vigilant flag already waves over our ground, but Zapatista trenches will now be only for those seeking democracy, justice, and freedom.

Ninth. Our just struggle continues; we are still willing to continue along the road to peace, but they want to deny it. The usurper and his servants want to bring war to our Mexican lands again.

Tenth. The EZLN reiterates to the entire world its commitment to respect the offensive cease-fire, not to impede the peaceful development of the upcoming elections, and not to carry out any offensive military action against governmental forces anywhere in national territory, as per the conditions established in our January 12, 1994, communiqué. If we are attacked, our forces will protect, up to the end, the just aspirations of all Mexicans.

If national history once again demands the blood and death of our people in order to move toward an honest peace with justice and dignity, we will not hesitate to give it. We, the faceless, will defend with dignity and courage the land in which our dead people sleep. We will never again return to the land with shame. We will never again speak without dignity. Our steps will continue to walk with truth even if—down the road—death is waiting.

Freedom! Justice! Democracy!

Respectfully,
Subcomandante Marcos
From the mountains of the Mexican Southeast
CCRI-CG of the EZLN

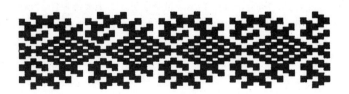

• 53 •
WHO PROFITS FROM COLOSIO'S ASSASSINATION AND A MESSAGE TO ZAPATISTA MOLES

To the national weekly *Proceso*
To the national newspaper *La Jornada*
To the national newspaper *El Financiero*
To SCLC's local newspaper *Tiempo*
To the national and international press

March 24, 1994

Sirs,

They . . . Why did they have to do that? Whom do they punish with this disgrace? If they are trying to justify a military action against us and against our flag, why not just kill one of us? That way the country would bleed less than with this infamy that is now shuddering through us. Whom did this man harm? Who was so worried that he would separate himself from the group that was trying to perpetuate itself through him? Who profits from his blood? Where were the people who should have been guarding him? Who could be behind the "pacifist" hand that opens once again the gigantic door of war? Is this the logic? Attributing a crime to peace in order to avoid the possibility of peace? Who's next? How many more must fall in order finally to have democracy, freedom, and justice?

We understand the message that this crime draws in the nation's sky. Is more of our blood necessary? Okay . . . we knew that. But he didn't. Come here. Here we are, where we were born and raised, where our great heart sustains us, where our dead people and our history still live. Here we are, in the mountains of the Mexican Southeast . . . come and get us . . . we'll welcome everyone in the manner they deserve . . . the good and the bad . . .

Be careful. Nothing is safe anymore, especially not the hope of peace. *Vale.*

From the mountains of the Mexican Southeast
Subcomandante Insurgente Marcos

P.S. FOR THOSE NO ONE SEES: Greetings, Zapatista moles.* We shine because of your patient work in the dark. The black night of infamy is coming once again. The end of our cycle is close. We promise you, before we completely disappear, we will shine so intensely that we will blind the sun. Until our last hour we will salute those of the dark side who are the backing of our mirror, the *interior* light that filters through us to light up this little piece of history. We will be at the front like those who preceded us. We will honor the dignity of our dead . . . brother and sister moles, we approach the end of our path . . . then it will be your turn, dear moles. Don't forget what our path was. We sincerely looked for other doors that might open to admit our timid light. You must now learn from this sad story. Never forget the words that made us important, although it was only for a moment: *everything for everyone, nothing for ourselves.*

Good-bye, beloved moles, have the flag ready and prepare now, without rest, for those who will follow you. It's your turn to hide your face, to erase your name, to deny your past, to prepare your tender fury, to watch over your arms, because peace is moving away as fast as it came. Allow us, distant moles, to extend our left hand to our forehead as a final salute, and also . . . *a gift and a lesson in politics:*

A little piece of the moon . . .
though really it's not one at all,
but two:
A piece from the dark side,
and one from the bright.
And what must be understood
is that the little piece of the moon
that shines
shines because there is a dark side too.
The dark side of the moon
makes possible the bright.

Us too.
When we are the dark side,
(and we must take turns)
it doesn't mean we are less,
only that it's time
to be the dark side,
so everyone can see the moon
(to tell the truth,
when it comes down to it, the dark side
is more important,
because it shines in other skies,
and because to see it
you have to learn to fly
very high).

And so it is,
only a few
are willing to suffer so
others won't,
and die
so others live.
And this is so,
given that boots and moon and etcetera
are there.

There you have it, faithful moles, we'll see you around underground.

Subcomandante Marcos

• 54 •
REQUIREMENTS FOR WAR CORRESPONDENTS

**Communiqué from the CCRI-CG of the EZLN
March 24, 1994**

To the national and international press

Sirs,

The CCRI-CG of the EZLN addresses all of you with honor and respect in order to establish the requirements for obtaining credentials as war correspondents so that you can enter territory under EZLN control:

First. The present situation in our country compels the CCRI-CG of the EZLN to end its policy of total and indiscriminate openness toward media covering the conflict within the territory under the control of our forces in Chiapas.

Second. Starting at 00:00 hours on March 25, 1994, only those media employees who have been authorized by the General Command [CG] of the EZLN as war correspondents will have access to our territory.

Third. To obtain the credentials as war correspondents, applicants must present a letter signed by them and one of their editors. In the letter the following must be specified:

(1) That the news media in question verifies that the applicant is an employee of that company, assigned to cover the conflict inside our territory.

(2) That for work within our territory, the reporter has not received or passed on any payment whatsoever, either in money or in kind,

either from the EZLN to the news media, or from the media to the EZLN.

(3) That the reporter will work within our territory at the company's and/or his or her own risk and expense.

(4) That the company and the reporter commit themselves to tell the truth about what is happening.

Fourth. The CCRI-CG of the EZLN reserves the right to give or deny authorization at all times, to any news agency or its reporters.

Fifth. All applicants must present a document with a current photograph of themselves, confirming their employment at the news agency in question.

Liberty! Justice! Democracy!

Subcomandante Marcos
From the Mexican Southeast
CCRI-CG of the EZLN, March 1994

• 55 •
THE SUP WRITES A LETTER TO A TEN-YEAR-OLD GIRL WHO LIVES IN MEXICO CITY

April 10, 1994

To Mariana Moguel

From Subcomandante Insurgente Marcos

Subcomandanta Mariana Moguel,

I greet you with respect and congratulate you for the new levels you have reached in your drawing. Let me tell you a story that one day, perhaps, you will understand. It's the story of—*Durito*.

I'm going to tell you a story that happened to me the other day. It's the story of a little beetle who wears glasses and smokes a pipe. I met him one day as I was looking for tobacco to smoke and couldn't find any. All of a sudden to one side of my hammock I saw that a little bit of tobacco had fallen and formed a little trail. I followed it to see where my tobacco was and to find who the heck had taken it and was spilling it all over. A few meters away and behind a rock I found a beetle seated at a small desk, reading through some papers and smoking a tiny pipe.

"Ahem—ahem!" I said so that the beetle would notice me, but he ignored me.

Then I told him: "Hey, that's my tobacco."

The beetle took off his glasses, looked me up and down, and said very angrily: "Please, captain, I beg you not to interrupt me. Don't you realize what it is I'm studying?"

I was a little taken aback and was about to kick him, but I calmed down and sat to one side to wait for him to finish studying. A little while later he gathered up his papers, put them away in the desk and, gnawing at his pipe, said to me: "All right, now. How can I help you, captain?"

"My tobacco," I answered.

"Your tobacco?" he said. "You want me to give you some?"

I started to get really annoyed, but the little beetle scooted the bag of tobacco over to me with his little foot and added: "Don't get angry, captain. Understand that you can't get tobacco around here and I had to take a little bit of yours."

I felt better. I liked this beetle and said to him: "Don't worry. I have more somewhere."

"Mmh," he answered.

"And what's your name?" I asked him.

"Nebuchadnezzar," he said, and continued: "But my friends call me Durito. You can call me Durito, captain."

I thanked him for his kindness and asked him what it was that he was studying.

"I'm studying about neoliberalism and its strategy for dominating Latin America," he answered.

"And what good does that do a beetle?" I asked him.

And he answered angrily: "What do you mean what good? I have to know how long your struggle is going to last and whether you are going to win. What's more, a beetle should concern himself with studying the world he lives in, don't you think, captain?"

"I don't know," I told him. "But why do you want to know how long our struggle is going to last and whether or not we're going to win?"

"Well, you haven't understood a thing," he said, putting his glasses on and lighting his pipe. After letting out a puff of smoke he continued: "So as to know how long we beetles have to be careful not to be squashed by your huge old boots."

"Ah!" I said.

"Mmh," he said.

"And what have you concluded from your studies?" I asked.

He took the papers out of his desk and began to leaf through them. "Mmh—mmh," he said as he looked over them.

After he was finished, he looked me in the eye and said: "You are going to win."

"I knew that," I said. And then I added, "But how long is it going to take?"

"A long time," he said with a sigh of resignation.

"I knew that too. Do you know exactly how long?" I asked.

"You can't tell exactly. You have to take into account many things: the objective conditions, the maturity of the subjective conditions, the correlation of forces, the crisis of imperialism, the crisis of socialism, etc., etc."

"Mmh," I said.

"What are you thinking about, captain?"

"Nothing," I answered him. "Well, Sr. Durito, I have to go. It was a pleasure to meet you. You know you can help yourself to all the tobacco you want, whenever you want."

"Thank you, captain. You can call me 'tu' if you want," he added.

"Thank you, Durito. Now I'm going to give orders to my compañeros that it is forbidden to step on the beetles. I hope that helps."

"Thank you captain, your order will be very useful to us."

"Even so, take good care of yourselves, because my boys are very distracted and they don't always watch where they put their feet."

"I will, captain."

"See you later."

"See you later. Come whenever you want and we'll talk"

"I will," I said, and left to go back to headquarters.

That's all Mariana, I hope to meet you personally some day and be able to exchange ski-masks and drawings.

Vale.

Be well and I hope you get some more markers soon, because I'm sure you used up all the ink in the others.

Subcomandante Insurgente Marcos
From the mountains of the Mexican Southeast
April 1994
Down with the haciendas! Up with the villages!

• 56 •
75TH ANNIVERSARY OF THE ASSASSINATION OF ZAPATA

Communiqué of the CCRI-CG of the EZLN
April 10, 1994

To the support bases of the EZLN
To the regular and irregular Zapatista combatants of the
   various branches and services of the EZLN

Compañeros,

Today, April 10, 1994, is the 75th anniversary of the assassination of General Emiliano Zapata and the 100th day of our righteous war against the bad Mexican government.

As in 1919, we Zapatistas must pay in blood for our cry for land and freedom. As in 1919, the land does not belong to those who work it. As in 1919, the bad government leaves those without land no other choice but to take up arms.

This is why we rise up in arms. This is why our compañeros died in the 100 days of our war. This is why today we pay homage to the heroes and martyrs of the Zapatista struggle, to the forever dead who live in us. This is why today we say again that we will not surrender, that we will not turn in our weapons, that there will be no peace until we have a fair and decent peace, that we will not stop struggling until all the peoples of Mexico have democracy, freedom, justice, independence, decent housing, well-paid work, land, good food, health, and education. Meanwhile, our armed steps keep marching forward, and our flag will continue to wave in the mountains of Mexico.

We salute you, Zapatista brothers and sisters!
Death to the almighty government!
Long live the EZLN!

From the mountains of Mexican Southeast
CCRI-CG of the EZLN

• 57 •
VOTÁN ZAPATA

**Communiqué of the CCRI-CG of the EZLN, Mexico
April 10, 1994**

To the people of Mexico
To the peoples and governments of the world
To the national and international press

Brothers and sisters,

The CCRI-CG of the EZLN addresses you in order to say its word. At this moment, tens of thousands of men, women, children, and elderly people, all of them indigenous Mexicans, can be found gathered in hundreds of *ejidos*, villages, their outlying areas, and communities in the Mexican countryside. Our hands even reach the heart of asphalt. All of us, all of these people, are gathered before a tricolor flag with the image of an eagle devouring a snake in its center. We are gathered by our common misery, by the collective oblivion in which we were relocated 501 years ago, by the useless death we suffer, by not having a face, by having our name ripped out of us, by having bet life and death on a foreign-owned future. We are all gathered before this flag by a collective longing: to change once and for all the skies and soils that oppress us.

To accomplish that, we, those without name and without face, the self-named "professionals of hope," the more-mortal-than-ever "transgressors of injustice"; we who are mountain, we of the nocturnal path, without voice in the palaces, strangers in our own land; we of eternal death, we who have been cast out of history, without country and without a tomorrow, we of tender fury, of the unveiled truth; we of the long night of insult, the true men and women—the smallest . . . the most dignified . . . the always last . . . the best. We must open the door to our brother's heart again so that it can receive our word.

Our mouth must speak truly; we must put our heart in our hands. Brothers and sisters, we want you to know who is behind us, who directs us, who walks on our feet, who dominates our heart, who rides in our words, who lives in our deaths.

We want you to know the truth now, brothers and sisters. And it is this:

From the first hour of this long night on which we die, say our most distant grandparents, there was someone who gathered together our pain and our forgetting. There was a man who, his word traveling from far away, came to our mountain and spoke with the tongue of true men and women. His step was and was not of these lands; in the mouths of our dead, in the voices of the old wise ones, his word traveled from him to our heart. There was, and is, brothers and sisters, someone who, being and not being seed of these soils, arrived at the mountain dying, to live again; the heart of his footstep which was ours and not ours lived dying when he made his home in the mountain with a roof of night.

It was, and is, his name in the named things. His tender word stops and starts inside our pain. He is and is not in these lands: Votán Zapata, guardian and heart of the people. Votán Zapata, timid fire that lived 501 years in our death. Votán Zapata, name that changes, man without face, soft light that shelters us.

He came coming, Votán Zapata. Death was with us always. Dying, hope was dying. Coming he came, Votán Zapata. Name without name, Votán Zapata looked out of Miguel, walked in José María, was Vicente, was named in Benito, flew inside the little bird, rode in

Emiliano, cried out in Francisco, clothed Pedro. Dying he lived, named without name in our land. Name without name, being here, Votán Zapata came to our land. Speaking, he silenced his word in our mouths. Coming, he is here. Votán Zapata, guardian and heart of the people.

He is and is not everything in us . . . He walks . . . Votán Zapata, guardian and heart of the people. He is one and many. No one and everyone. Being here, he comes. Votán Zapata, guardian and heart of the people.

This is the truth, brothers and sisters. Now you know: he will die no more in our life, in our death he lives now and forever. Votán, guardian and heart of the people. Without name he is named, face without features, everyone and no one, one and many, living dead. Votán, guardian and heart of the people. Tapacamino bird, ever before us he follows us. Votán, guardian and heart of the people.

He took his name from those who have no name, his face from those with no face; he is sky on the mountain. Votán, guardian and heart of the people. And our road, unnameable and faceless, took its name in us: Zapatista Army of National Liberation.

With this new name, the nameless are named. With this flag that covers the face, all of us have a face again. With this name, the unnameable is named: Votán Zapata, guardian and heart of the people.

Zapatista Army of National Liberation. Tender fury that arms itself. Unnameable name. Unjust peace that becomes war. Death that is born. Anguish made hope. Pain that laughs. Silenced scream. One's own present for another's future. Everything for everyone; for ourselves nothing. The unnameable, we, the forever dead. We, stubborn dignity, forgotten corner of our country. We, Zapatista Army of National Liberation. We, black-and-red flag under the tricolor eagle. We, red star finally in our sky, never the only star, just one more, the smallest one. We, nothing more than a gaze and a voice. We, Zapatista Army of National Liberation. We, Votán, guardian and heart of the people.

This is the truth, brothers and sisters. This is where we come from and where we're going. Being here, he comes. Dying, death lives. Votán Zapata, father and mother, brother and sister, son and daughter, old and young, we are coming . . .

Receive our truth in your heart dancing. Zapata lives, also and forever, in these lands.

Salud, Mexican brothers and sisters!
Salud, campesinos of this country!
Salud, indigenous peoples of all lands!
Salud, Zapatista combatants!
Zapata, being here, he comes!
Dying he lives!
Long live Zapata!
Democracy! Freedom! Justice!

From the mountains of the Mexican Southeast
CCRI-CG of the EZLN
Mexico, April 10, 1994

• 58 •
ZAPATA WILL NOT DIE
BY ARROGANT DECREE

**Communiqué from the CCRI-CG of the EZLN, Mexico
April 10, 1994**

To the people of Mexico
To the peoples and governments of the world
To the national and international press

Brothers and sisters,

The CCRI-CG of the EZLN addresses you in order to say the following:

Today, April 10, 1994, is the 75th anniversary of the assassination of General Emiliano Zapata. His betrayal by Venustiano Carranza was an attempt to drown out his cry of "Land and Freedom!" Today, the usurper Salinas de Gortari, who claims to be "President of the Mexican Republic," lies to the people of Mexico, saying that his revisions of

Article 27 of the Constitution reflect the spirit of General Zapata. The federal government lies! Zapata will not die by arrogant decree. The right to the land by those who work it cannot be taken away, and the warrior cry "Land and Freedom!" echoes restlessly through these Mexican lands. Beneath the cloak of neoliberalism, which casts its shadow over our soils, they are jailing and killing the campesinos who fight for their agrarian rights. The Salinas revisions of Article 27 of the Magna Carta represent a betrayal of the country, and the usurper of the federal executive branch of Mexico must be held responsible for this crime.

Brothers and sisters, today marks 100 days since the birth of our new voice. Out of the mouths of the guns of the faceless men and women spoke the voices of landless campesinos, agricultural workers, small farmers, and indigenous Mexicans. The voice of those who have nothing and deserve everything had to follow the path of the smallest, most humble, most persecuted, and most forgotten. All Mexicans dispossessed of their land, their dignity, and their history spoke in the voice of the true men and women.

Everything seemed to be lost during our people's long night. The earth bore nothing but pain and death. But ten years ago, a few good souls began to sow hope in our grieving earth, the hope that the true men and women would come back to life. The seeds—their words— found fertile soil in the Mexican mountains and grew silently, in the hour when the night takes its first step toward dawn.

Our cry "Enough!" was the daybreak, and in the new light the earth bore the fruits of our planting. Where there had been pain, rage was born; in place of humiliation, dignity surged forth; instead of sorrow, we harvested arms. Thousands of men and women unearthed, from the same soil that had brought them poverty, a tender flame that would fill their hands. They covered their faces, erased their past, left behind their names and land, and began to walk the steps of war. None of us men and women of the night path will have a tomorrow. Our anguish will never find peace; never more will we be able to rest our bones and blood.

For whom do these men and women walk? Who drinks their blood? For whom is the light of their words? For whom do they change their death to life? One-hundred days, ten years. Who will join hands with these men and women who cannot be with you here today, and take the flag that their blood snatched away from the hands of the powerful? Who will fall into step alongside them down the road of dignity? Who, along with us who are only eyes, voice and fierce tenderness, will speak? Who shouts with us? Who does not abandon us? Who fights with us? Who listens to our deaths?

Not the usurper, whose arrogance does business out of the National Palace. Not he who sells us. Not he who kills us. Not he who evicts us. Not he who humiliates us.

You, our brothers and sisters. For you, our blood. For your dark night, our timid light. For your life, our death. Our war for your peace. For your ears, our words. Your pain, brothers and sisters, will find relief in our fight. For you, brothers and sisters, everything; for ourselves nothing.

Brothers and sisters, right in front of you, in this palace where lies reign, lives he who denies us everything. No one good has asked for him to be there. This powerful man who snatches life from us every day must get out of there now. He must go, brothers and sisters! His voice shall no longer be our command. Nothing good ever comes from those doors. There are lies in his face, and deceit lives in his words. He must go, brothers and sisters! This is the cry that comes from the mountains, this is what our blood says, this is what our dead ask. He must go, brothers and sisters. Tell him, brothers: Go!

No one else shall come to this palace unless it is by mandate of the many! He who sits in this chair must command by obeying us; he who speaks from this balcony must have truth in his words; he who calls himself our leader must obey us. Tell him this, brothers and sisters, this is what we want!

We cannot be with you today, brothers and sisters; we must stay on our night path on the mountain. Our faces must remain hidden, our words come from far away. Lend us your voice for a moment, and let our words speak through your mouths. In this same instant, in the mountains of the Mexican Southeast, thousands of men and women who have denied their faces, who walk without name or past, renew in their breasts the first cry of the new year. Our hearts are joyful: Emiliano Zapata has come again to the Zócalo of Mexico City; he is in you; he walks in you. We, the small and forgotten, raise up the image of Zapata in the other heart of the country: in the mountains of the Mexican Southeast.

Salud, our Mexican brothers and sisters! Let our cry be your own:
Long live Emiliano Zapata!
Death to the almighty government!
Freedom! Justice! Democracy!

Respectfully,
From the mountains of the Mexican Southeast
CCRI-CG of the EZLN
Mexico, April 1994

• 59 •
COMPAÑERO FRANCISCO MENA LÓPEZ MURDERED BY COWARDLY ARMED RANCHERS

**Communiqué of the CCRI-CG of the EZLN, Mexico
April 12, 1994**

To the people of Mexico
To the peoples and governments of the world
To the national and international press

Brothers and sisters,

The CCRI-CG of the EZLN addresses you in order to denounce the following:

First: Thursday, April 7, 1994, when he went to gather for the harvest, the compañero Francisco Mena López was murdered by cowardly armed ranchers. The crime was committed near the Venustiano Carranza *ejido*, in the municipality of Altamirano, Chiapas.

Second: Francisco Mena López was killed with two bullets, one in the head and the other in the mouth, shot with a firearm they call the revolver, a .38-caliber special.

Third: Ranchers by the names of Arturo Espinoza, Juan Espinoza, and Jorge Espinoza, owners of the ranch El Miradero in Altamirano, Chiapas, are accused of this act of aggression.

Fourth: At the time of his death, compañero Francisco Mena López was in charge of the local committee of our EZLN. Since before January 1, 1994, he had received death threats from ranchers in Altamirano because of his participation in the struggle for agrarian justice.

Fifth: After the murder, the now-accused fled and were sheltered on the properties of their rancher accomplices in Altamirano in order to escape Zapatista justice. As of today, they are still fugitives.

Sixth: With the complicity of governmental authorities, the fine ranchers of Altamirano have spread the lie that the Espinoza family has been kidnapped by elements belonging to our EZLN. Accustomed to their own haughty arrogance, the ranchers and the government imagine that our EZLN must act unjustly as we fight against injustice. They are trying to damage the prestige our forces now have among the population. A good number of small property owners would like to shatter completely the already fragile and cracking process of dialogue, and create grounds for military action against us.

Seventh: The EZLN, unlike the bad government, does not make arbitrary arrests. The CCRI-CG of the EZLN has turned the case over to the Zapatista tribunal of justice so that it may carry out an in-depth investigation and clearly identify the person or persons responsible for committing this crime. Zapatistas will take no judicial action until we have solid and confirmed results from the investigation currently underway.

Eighth: We reiterate that we are not frightened by hollow arguments that seek to justify a military action against us. We are prepared to respond to any attack and to resist to the last man against whatever aggression the federal government may be preparing.

Ninth: The consulting process is still suspended. We will not speak of peace while the signs of war continue.

Tenth: The EZLN reiterates to the people of Mexico its commitment to conduct itself with dignity, truth, and honesty, weapons that the usurper government will never be able to acquire.

Respectfully,
From the mountains of the Mexican Southeast
CCRI-CG of the EZLN
Mexico, April 11, 1994

• 60 •
"OUR DIGNITY IS HELD CAPTIVE IN STATUES AND MUSEUMS"

EZLN, Mexico, April 10, 1994

To the signers of "The Declaration of Morelos"
Attention: Lt. Colonel Estanislao Tapia Sánchez
From CCRI-CG of the EZLN, Mexico

Brothers and sisters,

We have received the historic document called "The Declaration of Morelos," sent out on March 27, 1994, from a Mexican territory in struggle. We, small and forgotten men and women, have felt your word open our heart with its truth and dignity. In the grandest tradition of Mexican campesino struggle, "The Declaration of Morelos" keeps alive the dignified words of the Plan de Ayala and the Plan de Cerro Prieto, which in other times were lifted high by our greatest leader in history, Emiliano Zapata, and our Supreme General Rubén Jaramillo.*

Therefore, please accept the military honors our army solemnly bestows upon you. Our step is lightened and our flag is higher having read your words in support of our "Declaration of the Lacandon Jungle."

For years the federal government, now headed by the usurper of the National Palace, has drowned in prisons and blood the righteous words of all the campesinos and indigenous people. We have been stripped of land and water; not even the air belongs to us anymore. Our death is mute in today's world. Zapata and Jaramillo die in the Salinas revision of Article 27 of the Constitution. The hope that our people will be able to live well and govern ourselves, the inheritance our ancestors left us, walks on without rest. Our step is a stranger to our native soil, while the feet of foreigners offend our land. Papers full of lies stain our real and legitimate history. Our dignity is held captive in statues and museums. Vacationers from foreign countries take our voice and their poison kills the truth in our word.

We were alone, far from our own and forgotten to one another. Our death walked with deaf ears to the poor life that inhabits us. They thought, they of the double faces, that they had forever silenced our cries. They thought, they the usurpers of light and givers of darkness, that our dead were dead. They were already celebrating our downfall and their victory, in the haughty solitude of their palaces. Their lie danced upon the trampled truth. The world watched without seeing. The country and its hope were cornered. Nothing could move among so much oppression. In silence it was dying, living in silence.

But amidst the nothing-happening our step was walking across nights and mountains. Tenderly we cared for our fierce word. In the silence we were speaking. Patient companion was the night, lover and accomplice the mountain. We were small but growing; we were newly new. Our path was going in the right direction; it was mute and it was coming. During ten years of silence, slowly the broken hope was maturing; without speaking our word was speaking.

On the dawn of the year, nameless we once again had a name, faceless we again had a face. Emiliano Zapata, our father, gave us his name. Our brother, Emiliano Zapata, set an armed example. Our son Zapata asked us for a new future. It is a flag that clothes our warrior step. Emiliano Zapata of our land, dignity of our history, light of our night, always the clear morning of our hope. Brothers and sisters, the bad government is still deaf to our voice. Other voices are needed to open its ears. Your word has made our cry strong.

Viva Emiliano Zapata!

Death to the federal government!

We salute you, Zapatista and Jaramillista brothers and sisters of Morelos!
Democracy! Justice! Freedom!

Respectfully,
From the mountains of the Mexican Southeast
CCRI-CG of the EZLN
Mexico, April 1994

• 61 •
THE NATION MUST RECOGNIZE THE RIGHT OF THE INDIGENOUS TO GOVERN OURSELVES

**Communiqué from the CCRI-CG of the EZLN, Mexico
April 12, 1994**

To the people of Mexico
To the peoples and governments of the world
To the national and international press

Brothers and sisters,

The CCRI-CG of the EZLN addresses you in order to declare the following:

First: We have become acquainted with the document, dated April 8, 1994, called "Political Proposal of the Indigenous Organizations of Mexico," which is signed by a series of indigenous organizations, authentic representatives of various indigenous peoples of Mexico.

Second: This document demands the right of indigenous people to have direct representation in the federal houses of deputies and senators, in accordance with the percentage of indigenous Mexicans in the national population. These sister organizations justly claim the right of the indigenous peoples to 10 percent of all the representatives in the House of Deputies and the Senate.

Third: The EZLN announces its support of this initiative, which would return the rights to govern and to govern themselves to the original inhabitants of our country. The participation of indigenous people in all branches of government is a fair and legitimate aspiration. The nation must recognize this right.

Democracy! Justice! Freedom!

Respectfully,
From the mountains of the Mexican Southeast
CCRI-CG of the EZLN
Mexico, April 11, 1994

• 62 •
THE EZLN HONORS ITS WORD

**Communiqué from the CCRI-CG of the EZLN, Mexico
April 15, 1994**

To the people of Mexico
To the peoples and governments of the world
To the national and international press

Brothers and sisters,

The CCRI-CG of the EZLN addresses you in order to declare the following:

First: Today, April 15, 1994, in the morning, via radio transmission, we became aware of a shooting attack against a Federal Army military checkpoint in the immediate area of the city of Tuxtla Gutiérrez, Chiapas.

Second: The EZLN declares that it has no military position or troops in the zone where the attack happened.

Third: The EZLN does not have good weapons or sufficient ammunition, but it does have military honor and an honorable word. The

EZLN made the commitment not to initiate any offensive military action against federal troops or the positions they hold unless it is attacked first.

Fourth: The EZLN reiterates its commitment to respect the offensive cease-fire, to not carry out any offensive military action anywhere in national territory against governmental forces, as per the conditions established by our January 12, 1994, communiqué, and to continue the search for a peace with justice and dignity through dialogue. The EZLN hopes that favorable conditions are reestablished so as to begin the dialogue once again with the federal government.

Freedom! Justice! Democracy!

Respectfully,
From the mountains of the Mexican Southeast
CCRI-CG of the EZLN
Mexico, April 1994
Subcomandante Marcos

• 63 •
OLD ANTONIO TELLS MARCOS ANOTHER STORY

"Streams, when they begin to flow downhill, cannot turn back, except underground."

To the national weekly *Proceso*
To the national newspaper *La Jornada*
To the national newspaper *El Financiero*
To San Cristóbal de las Casas' local newspaper *El Tiempo*

May 28, 1994

Sirs,

Here comes a communiqué about the final goal—finally—of the consultations. Plus various letters with different destinations.

We are quite . . . besieged. Resisting "heroically" the storm of reactions after the occurrence of May 15. The ever vigilant planes are now joined, as of three days ago, by helicopters. The cooks complain that there won't be enough pots if they all drop in on us at the same time. The superintendent argues that there is enough wood for a barbecue, so why don't we invite over some Argentinean journalists, because those people really know how to do barbecues.

I mull it over, and it's not right: the best Argentineans are *guerrilleros* (for example, el Ché), or poets (Juan Gelman, for example), or writers (for example, Borges), or artists (Maradona, for example), or *cronopios** (forever, Cortazar); there are no Argentinean barbecuers of lasting fame.

Some innocent proposes that we wait for the unlikely hamburgers of the CEU. Yesterday we ate the *"console"* and two microphones from station XEOCH; they had a rotten, rancid taste.

The medics are handing out slips of paper with jokes instead of painkillers—they say that laughter heals too. The other day I came upon Tacho and Moi crying . . . with laughter. "Why are you crying?" I asked. They couldn't answer because they were laughing so hard they couldn't breathe. A medic explained with some embarrassment: "It's because they've got terrible headaches."

Day 136 of the siege . . . (sigh).

To top it off, Toñita asks me for a story. I'll tell her the story as it was told to me, by Old Antonio who wakes up in "Chiapas: The Southeast in Two Winds, a Storm, and a Prophecy . . . "

"When the world slept and didn't want to wake up, the great gods came together in their council to divide up the jobs and decided then to make the world and to make the men and women. And they reached a majority opinion on how to make the world and the people. They decided to make them very pretty and very durable, and so they made the first people out of gold, and the gods were very happy because the people they made were shiny and strong. But then the gods realized that the people made of gold didn't move. They were always sitting around, not walking and not working, because they were very heavy.

"And so the community of gods met to reach an agreement about how to solve that problem and so they reached an agreement to make other people. They made them from wood, and so these people were the color of wood. They worked a lot and walked a lot and the gods were happy again because now man worked and walked, and they were just about to go celebrate when they realized that the people of gold were making the people of wood carry them around and work for them. And then the gods saw that it was bad, what they had done, and so they searched for a good way to remedy the situation. And so it was that they decided to make the people of corn, the good people, the true men and women. Then they went off to sleep and the people of corn remained, the true men and women, coming to fix things because the gods went off to sleep. And the people of corn spoke the true language to reach agreements among them and went to the mountain to see that a good path was made for all the people."

Old Antonio told me that the people of gold were the rich people, the ones with white skin, and that the people of wood were the poor people, the ones with dark skin, who worked for the rich ones and always carried them around, and that the people of gold and the people of wood are waiting for the people of corn, the first with fear and the latter with hope. I asked Old Antonio what color skin the people of corn had and he showed me various kinds of corn, of a variety of colors, and told me that they were of all skins but nobody really knew, because the people of corn, the true men and women, didn't have faces ...

Old Antonio died. I met him ten years ago, in a community deep in the jungle. He smoked like no one else and, when the cigarettes ran out, he would ask me for tobacco and make cigarettes with a corn leaf "roller"; he used to look curiously at my pipe, and once when I tried to loan it to him, he showed me the cigarette made with the "roller" in his hand, telling me without words that he preferred his own method of smoking.

About two years ago, in 1992, when I was making the rounds of the communities calling meetings to see whether or not we were to begin the war, I arrived at Old Antonio's town. Young Antonio caught up with me and together we walked through pastures and coffee groves. While the community discussed the matter of war, Old Antonio took me by the arm and led me to the river, some 100 meters below the center of the town. It was May and the river was green, with a barely discernible current. Old Antonio sat on a log and said nothing. After a while he spoke: "See? Everything is calm and clear, as if nothing were happening."

"Mmmm," I said, knowing that he didn't expect either a yes or a no. Then he pointed out the top of the nearest mountain; clouds were bedded down, gray, on the peak, and lightning bolts shattered the soft blue of the hills. A real storm, but it looked so far away and harmless that Old Antonio began to roll a cigarette and to look, in vain, for the lighter that he didn't have, which gave me enough time to pass him mine.

"When everything is quiet down below, there is a storm on the mountain; the streams begin to gather force and they head for the ravine," he said after taking a puff. "In the rainy season, this river is fierce, a dark brown whip, an earthquake, out of control; it is pure force. Its power doesn't come from the rain that falls on its banks, but from the streams that feed it as they come down from the mountain. Destroying the riverbed rebuilds the earth; its waters will be corn, beans, and brown sugar in the flats of the jungle. It's the same with our struggle," Old Antonio says to me and to himself. "The force is born on the mountain, but it can't be seen till it comes down." And, answering my question about whether he thinks that now is the time to start, he adds, "It is time now for the river to change color . . ."

Old Antonio falls silent and gets up, supporting himself on my arm. We go back slowly. He tells me, "You all are the streams and we are the river . . . it is time to come down now . . ." The silence continues and when we arrive at the village meeting place, it is already beginning to get dark. Young Antonio comes back after a while with the Act of Agreement, which says, more or less:

"The men and women and children met in the community school to examine in their hearts whether it is time to start the war for freedom and the three groups separated, that is, the women, the children, and the men, to discuss it and then later we met again in the little school and the majority had reached the point in their thinking that the war should begin because Mexico is being sold to foreigners and hunger is occurring, but it is not occurring that we are no longer Mexicans, and in the agreement 12 men and 23 women and 8 children who already have their thoughts clear came forward and those who know how signed and those who don't, put down their fingerprint."

I left before dawn. Old Antonio wasn't there: he had gone early to the river.

But I saw Old Antonio again a couple months ago. He didn't say anything when he saw me, and I sat down at his side and began to shuck ears of corn with him. "The river grew," he said after a while. "Yes," I said.

Later during the same visit I explained to Young Antonio about the consultation and handed over to him the documents with our demands and the government's responses. We talked about how it had gone with him in Ocosingo and, again before dawn, I left with the others to go back. In a bend of the road Old Antonio was waiting for me; I stopped at his side and took off my pack, looking for tobacco to offer him. "Not now," he said, waving away the bag I held out to him. He took me away from the line of marchers and took me to the foot of a silk-cotton tree. "Do you remember what I told you about the streams in the mountains and the river?" he asked. "Yes," I answered in the same murmur with which he had asked me. "There was something else I should have told you," he says, looking at his bare toes. I answered in silence. "The streams . . ." he stops for the cough that wracks his body, takes a little breath, and continues, "The streams . . . when they begin to flow down . . ."

A new coughing attack makes me call the medic from the line, but he waves away the compañero with the red cross on his shoulder; the rebel looks at me and I signal to him to go back. Old Antonio waits until the medicine pack gets further away and, in the half-light, continues, "The streams . . . when they flow down . . . cannot turn back . . . except underground." He embraces me and quickly goes.

I stand there watching as his shadow moves away, lighting my pipe and hefting my pack onto my back. Once I'm on my horse again, I recall the scene. I don't know why, and it was very dark, but Old Antonio . . . seemed to be crying . . .

Now Young Antonio's letter reaches me with the village's response to the government's proposals. Young Antonio tells me that Old Antonio soon became very ill, that he didn't want them to let me know, and that he died that night. Young Antonio says that he only said: "No, I already told him what I had to tell him . . . leave him alone, he has a lot of work right now . . ."

When the story ends, Toñita, six years old and with holes in her teeth, says to me, with great solemnity, that she loves me but that she isn't going to give me kisses anymore because "it itches too much." Rolando says that when she has to go to sick bay, Toñita asks if the Sup is there. If they tell her that he is, she doesn't go to the infirmary, "Because that Sup wants nothing but kisses and it itches too much"; so says the inexorable logic of a six year old with holes in her teeth who from this side of the siege is named Toñita.

Here the first rains are beginning to make their presence known. All for the better, we were thinking we'd have to wait for the anti-riot trucks just to have water. Ana María says that the rain comes from the clouds that fight high in the mountains; they do it up there so that men and women can't see their squabbles. The clouds begin their fierce combat with what we call thunder and lightning; and there at the summit, armed to infinity with ingenuity, the clouds fight for the privilege of dying in rain to feed the earth. It's the same with us, without face like the clouds, like them without name, with no pay whatsoever . . . like them we fight for the privilege of being seeds in the earth.

Vale, salud, and a raincoat (for the rains and for the riots).

From the mountains of the Mexican Southeast
Subcomandante Insurgente Marcos
May 1994

Majority-which-disguises-itself-as-untolerated-minority P.S.: About this whole thing about whether Marcos is homosexual: Marcos is gay in San Francisco, black in South Africa, Asian in Europe, Chicano in San Isidro, Anarchist in Spain, Palestinian in Israel, Indigenous in the streets of San Cristóbal, bad boy in Neza,* rocker in CU,* Jew in Germany, ombudsman in the SEDENA,* feminist in political parties, Communist in the post-Cold War era, prisoner in Cintalapa,* pacifist in Bosnia, Mapuche in the Andes, teacher in the CNTE,* artist without gallery or portfolio, housewife on any given Saturday night in any neighborhood of any city of any Mexico, *guerrillero* in Mexico at the end of the twentieth century, striker in the CTM,* reporter assigned to filler stories for the back pages, sexist in the feminist movement, woman alone in the metro at 10 p.m., retired person in *plantón** in the Zócalo, campesino without land, fringe editor, unemployed worker, doctor without a practice, rebellious student, dissident in neoliberalism, writer without books or readers, and, to be sure, Zapatista in the Mexican Southeast. In sum, Marcos is a human being, any human being, in this world. Marcos is all the minorities who are untolerated, oppressed, resisting, exploding, saying "Enough." All the minorities at the moment they begin to speak and the majorities at the moment they fall silent and put up with it. All the untolerated people searching for a word, their word, which will return the majority to the eternally fragmented, us; all that makes power and good consciences uncomfortable, that is Marcos.

You're welcome, gentlemen of the PGR, I am here to serve you . . . with lead.

• 64 •

WE HOPE YOU UNDERSTAND THAT WE HAD NEVER RUN A REVOLUTION BEFORE . . .

Communiqué from the CCRI-CG of the EZLN, Mexico June 10, 1994

"Everything for everyone, nothing for ourselves."

The dialogue of San Cristóbal: "Over and out."
To the people of Mexico
To the peoples and governments of the world
To the Non-Governmental Organizations
To the Envoy for Peace and Reconciliation in Chiapas
To the Nationally Appointed Mediator
To the national and international press

The CCRI-CG of the EZLN addresses you to inform you of and declare the following:

First. The CCRI-CG of the EZLN, as it announced as soon as possible and in a timely fashion, has finished consulting with all of the people that constitute and support it. By way of acts passed by assemblies in *ejidos*, villages, and outlying areas, we have been informed of the heartfelt opinions of our people.

Second. The CCRI-CG of the EZLN has counted the votes regarding the peace agreement proposals made by the federal government to the EZLN in the dialogue at San Cristóbal de las Casas, Chiapas.

Third. The result of the free and democratic vote is as follows:

Of the total, 2.11 percent voted to sign the government's peace agreement proposal.

Of the total, 97.88 percent voted NOT to sign the government's peace agreement proposal.

Fourth. The voting results on the proposals regarding the next thing to do, in case the government's peace agreement proposal was not signed, were as follows:

3.26 percent of the total voted to renew hostilities.

96.74 percent of the total voted for resistance and the convocation of a new national dialogue with all honest and independent forces.

Fifth. Consequently, and as agreed by the majority of Zapatistas, the CCRI-CG of the EZLN hereby declares:

—That it rejects the federal government's peace agreement proposal;

—That the dialogue of San Cristóbal has now come to an end;

—That it calls all the people of Mexico to a new national dialogue, with all the progressive forces of the nation, with the central theme of democracy, freedom, and justice for all Mexicans;

—That, so as not to set back the search for a political way out of the conflict and not to interfere with the upcoming electoral process this August, the CCRI-CG of the EZLN orders all regular and irregular forces in all national and international territory to carry out a unilateral extension of the offensive cease-fire;

—That the EZLN guarantees that it will not take any offensive military action against the federal government as long as it is not attacked;

—That the EZLN will not impede the upcoming elections in territory under its control, and will allow the installation of election booths under the supervision of the NGOs and the International Red Cross;

—And that the EZLN will not accept any help from federal, state, or municipal governments and will resist the siege with its own resources and with the help of the Mexican nation only.

Sixth. The EZLN thanks the Envoy for Peace and Reconciliation in

Chiapas, Sr. Manuel Camacho Solís, for his sincere efforts to search for a political solution to the conflict. Unfortunately, the blindness of his federal government prevents it from seeing that its refusal to yield to the push for democracy will only lead the nation to a painful confrontation and unforeseen consequences.

Seventh. The CCRI-CG of the EZLN thanks the Nationally Appointed Mediator, Bishop Samuel Ruiz García and his staff for their efforts and sacrifices in the mediation between the parties in conflict, their integrity in resisting pressure and threats, and their willingness to listen.

Eighth. The CCRI-CG of the EZLN thanks the honest and independent media for their commitment to learn the truth and let it be known to the Mexican people, despite threats, pressure, and blackmail. We apologize if in our clumsy media policy we insulted or mistrusted your sense of professionalism. We hope you understand that we had never run a revolution before and that we are still learning. We reiterate that, thanks to the press, it was possible to stop the military phase of the war. We sincerely hope you will understand the difficult conditions we are working under, and will excuse the unfair selection process we used to determine which news agencies would have access to our territories. We hope you continue on your path of truth.

Ninth. The CCRI-CG of the EZLN especially thanks the NGOs, vanguards of civil society. The NGOs work disinterestedly in order to obtain the peace with justice and dignity that our people desire. At the moment, the government's willful ignorance impedes any agreement whatsoever. But we are still open to dialogue and ready to follow the path you have shown us with your committed work: the political route to the transition to democracy.

Tenth. The CCRI-CG of the EZLN salutes all men and women, children and elderly, all those faceless people, in this country as well as abroad, who have extended their hands in solidarity and allied themselves with our just cause. Our struggle, brothers and sisters, is for you; for you, our death. We will not rest until all Mexicans, indigenous, campesino, factory workers, clerks, students, teachers, artists and honest intellectuals, retired people, the unemployed, the marginalized, the men and women without voice or face, have everything necessary for a decent and true life. Everything for everyone, nothing for ourselves.

Until the national flag waves with democracy, freedom, and justice above the Mexican soil, we, the furious earth, will continue our struggle. Democracy! Freedom! Justice!

Respectfully,
Subcomandante Marcos
CCRI-CG of the EZLN
Main barracks, the mountains of the Mexican Southeast
Chiapas, Mexico
June 1994

• 65 •
THE EZLN SAYS NO

EZLN-CG, Mexico, June 10, 1994
Response to the government's peace proposal

To the people of Mexico
To the people and governments of the world
To the national and international press

Brothers and sisters,

The CCRI-CG of the EZLN addresses all of you with respect and honor to let you know our appraisal and reply to the proposals for a peace agreement that were placed on the table by the national government during the dialogue held at the Meetings for Peace and Reconciliation in Chiapas.

First. The EZLN, a Mexican military organization formed primarily by indigenous people, rose up in arms against the central government on January 1, 1994. The demands of the EZLN are summed up in the eleven points of the Declaration of the Lacandon Rainforest: jobs, land, housing, food, health, education, independence, freedom, democracy, justice, and peace. These demands are supported by the majority of the Mexican people, and the EZLN fights so that all Mexicans can achieve them.

Second. Following the bloody battles fought between our troops and elements of the federal police and the Mexican army, a nationwide popular movement obliged us to cease fighting and undertake a dialogue with the central government. This dialogue took place in the city of San Cristóbal de las Casas, Chiapas, in late February and early March 1994.

Third. At the San Cristóbal discussions, the EZLN presented a list of thirty-four demands, which if met would bring about a peace with justice and dignity.

Fourth. The EZLN's list of thirty-four demands refers to pressing needs at both the national and state levels, some of which concern the whole populace and some the campesino and indigenous people. The government attempted in vain to reduce the importance of our struggle to the concerns of the local indigenous community, and even to those of the four municipalities of southeastern Chiapas.

Fifth. Among our demands affecting all Mexicans are the following:

(1) Free and democratic elections, with full equality of rights and responsibilities for all existing political forces.

(2) As a guarantee of freedom and democracy, we demand the resignation of the president of the republic and of all of the illegitimately elected governors of the states. Upon the resignation of the president, a government of transition should be formed that will organize free and democratic elections. We also demand that citizens and groups of citizens, who are not members of any party, shall participate with full authority in the electoral process.

(3) We demand a new federal agreement which will put an end to centralism and permit the autonomy of the indigenous communities and municipalities.

(4) We demand a revision of the North American Free Trade Agreement signed with Canada and the United States, because it is not in accordance with Mexican reality.

(5) We demand decent jobs with reasonable wages for all workers, both rural and urban, and full compliance with the federal Labor Law for the benefit of both.

(6) We demand an end to the plunder of our national wealth.

(7) We demand the cancellation of all debts contracted through credits, loans, and taxes.

(8) We demand solutions to the national problem of hunger and malnutrition in the rural areas and the cities of Mexico.

(9) We demand immediate and unconditional freedom for all political prisoners and for all poor people unjustly detained in prisons around the country.

Sixth. The national government did not give a positive response to these demands of the EZLN, supported by wide sectors of the Mexican population.

The events following the dialogue of San Cristóbal de las Casas have proved the reasonableness of the democratic demands of the EZLN. The cowardly assassination of Colosio, the arbitrary designation of Zedillo as the new candidate of PRI, and the renewed energy with which the government is pushing its hard line all demonstrate that it would have been best for the nation if Sr. Salinas de Gortari had resigned from the presidency on the 1st of January. His insistence upon holding on to power has thrown our country into a climate of permanent insecurity; and his determination to continue his usurpation of power by means of a new electoral fraud to elect Zedillo has the nation at the edge of civil war.

Everyone agrees that the electoral reform was incomplete. The continuation of an electoral system that is shot through with defects permits electronic fraud and continues the usurpation of the popular will.

The reinforcement of the repressive apparatus of the government, and the attempt to force the Federal Army to do police work, makes it abundantly clear that the Salinas group is staking its fortunes not on a democratic transition, but on fraud and the arbitrary exercise of power.

The EZLN affirms what reality shows: there is no commitment to democracy in the almighty government. The official party system must be destroyed. The EZLN repeats demands One and Two of the document we presented in San Cristóbal:

(1) Free and democratic elections.

(2) Those who have illegally seized power in the state and federal governments must be thrown out.

The EZLN now expands upon our demands:

We need a government of national transition and a new constitution that guarantee, in law and in fact, the fulfillment of the fundamental demands of the Mexican people: democracy, freedom, and justice, demands that found a voice in the voiceless, a face in the faceless, a tomorrow in those who have no tomorrow, a life in our death.

Bad government tries to diminish the demand for the autonomy of the indigenous communities, while it leaves untouched a central power that gives dictator status to the federal executive. The government's responses ignore our demand for real municipal autonomy.

The law, promised by the government to acknowledge the political, cultural, and economic autonomy of indigenous communities, follows the usual procedure: a bill that fails to get to the root of the question, does not draw on the collective thinking of either specialists or the indigenous people themselves, and is pushed through as quickly as possible. Contradicting its own offer that the proposed "General Law of the Rights of the Indigenous Communities" would respond to the "demands, opinions, concerns, and political consensus of the Indian communities," and that it would be enriched conceptually by "a group of specialists," the law does no more than seek to implement the fourth article of the Constitution without consulting the opinions of any interested sector of the population.

To the demand for a revision of NAFTA, the government responds by stubbornly trying to implement an economic project that has done nothing but increase poverty in our country, and deceive foreign investors by promising economical stability and social peace. The government promised to do a careful evaluation of the impact of NAFTA within ninety days; this "evaluation" has not been done, but the Mexican people can save them the trouble of forming a commission to "evaluate the impact": NAFTA's impact can be observed on the table of any poor household in the country.

As an answer to the national demand for dignified jobs and fair wages, the government continues with economic policies that increase both unemployment and underemployment, and diminish the purchasing power of the workers. Trade union bossism continues to serve as the power base for the neoliberal economic project.

The demand for an end to the looting of national resources is passed over, and the government's response is limited to the ecological problem. There is no national policy for the defense of the natural resources of our country.

To the demand for a cancellation of all debts that affect the poor sectors of the nation, the government responds with a promise, still unfulfilled, to study the matter—which would undoubtedly have the effect of merely postponing consideration of the problem.

As in the cases mentioned above, the response to the demand for an end to the hunger and malnutrition of our people is intended to be limited to a few regions of Chiapas. They respond with promises for programs in our area, as if hunger and malnutrition were the lot only of Indians in the highlands and the rainforest, and as if the programs themselves could be eaten.

The freedom of all political prisoners and of all the poor unjustly jailed in the prisons of the country is made light of with the promise to form commissions to study these problems. The unjust Mexican judicial system, which favors only the rich and powerful, will remain intact.

In conclusion, the reasonable national demands of the EZLN were not responded to by the government in a satisfactory fashion. The EZLN therefore rejects the following points in government's peace proposal: 1, 2, 4, 7, 18, 20, 21, 22, and 23.

Seventh. Among the demands for the agricultural sector made by the EZLN, which would benefit all Mexican campesinos and farmworkers, are the following:

(1) The demand that Article 27 of the Mexican Constitution be implemented in the original spirit of Emiliano Zapata. The land belongs to those who work it.

(2) The construction of hospitals and clinics in all rural areas and communities of the country, to be supplied with doctors and medicines.

(3) A fair market price for farm products and the elimination of middlemen in their distribution.

(4) That the army and police force no longer act to defend the interests of landlords and political bosses in rural communities.

Eight. The government refused to respond in satisfactory fashion to the demands of the campesinos and farmworkers.

The government's refusal to reverse the Salinas regime's revision of

Article 27, returning the right to the land to its place in the Constitution, has been the occasion for protest among wide sectors of the rural population all over the country. These reforms, basic to the neoliberal policy for Mexican agriculture, must be eliminated. The Political Constitution of the United States of Mexico must take up Emiliano Zapata's struggle once more.

The government's response to the demand for hospitals, clinics, doctors, and medicines for all of rural Mexico is limited to the war zone of Chiapas. Rural Mexico will continue to be forgotten with respect to its right to health facilities.

To the demand for fair prices for farm products and the elimination of middlemen, the government responds by offering the services of Procampo, its vote-buying agency whose efficiency is measured by its ability to corrupt peasant leaders. The government's solution to the problems of rural Mexico is to promise another project.

To the demand for a departure of the army and police forces from rural areas, the government responded with a promise of changes in the administration of justice, with an increase in the presence of armed forces and military equipment in the zone of conflict, and with the effort to oblige the Federal Army to perform police functions. The excessive influence of cattle ranchers, operating with the economic support of the government, means constant harassment of peasants, *ejido* members, and indigenous communities in general.

In summary, the reasonable demands in favor of the agricultural sector made by the EZLN were not responded to with sincerity by the federal government, many of whose proposals are limited to partial and local solutions to problems. Therefore, the EZLN rejects points 8, 9, 19, and 24 in the government's peace proposal.

Ninth. Among the national indigenous demands of the EZLN are the following:

(1) The right of indigenous communities to have access to accurate and timely information through indigenous radio stations operated independently from the government, by the indigenous people themselves.

(2) A full course of free public education for all indigenous communities.

(3) That the languages of all indigenous communities be given

official status, and that instruction in them be obligatory at all levels of education.

(4) That the cultures and traditions of the indigenous peoples be respected.

(5) That discrimination and racism against the indigenous peoples be terminated.

(6) Cultural, political, and judicial autonomy for indigenous communities.

(7) Respect for the right to freedom and a dignified life for the indigenous communities.

(8) Economic and social support for indigenous women.

Tenth. The government gave an only partial response to these national indigenous demands made by the EZLN.

Though the government has promised to establish an independent indigenous radio station, its reply to the demand for education is limited to the selective method of granting scholarships, which deprive many young indigenous people of their right to an education at all levels. The rest of its answers on these points are limited to the promise of studies and programs within time periods, that in most of the cases have already expired.

In synthesis, the government's partial answer to our indigenous national demands and its failure to follow through on previous promises lead us to reject points 10, 12, 13, 14, 15, 16, 17, 27, and 29 in the government's peace proposals.

Eleventh. Among the demands regarding the state of Chiapas made by the EZLN are the following:

(1) The holding of general elections in Chiapas, and legal recognition of all the political forces within the state.

(2) Rural electrification of Chiapas paid for with a percentage of the earnings from the sales of the petroleum extracted from the state.

(3) Indemnification for the victims of war.

(4) Changes in the Chiapas penal code with respect to the limitations imposed upon political struggle.

(5) An end to evictions, a free and voluntary return of those evicted from their traditional lands, and indemnification for all damages.

(6) Investigation into the misconduct in public office of Patrocinio González Garrido, Absalón Castellanos Domínguez and Elmar Setzer M.

Twelfth. The government responded in unsatisfactory fashion to the demands regarding the state of Chiapas made by the EZLN.

The Chiapas electoral reform does not permit nonpartisan groups to organize for participation in elections; to the demand for rural electrification, it responds with programs and promises; the evictions still continue and those responsible have not been punished; there are only promises for economic support for the indigenous people of the state (and what promises there are, are in exchange for votes); the prosecution of the three most recent governors of the state, whose misconduct obliged us to rise up in arms, is omitted.

In summary, the unsatisfactory replies and our continuing distrust that government promises will be fulfilled, lead us to reject points 5, 6, 25, 27, 28, 29, and 30 in the government's peace proposal.

Thirteenth. Finally, the EZLN demanded to be recognized by the federal government as a belligerent force. The people of Mexico, through a wide variety of organizations, have already granted us that recognition.

To our demand for the recognition of the EZLN as a belligerent force and of our troops as authentic combatants, the federal government responds by offering guarantees of respect and dignified treatment for our members, and legal recognition to the EZLN.

Bad government cannot even guarantee the full security of its own members; much less can we expect that it treat with dignity and respect those who, interpreting the legitimate desire of the Mexican people for democracy, freedom, and justice, have risen in arms to fight.

The EZLN was formed as an army demanding respect for the will of the Mexican people. This respect continues to be denied, and the popular will is being trampled under foot by the usurper government.

The concerns that gave birth to the EZLN remain; and the EZLN remains in arms until the demand for democracy, freedom, and justice for all has been fulfilled.

The EZLN has promised to observe the international treaties that govern the conduct of war. We have stood by these treaties, and will continue to do so.

The EZLN reaffirms its demand to be recognized as a belligerent force, and its troops as authentic combatants. To this end, the EZLN will make use of the different international forums to demand this recognition from the peoples and governments of the world.

The recognition of the EZLN as a belligerent force is necessary to provide a firm basis for the development of our peace talks.

Fourteenth. In the discussions at San Cristóbal, the government presented its proposal for peace. The EZLN responded that a consultation with all of its members was necessary, since it was they who sent us to war and from them alone can come the order for peace. After many difficulties, the consultation has been completed; and this is our response to the government's proposals.

Fifteenth. For these reasons and on the basis of a free and democratic vote among its members, the Zapatista Army of National Liberation says NO to the request that we sign the government's peace proposal. The dialogue of San Cristóbal is at an end; but we reaffirm our disposition to continue the search for a political solution that will lead to peace with justice and dignity, and call upon all the progressive and independent sectors of the nation to join us in a national dialogue for peace with democracy, freedom, and justice.

We will not surrender!

Democracy! Freedom! Justice!

Respectfully,
From the mountains of the Mexican Southeast
CCRI-CG of the EZLN

• 66 •

HOW DO YOU SAY, "TO GIVE UP" IN REAL LANGUAGE?

To the national weekly *Proceso*
To the national newspaper *La Jornada*
To the national newspaper *El Financiero*
To the San Cristóbal de las Casas local newspaper *Tiempo*

June 10, 1994

Sirs,

Run! Go tell the Mazahuas, Amuzgos, Tlapanecos, Nahuatlacas, Coras, Huicholes, Yaquis, Mayos, Tarahumaras, Mixtecos, Zapotecos, Mayas, Chontales, Seris, Triquis, Kumiai, Cucapá, Paipai, Chochimi, Kiliwa, Tequistlatecos, Pame, Chichimecos, Otomies, Mazatecos, Matlatzincos, Ocuiltecos, Popoloca, Ixcatecos, Chochopopoloca, Cuicatecos, Chatinos, Chinantecos, Huaves, Pápagos, Pimas, Tepehuanos, Guarijios, Huastecos, Chuj, Jalatecos, Mixes, Zoques, Totonacas, Kikapus, Purépechas, and the O'odham of Caborca!

Let the CEU-istas and all its factions know! Let it be heard by the factory workers and landless peasants! Let those from El Barzón,* the housewives, the neighborhood residents, the teachers and students listen!

Let the Mexicans living outside our country hear the message!

Listen, bankers and dinosaurs of Atlacomulco! Let it resound in the stockmarket and in the gardens of Los Pinos!*

Let this voice reach the Mapuche and the authentic Farabundos!*

Let all the brothers and sisters in these lands open a space in their hearts for this cry!

Let the drums and the teletypes sound! Let the satellites go crazy!

What's that? What's the message? Only this: THE ZAPATISTAS. *STOP.* DO NOT GIVE UP. *STOP.* THEY RESIST. *STOP AND FINAL STOP.*

From the mountains of the Mexican Southeast
Subcomandante Insurgente Marcos
Mexico, June 1994

227

P.S. on the matter of our imprudence: We were advised to be prudent and sign a peace agreement. They say that if we don't sign this agreement, the government will finish us off within hours, in days if they take their time about it. They urge us to be satisfied with the promises that have been offered, and to wait. They think we should be prudent enough to give up in order to live. But who could live with that shame? Who exchanges dignity for life? So this reasonable counsel was useless to us. In this part of the world, both imprudence and dignity have ruled for many years now.

P.S.: We were discussing this question all afternoon in the Committee, trying to figure out how to say "to give up" in our language; and we couldn't find the words for it. The term can't be translated into Tzotzil nor Tzeltal; no one remembers if it exists in Tojolabal or in Chol. They've been looking for hours for some equivalent.

It is raining outside; a friendly cloud comes to stay with us. Old Antonio waits until everyone is quiet and only the complex drumming of the rain on the metal roof can be heard. Quietly, Old Antonio approaches me, coughing out his tuberculosis, and whispers in my ear, "That word doesn't exist in any real language, which is why our people never give up and would rather die. Because those who have gone before have ordered that words that don't go anywhere have no life."

Then he goes over to the fireplace to scare away the fear and the cold weather. I tell Ana María about this; and she looks at me tenderly and reminds me that Old Antonio is already dead.

The uncertainty of the last hours of last December has come upon us again. It's cold; the guards are relieved with a murmured password. Rain and mud shut everything down; human beings whisper and the water cries out. Someone asks for a cigarette and the match illuminates the face of the fighting woman who is standing guard—only an instant—but you can see her smile. Someone arrives with his hat and rifle dripping with water. "There's coffee made," he says. As is customary here, the Committee takes a vote to see if they should go drink the coffee or keep on searching for an equivalent for the verb "to give up" in real language. The coffee wins hands down: it's unanimous. No one is giving up!

Will we keep on struggling alone?

• 67 •
SECOND DECLARATION
OF THE LACANDON

EZLN, Mexico

Today we say:
We will not surrender!

"... It is not only those who carry the swords that make blood flow and shoot out fleeting rays of military glory, who are privileged to choose the personnel of the government of a people who want democracy; it is a right as well of the citizens who have fought in the press and in the tribunals, who are identified with the ideals of the revolution and have combated the despotism that fouls our laws. For it is not just shooting off missiles on battlefields that sweeps away tyranny. It is also by hurling ideas of redemption, slogans of freedom and terrible anathema against the executors of the people that dictatorships are toppled and empires brought down ... And if the deeds of history show us that the demolition of all tyranny, that the overthrow of all bad government, is a combined work of the idea and the sword, then it is an absurdity, it is an aberration, it is unheard-of despotism to want to exclude the healthy elements that have the right to elect the government. The sovereignty of the people is constituted by all the healthy elements that have full conscience, who are conscious of their rights, whether they be civilians or accidentally armed, but love freedom and justice and labor for the good of the country."—Emiliano Zapata, as spoken by Paulino Martínez,

Zapatista delegate to the Supreme Revolutionary Convention, Aguascalientes, Ags., Mexico, October 27, 1914

To the people of Mexico
To the peoples and governments of the world

Brothers and sisters,

The EZLN, steadfastly at war against the bad government since January 1, 1994, addresses you in order to let its thoughts be known:

(1) Mexican brothers and sisters,

In December 1993, we said *Enough!* The 1st of January 1994 we called upon the legislative and judicial powers to assume their constitutional responsibilities in order to stop the genocidal policy that the federal executive imposes on our people, and we founded our right on the application of Article 39 of the Political Constitution of the United States of Mexico:

"National sovereignty resides, essentially and originally, in the people. All public power emanates from the people and is constituted for the benefit of the same. The people have, at all times, the inalienable right to alter or modify the form of their government."

The response to this call was a policy of extermination and lies; the powers of the Union ignored our just demand and let loose massacre. But this nightmare only lasted twelve days, as another force, superior to any political or military power, imposed itself on the conflicting sides. Civil society assumed the duty of preserving our country; it demonstrated its disagreement with the massacre and forced a dialogue.

We all understand that the days of the party eternally in power, which uses the product of the work of all Mexicans to its own benefit, can no longer continue; that the *presidencialismo** that sustains it impedes liberty and must not be allowed; that the culture of fraud is the means by which they impose themselves and block democracy; that justice exists only for the corrupt and the powerful; that we must make whoever commands do so obediently; that there is no other way.

All honest Mexicans of good faith, the civil society, have come to understand this. The only ones who oppose it are those who have based their success on robbing the public treasury; those who, prostituting justice, protect the traffickers and murderers; those who resort to political assassination and to electoral fraud in order to impose themselves. It is these political fossils who plan, once again, to turn back the history of Mexico and erase from the national consciousness the cry that gripped the whole country on the 1st of January 1994: "Enough!"

But we will not allow it. Today we do not call on the failed powers of the Union who didn't know how to fulfill their constitutional duty, thus allowing the federal executive to control them. The legislature and the magistrates had no dignity, so others will come forward who do understand that they must serve the people and not one individual. Our call transcends one single presidential term or an upcoming presidential election. Our sovereignty resides in *civil society*. It is the people who can, at any time, alter or modify our form of government, and who have already assumed this responsibility. We now make a call to the people, in this *Second Declaration of the Lacandon Jungle*, in order to say:

First. We have without fail carried out our military actions within the international conventions of war; we have received tacit recognition as a belligerent force, nationally and internationally. We will continue to comply with said agreements.

Second. We order our regular and irregular forces everywhere in national and foreign territory to carry out a unilateral extension of the offensive cease-fire.

We will continue to respect the cease-fire in order to permit civil society to organize itself in whatever forms it considers necessary in order to achieve the transition to democracy in our country.

Third. We condemn the threat hanging over civil society by the current militarization of the country, complete with specialized personnel and modern equipment of repression, on the eve of federal elections. There is no doubt that the Salinas government is trying to impose itself via the culture of fraud. We will not permit it.

Fourth. We propose to all independent political parties that they now recognize the state of intimidation and the lack of political rights that our people have suffered for the past sixty-five years and that they declare themselves ready to form a government capable of the political transition to democracy.

Fifth. We denounce all the manipulation and the attempts to dissociate our just demands from those of the people of Mexico. We are Mexicans and we will not lay aside our demands nor our arms until democracy, freedom, and justice are achieved by everyone.

Sixth. We reiterate our preference for a political solution in the transition to democracy in Mexico. We call upon civil society to take on once again the central role it played in stopping the military phase of the war and to organize in order to conduct peaceful efforts toward democracy, freedom, and justice. Democratic change is the only alternative to war.

Seventh. We call the honest elements of civil society to a National Dialogue for democracy, freedom, and justice for all Mexicans.

Therefore we say:

(2) Brothers and sisters,

Once the war started, in January 1994, the organized outcry of the Mexican people stopped the confrontation and called for a dialogue between the contending sides. To the just demands of the EZLN, the federal government responded with a series of offers that did not touch the essential point of the problem: the lack of justice, freedom, and democracy in Mexican territory.

The federal government's limited capacity to follow through on its offers is what characterizes the political system of the party in power. This system is what has made it possible for another power to thrive and override constitutional law in rural Mexico, a power whose roots, in turn, make it possible for that same party to stay in power. It is this system of complicity which makes possible the existence and belligerence of *cacicazgos*,* the omnipotent power of the cattle ranchers and businessmen and the penetration of drug traffic . . . The mere offer of the so-called "Commitments Toward a Dignified Peace in Chiapas" provoked a massive revolt and open defiance by these sectors.

The single-party political system tries to maneuver within the limited horizon that its own existence imposes; it cannot affect these sectors without attacking itself, and it cannot leave things as they were without provoking an increase in the belligerence of the campesinos and indigenous people.

In sum: the fulfillment of the commitments implies, necessarily, the death of the state-party system. Whether by suicide or by firing squad, the death of the current Mexican political system is a necessary, although insufficient, condition for the transition to democracy in our country. There is no solution to the problems of Chiapas separate from a solution to the problems of Mexico.

The EZLN understands that the problem of Mexican poverty is not just a lack of resources. All efforts to combat Mexican poverty will only postpone a solution if they do not take place within a new framework for national, regional, and local political relationships: a framework of democracy, freedom, and justice.

In this new framework, the problem of power will not be a question of who the incumbent is, but rather of who exercises the power. If the majority of the people exercise the power, political parties will see themselves as obliged to confront that majority instead of each other.

A new way of approaching the problem of power in this framework of democracy, freedom, and justice will create a new political culture within the parties. A new kind of politician must be born and, no doubt, a new type of political party.

We are not proposing a new world, but rather a preliminary stage: an entryway to the new Mexico. In this sense, this revolution will not conclude in a new class, fraction of a class, or group in power, but rather in a free and democratic "space" for political struggle.

This free and democratic "space" will be born on the grave of *presidencialismo* and the putrid cadaver of the state-party system. A new political relationship will be born. It will be a new politics, based not on the confrontation among political organizations, but rather on the confrontation between different social classes over various political proposals. Political power will depend on the *real* support of these social classes, not on the exercise of political power itself.

Within this new political relationship, each of the different groups with proposals for differing systems or directions (socialism, capitalism, social democracy, liberalism, Christian Democracy, etc.) will have to convince the majority of the nation that its proposal is the best for the country. Moreover, they will be aware that they are being "watched" by the country, and will be obligated to account for themselves on a regular basis, and the judgment of the nation will determine if they stay in office or are removed. The plebiscite is a regulated form of power-party-politician-nation confrontation, and it deserves an important place in the highest law of the land.

Current Mexican legislation is too narrow for these new political relationships between the governed and their governors. A *democratic national convention* is necessary, out of which should emerge a *provisional* or *transitional* government, whether by means of the resignation of the federal executive or by the electoral process.

The *democratic national convention* and *transitional government* must produce a new Magna Carta which convenes new elections. The pain of this process will be less than the damage produced by a civil war. The prophecy of the Southeast is valid for the whole country; we can learn now from what has happened and make the birth of the new Mexico less painful.

The EZLN has an idea of what system and direction the country should have. But the political maturity of the EZLN, its coming of age as a representative part of the nation's sensibilities, depends on the fact that it doesn't want to impose its idea on the country. The EZLN hereby declares what is already evident: Mexico has come of age and has the right to decide, freely and democratically, the direction it will take.

From this historic entryway will emerge not only a better and more just Mexico, but a new Mexican as well. On this we bet our lives, so that the next generation of Mexicans will have a country in which it is not a disgrace to live.

The EZLN, in an unprecedented democratic exercise within an armed organization, consulted its entire membership on whether or not to sign the federal government's proposal for peace agreements. Seeing that the central questions of democracy, freedom, and justice had not been resolved, the bases of the EZLN, primarily indigenous people, decided to refuse to sign the government's proposal.

Under conditions of siege and pressured on various fronts by those who threatened us with extermination if the peace agreements were not signed, we Zapatistas reaffirm our pledge of life and death to achieve a peace with justice and dignity. In us, our ancestors' history of dignified struggle has found a place. The rebel Vicente Guerrero's cry of dignity, "Live for country or die for freedom," sounds again in our throats. We cannot accept an undignified peace.

We embarked upon our path of fire when we faced the impossibility of a peaceful struggle for our essential rights as human beings. The most valuable of those is the right to decide, with liberty and democracy, on our own form of government.

Now the possibility of peaceful transition to democracy and liberty faces a new test: the electoral process of August 1994.

There are those who are betting on the post-election period, preaching apathy and disillusionment from the pulpits of their own immobility. They would exploit the blood of the fallen on all fronts of combat, violent and peaceful, in the city and the countryside. They base their political project on the pre-electoral conflict and, doing nothing, wait for political demobilization to open once again the gaping doorway of war. They will save, they say, the country.

Others bet even now that armed conflict will begin again before the elections, and that they will be able to take advantage of the ungovernability of the country in order to stay in power. Yesterday they usurped the popular will with electoral fraud; today and tomorrow, with the river churning from a pre-election civil war, they will try to prolong the agony of a dictatorship which, masked by the state-party, has already lasted decades. Still others, sterile prophets of the apocalypse, reason that war is now inevitable and they sit down to wait, watching for their enemy's corpse to pass by . . . or their friend's.

The sectarians erroneously suppose that the mere shooting of guns will be enough to crack open the dawn that our people have awaited since the night fell—with the deaths of Villa and Zapata—over Mexican soil.

All of these thieves of hope suppose that behind our arms there is ambition and self-interested leadership, and that this will determine our path in the future. They are mistaken. Behind our firearms there are other arms—those of reason. And both are motivated by hope. We will not let them rob us of it.

Hope with a trigger had its place in the beginning of the year. Now it is crucial to wait. The hope that always accompanies great mobilizations must regain the central leadership role that belongs to it by right and reason. The flag is now in the hands of those who have name and face, of good and honest people who travel by routes that are not ours, but whose goal is the same one we yearn for. We salute these men and women, we salute them and we hope that they carry that flag to the place where it ought to be. We will be waiting, at attention and with dignity. If that flag falls, we will know how to raise it again...

May hope get organized, may it travel now through the valleys and cities as it did yesterday in the mountains. Fight with your own weapons; don't worry about us. We will know how to resist to the last. We will know how to wait ... and we will know how to return if all the doors to dignity close again.

Therefore we address our brothers and sisters of the Non-Governmental Organizations, of the campesino and indigenous peoples' organizations, workers of the countryside and of the city, teachers and students, housewives and neighborhood residents, artists and intellectuals, those of the independent parties, Mexicans:

We call you to a national dialogue with the theme of democracy, freedom, and justice. For this we send out the present call for a Democratic National Convention.

We, the EZLN, struggling to achieve the democracy, freedom, and justice that our country deserves, and considering:

First. That the federal government has usurped the legitimacy—left to us by its heroes—of the Mexican Revolution.

Second. That the Magna Carta that rules us no longer represents the popular will of Mexicans.

Third. That it is not enough for the usurper of the federal executive to step down; our country needs new laws which must be born of the struggles of all honest Mexicans.

Fourth. That all forms of struggle are necessary to achieve the transition to democracy in Mexico.

Therefore, we call for a Democratic National Convention, supreme and revolutionary, from which must emerge the proposals for a transitional government and a new national law, a new constitution that guarantees the legal implementation of the popular will.

The fundamental objective of the Democratic National Convention is to organize civil expression and the defense of the popular will.

The revolutionary convention will be national in terms of its composition—representation must include all the states of the federation; plural in the sense that all patriotic forces will be represented; and democratic in decision-making, deferring always to consultations throughout the nation.

The convention will be presided over, freely and voluntarily, by civilians: public figures of recognized prestige, regardless of their political affiliation, race, religious creed, sex, or age.

The convention will be formed via local, regional, and state committees, in *ejidos*, neighborhoods, schools, and factories, by civilians. These committees will be entrusted with arguing for their own grassroots proposals for the new constitutional laws and for the demands which the new government, once it emerges from the convention, will have to meet.

The convention must require that free and democratic elections must take place, and they must struggle, without rest, to see that the popular will is respected.

The EZLN will recognize the Democratic National Convention as the authentic representation of the interests of the Mexican people in its transition to democracy.

The EZLN is already present throughout the nation, and is able to offer itself to the people of Mexico as a security guard for the implementation of the popular will.

For the first meeting site of the Democratic National Convention, the EZLN offers a Zapatista village and all the facilities it includes.

The date and place of the first session of the Democratic National Convention will be announced when possible and appropriate.

(3) Mexican brothers and sisters,

Our struggle continues. The Zapatista flag still waves over the Mexican Southeast and today we say: We will not surrender!

Facing the mountain, we speak with our dead so that they will reveal to us in their word the path down which our veiled face should turn.

The drums rang out and in the voice of the earth our pain spoke and our history spoke.

"For everyone everything," say our dead. "Until it is so, there will be nothing for us.

"Speak the word of other Mexicans, find in your heart an ear for their word. Invite them to walk down the honorable path of those who have no face. Call everyone to resist, so that nobody accepts anything from those who command commanding. Convince them not to sell out a flag that belongs to everyone. Ask that we receive more than just words of hot air to alleviate our pain. Ask that they share, ask that they resist, that they reject all the handouts that come from the powerful. Ask that today all the good people of these lands organize the dignity that resists and does not sell itself out, that tomorrow that dignity organize itself to demand that the word that lives in the heart of the majority is met with truth, and is welcomed by those who govern, that the good road is imposed, in which the person who commands, commands obeying.

Do not surrender! Resist! Do not let down the honor of the true word. Resist with dignity in the lands of the true men and women; may the mountains blanket the pain of the men of corn. Do not surrender! Resist! Do not sell yourselves! Resist!"

So spoke the word of the heart of our forever dead. We saw that our dead's word was good; we said, there is truth and dignity in their counsel. Therefore we call upon all our Mexican indigenous brothers and sisters to resist with us. We call upon all the campesinos to resist with us, upon the factory workers, the clerks, the neighborhood residents, the housewives, the students, the teachers, those who make thought and word their life, all of those who have dignity and pride, we call everyone to resist with us, since the bad government is opposed to having democracy on our soil. We will accept nothing that comes from the rotten heart of the bad government, neither a single coin nor a medicine nor a stone nor a grain of food nor a crumb from the handouts that it offers in exchange for our dignified path. We will take nothing from the federal government. Even if our pain and our grief deepen; though death may still be with us, at the table, in the land and on the roof; though we may see that others sell themselves to the hand that oppresses them; though everything might ache, and grief weeps even from the stones . . . we will take nothing from the government. We will resist until the person who commands, commands obeying.

Brothers and sisters: Do not sell yourselves. Resist with us. Do not surrender. Resist with us. Repeat with us, brothers and sisters: "We will not surrender! We will resist!" So that it is not only heard in the mountains of the Mexican Southeast, but in the north and out on the peninsulas, so that on both coasts it is heard, so that in the heartland it is heard, so that in the valleys and the mountains it becomes a cry, so that it resounds in the city and in the country. Join with your voices, brothers and sisters, cry out with us, make our voice yours: "We will not surrender! We will resist!"

May the dignity break the siege with which the bad government's dirty hands are smothering us. We are all besieged: they don't allow democracy, freedom, and justice to enter Mexican territory. Brothers and sisters, we are all besieged; don't surrender! Resist! Be dignified! We must not sell ourselves out!

What good are the riches of the powerful if they can't buy the most valuable thing in these lands? If the dignity of all Mexicans has no price, what is the power of the powerful for?

Dignity does not surrender!
Dignity resists!
Democracy! Freedom! Justice!

From the mountains of the Mexican Southeast
CCRI-CG of the EZLN
Mexico, June 1994

❀❀❀❀❀❀❀

HERE IS YOUR FLAG, COMPAÑEROS

SPEECH TO THE NATIONAL DEMOCRATIC CONVENTION

Nobody, not a single person from the National Organizing Committee, has been able to say how many delegates, guests, observers, journalists, sponges, nut cases, spooks, and lost souls have come here to Aguascalientes. So we don't know how many of us there are. But since we have press here from all over Mexico and the world, we have to come up with a figure. The National Organizing Committee is stumped, so we had to solve the problem ourselves; using our sophisticated system of computation we have counted and come to the conclusion that there are a hell of a lot of us here. So, it is now official: we are a hell of a lot of people.

I think it is no longer necessary for the Zapatista patrols to ask, "Who lives?" I sincerely believe that one of the first resolutions of this National Democratic Convention (CND) will be to declare with pride that the answer to "Who lives?" is none other than "Our country."

In 1985, for the first time, we took over a village—a few plots of corn, some seedlings, a couple of banana trees, a small coffee plantation, and several little *champada* trees, all of which had cheerfully been designated an *ejido*. It was the village of Old Antonio. Nine years before death embraced him, Old Antonio had invited us to visit his *ejido*. Together we made a plan to take it, to take over the *ejido*. After getting lost in a coffee grove, we managed to take over Old Antonio's small village. But we were a poor excuse for a guerrilla operation: when we arrived we found the villagers had already gathered in the middle of the town. The "middle of the town," as a jungle city-planner would explain, is located between the church, the school, the basketball court, and the coffee grove. There we were standing in front of the people, to whom Old Antonio introduced us, saying something like, "here are the compañeros who come from the mountain." The people started to applaud. I thought: " Man, I'm not doing too bad this year, I haven't even said anything and they are already applauding."

When they stopped clapping, Old Antonio said to me, "Now that we have welcomed you, you can say your word." It was then that I realized that in these parts, when people want to greet someone, they clap. So I want to begin by asking you, not for applause, but for a welcome. A welcome to all the men, women, children, and old folks who at this moment, in the countryside and the cities of Mexico, are asking, praying, begging, keeping their fingers crossed, anxiously hoping that this first session of the National Democratic Convention will go well. If there are a hell of a lot of us here, out there we are at least a hell of lot times two.

[Applause]

I also ask that you welcome the gathering of people that is taking place at this very moment in some part of Mexico, people getting together to talk about our nation's problems—I ask for a welcome to the National Democratic Convention that we are celebrating right now in Aguascalientes, Chiapas, Mexico.

[Applause]

Our Zapatista Army of National Liberation wants to honor our flag and the National Democratic Convention. I would like to ask your permission for the Zapatista troops, who are in charge of security here, to present you with a Zapatista salute. On the Zapatista guns you will see white ribbons. Those ribbons signify the purpose of our weapons; they are not arms to be used in confrontation with civil society. Those ribbons on the guns represent, like everything else here, a paradox: weapons that aspire to uselessness.

So I ask permission from the collective leadership and the convention for the combat troops to march before you. What Comandante Tacho presented were our bases of support, the Zapatistas' secret weapon. [Before Marcos' speech, Comandante Tacho had presented a parade of civilians—men, women, children, and elderly who had provided food and shelter to the Zapatistas.] There is no higher technology than the Zapatista technology: the support of the people. Now give them a military salute.

[Zapatista troops parade before the assembly, and Marcos resumes his speech.]

Honorable Democratic Convention:

To the Collective Presidency of the Democratic Convention, delegates, guests, observers, brothers and sisters:

Through my voice speaks the EZLN.

Aguascalientes, Chiapas: headquarters, bunker, arms factory, military training center, ammo dump.

Aguascalientes, Chiapas: Noah's Ark, the Tower of Babel, Fitzcarraldo's jungle boat, neozapatista pipedream, a pirate ship; an anachronistic paradox, the tender madness of the faceless, the absurdity of a civilian movement in dialogue with an armed one.

Aguascalientes, Chiapas: graded terraces of hope, hope in the little palm trees that line the steps, reaching for the sky, hope in the conch shell that calls out from the jungle through the breeze, hope in those who didn't come but are with us, hope that the flowers that die elsewhere will flourish here.

Aguascalientes, Chiapas: for the EZLN, 600 men and women putting in 28 days of labor, 14 hours a day: a total of 235,200 hours of labor; 9,800 days of labor; 28 years of labor; 60 million old pesos, a library, a stage the size of the bridge on a transatlantic liner, wooden benches for 8,000 participants, 20 houses for shelter, 14 fire pits, parking for 100 vehicles, and even strategic spots for sniper-assassins.

Aguascalientes, Chiapas: a joint military/civilian effort, a collective effort for change, a peaceful effort by armed people.

And before Aguascalientes, they said it was madness, that it couldn't be done, that this call for a convention on the eve of the elections from behind a frontier of guns and ski-masks couldn't work.

And before Aguascalientes, they said nobody in their right mind would answer this call from a rebel group, outlaws, who whether well-known or little known, were the flash that lit up January, but whose obsessive language is now trying to recover old, used-up words: democracy, freedom, justice. They said nobody would answer this call from shrouded faces, the night path, the mountain dressed as hope, from the Indian's lonely gaze that for centuries has watched the disastrous attempt at modernization. Nobody would answer from those who stubbornly refuse to accept hand-outs, insisting instead on the seemingly absurd: everything for everybody, nothing for ourselves.

And before Aguascalientes, they said that there was too little time, that no one would risk embarking on a project which, like the Tower of Babel, at the very moment and place of its conception announced its own failure.

And before Aguascalientes, they said that the fear, the sweet terror that nourishes the good people of this country from the moment they are born, would prevail, and that the obvious and comfortable route of doing nothing, of sitting and waiting to see what happens, of applauding or booing the actors in this bitter comedy that is called our country, would continue to reign in the newly renamed people of Mexico: civil society.

And before Aguascalientes, they said that irreconcilable differences that fragment us and turn us against one another would prevent us from uniting against our common enemy, the omnipotent state party and everything that surrounds it and gives it power: *presidencialismo*; the sacrifice of liberty and democracy on the altars of stability and economic bonanza; the fraud and corruption that have become our national idiosyncrasy; justice prostituted by handouts; hopelessness and conformism elevated to the status of national security doctrine.

And before Aguascalientes, they said not to worry, the call for a dialogue between a group of "transgressors of the law" and a shapeless, disorganized mass, fragmented down to the family microcosm, the so-called civil society, would find no echo or common cause, that a gathering of such scattered groups could only lead to more scattering and to immobility.

And before Aguascalientes, they said there would be no reason to oppose the celebration of the National Democratic Convention, that it would abort by itself, that open sabotage wouldn't be worth the effort, that is was better to let it explode from the inside, so that Mexico and the world could see that those who dissent are incapable of agreeing among themselves, and therefore incapable of offering the country a national project any better than the one the institutionalized, stabilized revolution has given us, along with the pride of having twenty-four billionaire heroes who now belong to the international country of money.

They are betting on all that. That's why they let us have our convention, and did not prevent you from coming here, so that the predictable failure of the CND would not be attributed to the powerful; so that it would be clear that the weak cannot be anything else but weak, that they are weak because they deserve it, because they desire to be so.

And before Aguascalientes, we said yes it's crazy, but from the horizon opened by guns and ski-masks, we can call a national gathering right before the elections—and we can succeed.

Do you want a mirror?

[Extended applause]

One sits on the painful threshold of history to lament that which prudence now demands: the constant pain of doing nothing, of waiting, of despairing that the boundless and tender fury of "everything for everyone, nothing for ourselves" will ever be heard by the Others, the Others who are falsely made out to be you and us.

And before Aguascalientes, we said that there was more than enough time, that what we lacked was shame at our own fear of trying to be better, that the problem of the Tower of Babel was not in the project itself, but rather the absence of a good system of linking people up, and a team of translators.

The failure was the weak attempt itself, sitting by and watching how the Tower went up, how it was supported, how it fell down. The failure was in sitting by and waiting to see what history would say, not about the Tower, but about those who sat by, waiting for failure.

And before Aguascalientes, we said that the fear, the seductive terror that gushes from the sewers of power and has nourished us since birth, could be and should be put to one side—not forgotten, not completely overcome, but simply put aside. That the fear of being just spectators should be greater than the fear of trying to find common ground, trying to find something that would unite us, something that would transform this comedy into history.

And before Aguascalientes, we said that the differences that divide us and turn us against one another will not prevent us from uniting against a common enemy: the system of abuses so open and obvious that they make us impotent. The common things that kill: the state/party system and the absurdities that it validates and institutionalizes; the hereditary dictatorship; shoving the struggle for democracy, liberty, and justice into the corner reserved for utopias and impossibilities; the electoral farce, now in the form of computer alchemy, elevated to the status of a national monument; misery and ignorance as the historical lot of the dispossessed; democracy whitewashed with imported detergent and the water from anti-riot tanks.

And before Aguascalientes, we said not to worry, that a dialogue between armed people without faces and the disarmed facelessness of civil society would find common ground, that a meeting and dialogue between scattered groups could provoke a movement that would finally turn this page of shame, this page in the history of Mexico.

And before Aguascalientes, we said that we would not oppose a celebration of the CND which would be exactly that, neither more nor less than a celebration, a celebration of broken fear, of a first, shaky step toward the possibility of offering the nation an "enough" that would not only be said in an indigenous and campesino voice, but an "enough" that would unite, multiply, reproduce, triumph. We might be able to celebrate a discovery: understanding ourselves, no longer as masters of defeat, but rather with the possibility of victory on our side.

We bet on that, and that's why the collective, anonymous will that has as its face only a five-pointed red star, symbol of humanity and struggle, and for its name only four letters, symbol of rebellion, constructed in this forgotten place in the history of governmental studies, international treaties, maps, and fiscal currents, a new place we call Aguascalientes in memory of past attempts to unite hope.

That's why thousands of men and women, with their faces covered, the vast majority of them indigenous people, raised this tower, the tower of hope. That's why we put to one side, for a time, our guns, our grudges, our grief for our dead, our warrior convictions, our armed path. That's why we built this place for this gathering, that if it should be successful will be the first step to making us unnecessary as a political alternative. That's why we raised up Aguascalientes, as the heart of a gathering, that if it should fail will oblige us again to carry forward with fire the right of all people to a place in history.

That's why we invited you, that's why we are happy you arrived, that's why we expect that your maturity and wisdom will lead you to discover that the main enemy, the most powerful and terrible enemy, is not here seated among you.

That's why, with great respect, we address this CND and ask in the name of all the men and women, of all the children and elders, in the name of all the living and dead of the EZLN that you prove wrong those who predicted the failure of this convention, that you look for and find that which unites us, that you speak truthfully, that you don't forget the differences that separate us, and all too frequently set us against each other, but that you save a moment, a few days, a few hours, enough minutes to find our common enemy. We respectfully ask that you do not betray your ideals, your principles, your history, that you neither betray them nor deny them; we respectfully ask that you carry forward your ideals, your principles, your history, and that by affirming them you will say "enough" to the lie that today governs our history.

The EZLN has twenty delegates to the CND, with one vote each, and we want to make two things clear: one is our commitment to the CND; the other is our decision not to impose our point of view. We have also refused to be a part of the collective leadership of the CND, as this is a convention that is looking for a peaceful road to change and should not be led by armed people. We are grateful that you have give us a place, as one among all of you, to say our word.

We want to say, in case anyone doubts it, that we do not regret rising up in arms against the federal government, and we say again that they left us no other way, and that we neither deny our armed path nor our covered faces; that we do not lament our dead, that we are proud of them and that we are ready to shed more blood and suffer more deaths if that is the price we must pay for democratic change in Mexico.

We want to say that we are unmoved by the accusations that we are priests of martyrdom, that we are war-makers. We are not tempted by the songs of sirens and angels to enter a world that looks upon us with disrespect and mistrust, that does not value our blood and offers us fame in exchange for dignity. We are not interested in living life as it is now lived.

Many have asked themselves, with the perverse inquisitiveness of those who look to confirm their own suppositions, what is it that the Zapatistas are trying to do with the CND, what is it that they hope to get out of this convention? A civic pact, some answer; full-page coverage in the national and international press, argue others; a new justification for their eagerness to go to war, say some; a civil endorsement of war, venture others; a platform for the resurrection of a world forgotten by the system, fear those in a certain official party, even as they prepare to sell out that certain official party; a space to enjoy the leadership of a left that has no apparent life of its own, murmurs the opposition; an endorsement of our surrender, say those who would silence us with a ghostly conspiratorial bullet; a platform so that Marcos can negotiate a place in the next administration of modernity, concludes some brilliant column of some oh so brilliant analyst of opaque political intrigues.

Today, in front of this CND, the EZLN responds to the question, What do the Zapatistas hope to get from the CND? Not a civilian political branch to extend the macabre arm of war into all corners of the country; not a media event that reduces the struggle for dignity to a sporadic article on the front page; not more arguments to dress up our suit of fire and death; not a scale by which to rank the power of politicians, groups, and sub-groups; not the doubtful honor of being the historical vanguard of the multiple vanguards that plague us; not the pretext for betraying the ideals and the deaths that we carry with us as our heritage; not a trampoline to land at a desk in an office of some department in some government in some country.

Not the designation of an interim government, not the writing of a new constitution, not the formation of a new constituency, not the endorsement for a candidate for the presidency of this republic of pain and conformism, not war.

Yes to the first steps in the construction of something greater than Aguascalientes, to the construction of peace with dignity. Yes to the beginning of an effort greater than the one that has produced Aguascalientes. Yes to the effort for democratic change that includes freedom and justice for the forgotten people, the majority of our country. Yes to the beginning of the end of this long, grotesque nightmare that is called the history of Mexico.

Yes, the moment has come to say to everyone that we neither want, nor are we able, to occupy the place that some hope we will occupy, the place from which all opinions will come, all the answers, all the routes, all the truths. We are not going to do that.

What we hope from the CND is simply this: the opportunity to look for and find someone to give this flag to, the flag that we found alone and forgotten in the palaces of power, that flag that we took with our blood, yes, with our blood, from the prison of the museums, the flag that we take care of day and night, that accompanies us in war and that we want with us in peace, the flag that we give today to this CND.

We don't give it to the CND to hold it back or hoard it from the rest of the nation, or to supplant other probable armed or proven civic leaders. We give it to the struggle so that all Mexicans will make it theirs once again, so that again it will be the NATIONAL FLAG. Here is your flag, compañeros.

[Marcos unveils the national flag and holds it up before the convention.]

What we hope from this CND is the peaceful and legal organization of struggle, the struggle for democracy, freedom, and justice, the struggle that saw us obliged to travel on an armed path and deny our own faces.

We hope from this CND to receive the true word, the word of peace, but not the word that would halt the struggle for democracy; the word of peace but not the word of renunciation of the struggle for freedom; the word of peace, but not the word of pacifist complicity with injustice.

We hope from this CND the capacity to understand that the right to consider ourselves the representative of the sentiments of the nation cannot come from a resolution that can be approved by a vote or by consensus, it is something that has to be won in the *barrios, ejidos, colonias,* indigenous communities, in the schools and universities, factories, businesses, centers of scientific investigation, in the cultural and artistic centers, in all the corners of this country.

We hope from this CND the clarity to realize that this is only one step, the first of many that will have to be taken, in conditions much worse than we face here.

We hope from this CND the courage to take on the color of hope that many Mexicans, including us, now see; the courage to demonstrate that the best men and women of this country are using whatever resources and forces they have for the change that is the only possibility for the survival of this people: the change to democracy, freedom, and justice.

We hope from this CND the maturity not to convert this space into a sterile and sterilizing adjustment of internal accounts. We hope from this CND, finally, a collective call to struggle for that which belongs to us, that which is reasonable and right for all good people: our place in history.

It is not our time now, it is not the hour of arms. We have moved to one side, but we are not gone. We will wait until a new horizon opens, or until we are no longer necessary, until we are not even possible, us, the forever dead, those who must die once again in order to live.

We hope from this CND an opportunity, the opportunity that the government of this country has denied us, the opportunity to return with dignity after we have paid the debt we owe to our dead. The opportunity to return again to silence, to the night from which we came, to the death in which we live. The opportunity to disappear in the same way we appeared: at dawn, without faces and without a future. The opportunity to return again to the center of our history, our dream, our mountain.

It has been said, incorrectly, that the Zapatistas have put a deadline for a new beginning of war; that if things don't come out like the Zapatistas want them to on August 21, the war will begin again. They lie. They lie to the Mexican people. No one, no one, not even the EZLN, can place deadlines and ultimatums on the Mexican people. The only deadlines for the EZLN are the ones that are determined by the peaceful, civic mobilizations. We subordinate ourselves to them, and if called upon to do so, we will even disappear as an alternative.

A new beginning of the war will not come from us. There is no Zapatista ultimatum to civil society. We will wait, we will resist. We are experts at that.

You must struggle. Struggle without rest. Struggle and defeat the government. Struggle and defeat the government. Struggle and defeat us. If the peaceful transition to democracy, dignity, and justice wins, never will there have been a defeat so sweet.

The General Command of the Revolutionary Indigenous Clandestine Committee of the EZLN has given you Aguascalientes so that you could meet and agree not on immobility, not on sterile skepticism, not for an interchange of reproaches and allegations, not as a tribune for personal promotion, not as a pretext for war tourism, not for unconditional pacifist blackmail, not for war—but neither for peace at any price.

We give you Aguascalientes to debate and agree on the organization of a civil, peaceful, popular, and national struggle for democracy, freedom, and justice. The CCRI-CG of the EZLN now gives you the national flag in order to remind you of what it means: Country, History, and Nation. And we commit ourselves to that which it ought to mean: Democracy, Freedom, Justice.

Salud, brother and sister conventioneers. For you we created Aguascalientes. It was built for you, in the middle of a territory of war, this space for a just and dignified peace.

Thank you very much.

Democracy, Freedom, Justice.

From the mountains of the Mexican Southeast
The General Command of the Revolutionary Indigenous
Clandestine Committee of the Zapatista Army of
National Liberation
August 1994

DEAR SUP, MUCH OBLIGED

AN AFTERWORD
BY FRANK BARDACKE

Subcomandante Insurgente Marcos begins his National Democratic Convention speech—a medley of his greatest hits, a hymn to the Mexican "patria," and a warning against sectarianism—with a story about Old Antonio. It is another self-deprecating anecdote; the wise old man of the mountain was, as always, two jumps ahead of the would-be guerrilla fighter. When the Marcos-led Zapatistas enter the *ejido* to take it over, the villagers are already assembled in the middle of town, well organized and ready to join the fight. Civil society is once again more advanced than those—even the Zapatistas—who would lead the way.

Add "civil society" to the already overburdened shoulders of Old Antonio. Think of all the other things he has to represent: the early determination to go to war, the contemporary relevance of Mayan mythology and social organization, the refusal to approve an undignified peace, death from curable disease. Not that his death much diminishes his presence. The last time we heard of Old Antonio—that is, the last time before the jungle convention—he was a dead man, but still working as the traditional counselor to our comic prince, telling Marcos not to sign the dirty peace because it is impossible to say "give up" in real language.

In Marcos' world, as in the world of the Posada drawings that illustrate this book, the dead are still living and the living are already

---

This Afterword was helped along by Jeff Lustig's manuscript, "Neither Submission nor Estrangement: An Inquiry into Political Obligation," and conversations with Ted Bardacke, Leslie López, David Sweet, and John Ross. For a full discussion of the revolutionary potential of democracy, see Doug Lummis, *The Art of the Possible: Toward a Philosophy of Radical Democracy* (Ithaca, NY: Cornell University Press, 1995).

dead. Such a view is useful to the Sup, who often urges people to political action in the name of what we owe our ancestors. If our dead are still around, actually still here, it is harder to betray our inheritance.

And what do we inherit from our ancestors? The Chiapans—not just the Chiapans, says Marcos, but all the Mexican people—inherit a tradition of resistance. Some of their ancestors drowned themselves in the river rather than submit to the oppressors. Knowing that, says Marcos, the living have no choice but to "honor this lesson in dignity." People fight to keep a tradition alive; they fight to honor the generations that went before them and as an example for those yet to come.

The people fight to win, but they usually lose. Marcos makes fun of those who would base their decision on whether or not to begin the war on some abstract calculation of the alignment of forces. The primary consideration is not what chance you have to win (the chances are usually slim), but what is the most dignified path. "The true choice for us," Marcos says, "is a dignified peace or a dignified war."

Winning or losing, usually considered the unquestionable measure of success in politics and war, is here relegated to a near minor theme. Oh sure, we will win eventually, but only because our cause is just, not because of any scientific certainty of human progress. The major concern is not to find the winning strategy, but the dignified one. Here we are, watched closely by our dead and our children, trying to write our story, knowing that we will probably lose. "Dying in order to live" is not a foreign idea to anyone raised in a Catholic world, but Marcos is talking about something other than resurrection. We fight and we die so that the tradition will live.

"We"? Does Marcos speak to us? Certainly the U.S. left can take heart from his argument about tradition; it is comforting to encounter a theory that makes sense of our losing, that gives value to struggle regardless of its immediate outcome. And any of us who have worked in popular movements have found our own Old Antonios: the old folks who first built the unions and now want to fight again; the civil rights and black power survivors who know how much has been won and how much has been lost; the veteran comrades who somehow came through the Cold War and the rise and fall of actually existing socialism with their dignity intact. We too have a tradition of resistance. Is it not worthy of our loyalty? And if we are loyal to it, are we not obliged to fight on? Perhaps we might mimic

Marcos and try to build a politics that bases itself (at least somewhat) on our mutual obligations and not exclusively on our sense of violated rights.

It is the self-assigned task of this essay to do what I just did: draw out of Marcos lessons for the U.S. left. But there are many dangers in such an assignment, many ways of getting Marcos wrong. So let's start with two essentials about the Sup that might serve as warnings against some over-analysis yet to come.

One. Marcos is a master pamphleteer writing in the midst of war. His purpose is to inspire, mobilize, amuse, touch, anger. He is capable of magnificent description, but he is not an explainer. (In his boilerplate prologue to this book he uncharacteristically takes on the task of explanation with disastrous results: in explaining the origin of the communiqués, he first says that they were thoroughly discussed and debated and that he was instructed to write up the results of the debate; then he says that he wrote them according to the "Zapatista editorial line," by which he means he put down whatever came into his head.) Marcos is in the literary/political tradition of Tom Paine and Ricardo Flores Magón. They wrote in the midst of revolution; their purpose was to move people to action. But neither of them were fully developed theorists. Their attempts at large architectonic theory were weak, and added nothing new to the grand explanations of their times. Nevertheless, their pens became true swords, their words filled the hearts and mouths of generations of fighting men and women who hoped to change the world.

A complete theory of politics—even to the extent that one is possible or desirable—is not going to come from letters and communiqués that primarily are meant to inspire. Marcos is not that interested in having an intellectually consistent and complete answer to everything. He is not El Durito, the little beetle who spends his time in deep analysis of the world situation. Marcos is looking for words that will bring him supporters and recruits. Any reconstruction of his thought into a formal theory is at war with his original intention.

Two. Marcos comes out of a particular Mexican situation (yes, a *coyuntura*) in which he is trying to do revolutionary politics. It is not automatically true that his politics will make sense in other countries and other cultures. It may not even be likely. After all, part of what makes Marcos so good at what he does is his mastery of Mexican popular culture, his ability to play with Mexican cultural themes, his wonderful way with the Mexican media. That is why it was so hard to translate his language. It also makes it hard to translate his politics.

The essence of Marcos' voice and politics is his deft combination of traditions of indigenous resistance with the cosmopolitan (and somewhat left) culture of contemporary Mexico City. This particular fusion of the traditional and the contemporary (Marcos is, among other things, a translator between the two) helped build powerful support for the EZLN throughout Mexico. Whether it can serve as a future guide for the Mexican left, no one knows. Whether it can help orient the left in the United States—where indigenous cultures have neither the numerical weight nor the symbolic importance that they have in Mexico, and where our left intellectuals do not have as great an impact on cosmopolitan culture as do Mexican leftists like Monsiváis, Gilly, and Poniatowska, who regularly write in Mexico City's mass circulation press—is even more questionable.

With those warnings out of the way, but not out of mind, what can the U.S. left learn from the Sup?

Let's return to the idea of obligation. It recurs throughout these letters and communiqués. In number 46, a letter to Miguel Vazquez, the thirteen-year-old boy from La Paz who sent the Sup a picture of his dog, Marcos says, "We must cultivate among us the tree of love and hate, and the tree of obligation." He speaks to the boy about what "we" are obliged to do: "And we must not be afraid during the rise and fall of red stars, not be afraid of anything but surrender, of remaining in our seats and resting while others continue on, of taking a break while others struggle, sleeping while others are on watch."

Marcos wants Miguel to feel obligated to his fellow struggling Mexicans—and to Mexico. Subcomandante Insurgente Marcos is a patriot. He almost literally wraps himself in the national flag. In his speech to the National Democratic Convention, he unfurled the flag and held it before him while he told the audience that the whole point of calling the convention was to find someone to give the flag to. At the end of the speech he formally presented it to Rosario Ibarra, founding member of the Mexican Mothers of the Disappeared and moral leader of the Mexican left. Similarly, Marcos unfolded the national flag and held it silently at the dramatic beginning of the Dialogue for Peace. Marcos is an unapologetic

Mexican nationalist. It is the nation (the actual inheritance of the ancestors?) that binds and obliges.

Should we learn patriotism from Marcos? Not exactly. The nationalism of a country that is a victim of imperialism has quite a different meaning from the nationalism of the imperial giant. Marcos' Mexico is a nation of resistance in a way that the U.S. nation could never be. Moreover, the vehemence of the Sup's nationalism is partially a consequence of the current changing relationship between the United States and Mexico: Salinas de Gortari and the PRI have jettisoned the democratic nationalist economic policies that were meant to protect the Mexican economy from U.S. capitalism and have replaced them with policies meant to integrate U.S. and Mexican capital. That is a policy which not only means more misery for the have-nots of Mexico, but which threatens a kind of cultural annexation of Mexico to the United States. It is against the background of this threat that Marcos' proud Mexican identity and deep understanding of Mexican popular culture play so well.

But the word that we have translated as "nation," or sometimes as "country," does not exactly mean either of those two ideas. The word is *patria*. The translation most true to the Latin root of the word would be "fatherland." But that won't do, as it is impossible to seal off "fatherland" from connotations of German statism. "Motherland" would be softer, of course, but not by much, and furthermore the "nation" is not the typical realm of the mother in Mexico, but rather of the father. (The mother's typical places outside the home would be the church and the village marketplace.) Perhaps the best translation of the word—in terms of what it actually means to a Mexican speaker—is "homeland." We did not translate it that way because the other forms of the word—"homelandism" for instance—are hopelessly awkward, if not nonexistent. So to say that Marcos is a Mexican patriot is not only to say that he is a classic Latin American democratic nationalist, but also that he is loyal to the homeland.

And it is even more particular than that. Marcos is a man of many homelands. *Patria* for him begins in the Mountain. And in Spanish *la montaña* doesn't mean just a high place, it means the place outside political jurisdiction, the place of outlaws, what is called "the bush" in Africa. Marcos is one of the thousands of Latin American intellectuals who have gone to the Mountain since Castro's triumphant entry into Havana on January 1, 1959. Marcos is loyal to the *patria* of the left; he lives in the Mountain with all the guerrillas—most of whom died in obscurity—who went before him, and especially with the great Mexican revolutionaries, Zapata, Villa, Flores Magón. From the Mountain his loyalty extends to the homeland of Mayan Chiapas, and from there to the Mexican *patria* that is the victim of imperialism.

Marcos is loyal to the home "land." He knows it, he respects it, he describes it in loving detail. Part of the power of this political writing is how well Marcos knows the local map. Like the old Zapatistas, the new ones believe in "Land and Freedom." The two ideas are very close. The land should belong to them—they know it, they work it, they could make their world from it—but it has been taken away by the "bad government." Freedom would get them their land back, and give them the power to create their own world and their own history.

We are now somewhere closer to home. We need not be loyal to U.S. imperialism to be loyal to various home lands. All the attempts to build local left politics, to define and defend regional identities, are in the spirit of the Sup. As our cities and towns, our land and our water, become nothing but inputs in a worldwide system of exploitation, loyalty to the home land, to local communities, becomes an act of resistance. And there are national home lands that could command our loyalty as well: the *patrias* of Sojournor Truth, Eugene Debs, Dorothy Day ... take your pick, it is a long and honorable list.

But there is no way of building these loyalties without active participation in popular movements. Marcos is uncompromising on that. The purpose of the left intellectual is to help people figure out what to do. In Marcos' universe, it is either that or empty theorizing.

It is a measure of how far we have strayed from our own left tradition that people would have to be reminded that theory is supposed to be a guide to action. Some of the very best work now being done by left intellectuals (especially academic ones) is nothing more than brilliant analysis of the contemporary disaster. Traditions and possibilities of resistance seldom appear. These days I often put down a left book even more depressed than before I picked it up. Sure the situation is grim and getting worse. It is usually thus, says Marcos. Says his American soulmate, Tom Paine: "This is no time for summer soldiers or sunshine patriots." What time ever was?

It is not a question of cheerleading. It is a question of becoming, along with Marcos and the Zapatistas, professionals of hope. The basis of that hope is the belief in the ultimate value of political action. There is no talk in Marcos of "pessimism of the intellect and optimism of the will." There is rather a commitment of the whole person to the proposition that in any situation, no matter how bad, together with other people you can figure out a few things to do. If you don't have that belief, then go into another line of work; you don't belong on the Left. Marcos is an activist. We might call him a mindful (as opposed to mindless) activist. It is a way we could think of ourselves.

This is not a good time for revolutionary hope. That is part of the *coyuntura* that we share with Marcos. The new Zapatista guerrilla war takes place after the Fall. Ours is a time of actually nonexisting socialism, and doubt about the whole revolutionary socialist project. Marcos knows that. The word "socialism" appears twice in the 60,000-some words of these writings. Socialism is not rejected outright by Marcos, it just doesn't seem to matter much. "Freedom, Democracy, and Justice" will do well enough as a salutation at the end of the communiqués.

This is not a casual shift from one slogan to another. Nor is it opportunism. Marcos has described in several interviews the process through which his small (they began with eleven, he says) band of Marxist revolutionaries were transformed by their experience in the Mayan communities of Chiapas. He says that when he and his group went to the Mountain, they carried in their heads "the political-military organizations of the guerrilla movements in Latin America during the sixties and seventies." This model had at its core, he says, "a vertical, authoritarian structure." It depended on a clear distinction between the guerrillas ("a group of strong men and women, with ideological and physical strength") and the people in general, whose role it was to support the guerrilla vanguard.

But in the course of trying to survive, the young Marxist intellectuals became integrated into the communities in ways that their theory had not predicted. During a near decade of interchange, dialogue, and consultations, Marcos and his comrades changed. Marcos describes how it happened in an August 1994 interview with the magazine *Love and Rage:*

"Finally, I can't say exactly when—it's not something that's planned—

the moment arrived in which the EZLN had to consult the communities in order to make a decision. At first, we only asked if what we were doing was going to cause problems for the compañeros. And later, when we left the jungle and entered the mountains, we also entered the assemblies and discussions in the communities. A moment arrives in which you can't do anything without the approval of the people with whom you work. It was something understood by both parties; they understood that we wouldn't do anything without consulting them, and we understood that if we did anything without consulting them, we would lose them. And this flow, this increase of men and women who left the communities in order to enter the mountains, made us realize that we couldn't draw a solid line between combatant forces and civilian forces. Even geographically, this line had broken down. There were military units that didn't live in the mountains but instead lived in the communities and participated in communal labors. They gave military instruction, but they also participated in the work of the communities. When we reflect on this now it isn't a question of 'us' and 'them'—now 'we' are the entire community."

This was not a superficial change. Marcos even found it necessary to slip it into his famous list (number 13) of sarcastic questions about what the Zapatistas should be pardoned for. "... Of having called on the people of Mexico to struggle, in all possible ways, for that which belongs to them? Of having fought for freedom, democracy, and justice? Of not following the example of previous guerrilla armies? Of not giving up? Of not selling out? Of not betraying ourselves?" And what changed was more than the EZLN's organizational structure. By the time the Zapatistas burst onto the world scene, they were thoroughgoing revolutionary democrats, explicitly rejecting vanguardism, sectarianism, and any notion of dictatorship as the goal of their revolution.

These three ideas have come under explicit attack in most of the theoretical attempts by socialists to explain "what went wrong." What we have in the Zapatistas is the rejection of these ideas in the actual practice of trying to make revolution. And what we can see from their experience is how the ideas are linked: vanguardism, sectarianism, and dictatorship all reflect a basic idea about the relationship between the revolutionary group and the people.

Whether it is the revolutionary group on the rise (vanguardism), defeated (sectarianism), or in power (dictatorship), the relationship is the same, and forever the same: not only do the revolutionaries know better than the people what's good for the people, but also they have no theoretical understanding or institutional structure that can overcome this hierarchy of knowledge.

But the Zapatistas' biggest break with conventional revolutionary theory is their attitude toward state power. "And what would triumph be?" Marcos rhetorically asks. "Seizing power? No, something ever harder to win: a new world." The heresy of this formulation is that most modern revolutionaries have seen the seizing of state power by their group as the major step in making that new world. The Zapatistas do not. In a formulation that has the feel of a carefully worked-over idea, Marcos describes the Zapatista revolutionary goals (number 14):

"And the result [of the revolution] will not be the triumph of a party, organization, or alliance of organizations with their particular social programs, but rather the creation of a democratic space for resolving the confrontations between different political proposals. This democratic space will have three fundamental premises that are already historically inseparable: the democratic right of determining the dominant social project, the freedom to subscribe to one project or another, and the requirement that all projects must point the way to justice."

Once again, this time on the level of the national government rather than a village community, democracy and justice are inextricably linked. Not just any argument can be made in the democratic space. You can't legitimately push your own interests or what is best for your group. You must argue about justice, which in the Zapatista lexicon means primarily economic justice. This is the kind of democracy that frightened the original theorists of liberal capitalism: the kind where once the poor have political power, they will use that power to take property and wealth away from the rich.

The new Zapatistas have in mind a great redistribution of wealth; much of the power of their appeal depends on the depth of their poverty. But democracy is not simply the instrument through which economic justice is achieved. Democracy itself is primary. There will be no "dictatorship of the proletariat" or any other kind of dictatorship proposed by these people.

How could it be different coming from Mexicans who have lived under the "perfect dictatorship" of the Party of the Institutionalized Revolution? But the kind of nationwide democratic space that Marcos is proposing is not an imitation of the 'democracy' we suffer from in the United States. Yes, we have a deep tradition of civil liberties that allows the "freedom to subscribe to one project or another." We have competing parties and free elections. All those things are part of the democracy that the Zapatistas want. But the Zapatistas want more. On a local level they want true communities, where (in Marcos' traditional language) "those who command, obey." On the national level they want (in Marcos' ever so contemporary language) "the democratic right of determining the dominant social project." Zapatista democracy depends on both the existence of democratic local communities and true choices between alternative national "social projects."

Does Zapatista democracy have anything to do with contemporary U.S. politics and the situation of the left? "Democratic local communities" are a reasonable goal, but they won't happen by themselves. They will have to be built, and it is a long way from here to there. Just how far we are from "true choices" nationally can best be explained by comparing the Democratic and Republican parties to the PRI. Inside the PRI there is a far greater range of opinion and interest than there is within the Democratic and Republican parties combined. That is, the PRI is more representative of the various interests and social classes within Mexico than are the Democrats and Republicans, taken together, representative of the full range of U.S. society. This is not meant to be a defense of the PRI. Rather, it suggests a different way of looking at (even) the formal democracy of the United States. Since our political power is limited to choosing between Democrats and Republicans, and since the differences between them are relatively narrow ("not a dime's worth of difference" was a good way to put it), then why shouldn't we think of U.S. democracy as an even "more perfect" dictatorship?

State power, moreover, is not the only space for democratic political activity, according to the Zapatistas. There is also "civil society." Marcos argues not only that civil society never fully relinquishes ultimate legitimacy to the state, but that the institutions and social forms of civil society exert a kind of perpetual dual power alongside the state. That such a theory would come from Marcos is not surprising. Civil society is one of the most popular terms in current political talk (even though it often seems to mean little more than the weight of public opinion) and some kind of social force that could be called "civil society" helped protect the EZLN from the Mexican government.

But civil society also has a specific Mexican meaning, and Marcos' emphasis on the idea is neither a simple reflection of what happened after January 1994 nor a slavish imitation of contemporary intellectual fashion. In Mexico, after the brutal repression of the student movement in 1968, thousands of radical students entered labor unions and neighborhood groups carrying their particular brand of Mexican New Left/Old Left student politics. These people helped build various movements and organizations that became relatively powerful in the late 1970s and the early 1980s, and are often called the "legacy of '68." It was these specific groups that were identified by some Mexican left intellectuals—most importantly, Carlos Monsiváis—as civil society.

Monsiváis defined civil society as "el esfuerzo comunitario de autogestión y solidaridad, el espacio independiente del gobierno" ("self-generated community power and solidarity, the space independent of the government"). It's crowning moment was after the 1985 Mexican City earthquake, when "self-generated community power and solidarity" organized the rescue and recovery efforts, independent of and in opposition to the Mexican government. Civil society's rescue of the Zapatistas was just the most recent expression of its power.

The institutions of Mexican civil society are something quite different from their pretenders north of the border. Most U.S. voluntary organizations do not qualify because they are not expressions of active solidarity and they do not exist as a check on governmental power. And our left popular movements are weak in comparison to the popular movements of Mexico. It is a measure of the relative failure of the U.S. New Left that it bequeathed no "legacy of '68," that is, the student movement failed in its attempt to bring its ideas and institutions into the arenas of popular struggle outside the college and university communities. (The possible exception to this is the continuing power of the antiwar movement inherent in the idea of the "Vietnam syndrome," and perhaps the partial success of some rank-and-file union groups.) A recognition of our failure to build popular movements of opposition that would give the idea of civil society real substance in the U.S. context might be a place to start formulating our own contemporary radical agenda.

This, finally, brings us to the question of Marcos' literary style. It would be wrong to talk about these writings as if Marcos had figured out how to put left ideas into popular language. It is not a question of grafting a new way of writing about politics onto the same old ideas. The Sup's words are affectionate, eclectic, flexible, fun-loving in the face of death, tenderly furious, and committed—and so are his politics. Yes, the Zapatistas went to war, suffered casualties, made what we consider the ultimate sacrifices. But without ignoring the death of his comrades (Marcos never ignores death), the dramatic center of Marcos' report on the days of fighting is a joke: military and political advice given to him by drunks. Yes, the Zapatistas went to war, but it was twelve days of war, followed by several months of theater. That wasn't all their own doing, of course. They had a good deal of luck, tremendous support from Mexican civil society, and from worldwide human rights organizations. But the ratio of war to theater is not inconsistent with who they are. Marcos and the Zapatistas will lead no one down the road to the protracted revolutionary wars of Guatemala, El Salvador, or Peru. They didn't shoot Castellanos. They let him go. Isn't that part of their genius? Isn't that part of why they continue to be a leading Mexican political force?

It is a mistake to ask too much of Marcos and the Zapatistas. Marcos tells the convention, "We neither want, nor are we able, to occupy the place that some hope we will occupy, the place from which all opinions will come, all the answers, all the routes, all the truths." The Mexican left must accept that, and the U.S. left even more so. It is inspiring to witness the persistence of revolutionary will and action. It is encouraging to see a promise of what a democratic revolutionary movement might look like and sound like. That is what Marcos and the Zapatistas can do for us: inspire and encourage. There is no Supism. We are obliged to make our own way, to live our own loyalties, to build our own movement.

—Watsonville, California
October 12, 1994

264

Postmodern Postscript: I managed to get through this whole essay without using the term "postmodern." It is applied often to Marcos, even more in Mexico than here, in reference to his lack of an overriding theory, constant jokes on himself, epigrammatic style, and self-conscious distancing from his own "text." There is a good dose of all of that in Marcos; but what do the postmodernists (who claim him as their own) say about his old-fashioned commitment to the "truth"? Although it is unclear whether Marcos believes in "*the* truth," he certainly believes in "truthfulness," and in the difference between people who speak the truth and people who lie. "The Lie" is one way Marcos names the Mexican political system, and it is clear that within all his talk of masks, there is an idea of a face behind the mask, a "truth" that can be unmasked and revealed. A truth that is not just text.

Postmodern is an idea that the left ought to avoid. "Modern" was a bad enough way to name an age, saying nothing about it except that it is "now," and "postmodern" is even worse, giving us as the naming characteristic of our time nothing more than "after now." I continue to think of our age as "Late Capitalism," even if it doesn't seem to be as late as we hoped. Calling it "late" suggests that it has an end, and as we no longer believe in the inevitable progressive march of history, the term "Late Capitalism" is not only a theoretical naming, but a call to action . . . which is a good way to end an essay about Subcomandante Insurgente Marcos.

GLOSSARY

Article 27. The section of Mexico's revolutionary 1917 Constitution that establishes the state's ownership of all land and water resources, forests, and mineral deposits and gives it the power to limit private ownership and break up existing large estates. This was the basis for the land-reform program and creation of the *ejido* (see below). The Salinas government revised this article in 1991 to enable the buying and selling of any parcel of land, including *ejido* land, and the reestablishment of large estates.

". . . as the times favor the little ones." Line from a song by the popular Cuban *nueva canción* (protest) singer Pablo Milanós: "El tiempo está a favor de los pequeños."

authentic Farabundos. Presumably a reference to the Salvadoran revolutionary hero Farabundo Martí, an organizer of peasants and workers in the late 1920s who was martyred in the massive repression known as La Matanza in 1932 and gave his name to the Salvadoran guerrilla movement of the 1980s, the FMLN.

El Bajío. Rich agricultural region of central Mexico, mostly in the state of Guanajuato, where U.S. agribusiness now plays a large role.

El Barzón. A town in northern Mexico where small farmers demanded agricultural subsidies, sparking a national movement. It is also the name of an organization of farmers who were early supporters of the EZLN.

Boy Heroes of Chapultepec. Cadets at the Military Academy at the Castle of Chapultepec who gave their lives in the unsuccessful defense of Mexico City against the U.S. forces in 1847, the event recalled in the United States by the first words of the Marines' Hymn ("From the halls of Montezuma . . . "). In Mexico the cadets are the principle symbols of patriotic heroism.

Cacique/caciquismo/cacicazga. A pre-colombian indigenous title denoting regional lord; now refers to a local or regional-level political boss. Often a major landowner, this person is accorded almost mystical powers by the peasants in his domain, and controls things behind the scenes as well as from his balcony; he is also the unofficial but principal local representative of the PRI. /The phenomenon of political control by *caciques*. /The reign of a *cacique*.

Caudillismo. A *caudillo* is a charismatic political leader who derives his power from his military experience, prowess, and bearing; *caudillismo* is the phenomenon of such leadership.

CEU. Consejo Estudiantil Universitario, the student organization at the National University of Mexico (UNAM); it is made up of factions that are essentially divided over their willingness to work with the PRD, the left-center party led by Cuauhtémoc Cárdenas, who is widely believed to have won the presidential election of 1988.

científicos porfiristas. Members of the business/technocratic elite during the dictatorship of Porfirio Díaz (1876-1910), so-called satirically because of their education in scientific positivism, the prevailing educational philosophy at the National Preparatory School, which they all attended.

Cintalapa. Town in Chiapas on the road between the coast and Tuxtla Gutiérrez.

CNTE. Coordinador Nacional de Trabajadores de la Educación, the National Coordinating Committee of Educational Workers, a dissident faction of the Mexican national teachers' union.

coletos. Non-Indian residents of San Cristóbal de las Casas; the name refers to the ponytails sported by their colonial ancestors.

coyotes. Mercenary middlemen who extract a high toll from the poor and vulnerable for transporting products to market or people across a border.

cronopios. A reference to Argentine novelist Julio Cortazar's *Historias de Cronopios y de Famas*.

CTM. Confederación de Trabajadores Mexicanos, the Mexican Workers' Confederation, the officially sanctioned and corrupt labor federation that is a branch of the PRI and more often represents the interests of the state than the interests of the workers in the conduct of labor conflicts.

CU. The enormous Ciudad Universitaria (University City) built to house the expanded National University of Mexico (UNAM) in the early 1950s and attended daily by perhaps 100,000 students and faculty. The interior circuit is the on-campus road system.

Díaz, Porfirio. Dictator of Mexico from 1876 to 1910; presided over the rapid consolidation of huge landed estates, the construction of a railroad network, the development of mines and oilfields, the beginnings of export agriculture and industrialization, and the urbanization of Mexico City. Governed through the *cacique* system (see above); used repression to suppress political opposition and guarantee labor peace as a means of attracting significant foreign capital investment.

ejido/ejidatario. System of communal land tenure institutionalized by the Mexican agrarian reform program since 1915. Peasants enjoy non-transferable usufruct rights to individual plots, unless they decide collective use is preferable. Communal ownership and administration existed "in perpetuity" until the guarantee was abolished under neoliberal pressure by the Salinas regime in 1991. /Members of an *ejido* known as *ejidatarios.*

Federales. All-purpose term of opprobrium inherited from the revolutionary struggle against the Federal Army of Porfirio Díaz; refers to federal police agents or soldiers, or to the federal authorities in general.

FONAPO. Fondo Nacional de Población, the National Population Fund.

grillos. Literally "crickets"; refers here to political discourse and is a common expression used to describe noisy, hard-line political speech-making.

Guerrero, Vicente. Leader of the independence struggle against Spain in the area south of Mexico City; president during the 1820s.

INEGI. Instituto Nacional de Estadística, Geografía, e Informatíca, the National Institute of Statistics, Geography, and Data. The federal department in charge of census and mapmaking.

Jaramillo, Rubén. Methodist pastor and peasant leader in the struggle for effective land reform in the state of Morelos. As a young man, he was a Zapatista soldier and was politically active for nearly fifty years, until he was assassinated by government forces in 1962.

Los Piños. The presidential mansion in Mexico City's Chapultepec Park, where political deals important to the nation are frequently made behind closed doors.

ladino. In Chiapas and other regions of Mesoamerica with large indigenous populations, a non-Indian or Spanish-speaking person of European or *mestizo* (see below) extraction. In Chiapas, *ladino* is the word for *mestizo.*

latifundistas. Owners of great agricultural or stock-rearing estates; many latifundistas have put together holdings more extensive than allowed by the law by acquiring parcels in the names of family and friends.

mestizo. Person of mixed indigenous and European racial and cultural heritage. Applies to the overwhelming majority of Mexico's people.

moles. Refers to people involved in underground political work.

neoporfiristas. Defenders of government economic policies reminiscent of those operative during the dictatorship of Porfirio Díaz (see above); applies today to the proponents of neoliberalism.

Neza. Ciudad Nezahualcóyotl, a giant shantytown on the outskirts of Mexico City, which rose from nothing in 1950 to a population of over 4 million today. Characterized by severe shortages of housing, electricity, running water, and public transportation, it is a much-publicized incubator of social unrest and has produced youth gangs, protest rock, and remarkable neighborhood survival organizations.

Pérez, Jacinto. An Indian leader of forces from the highlands of Chiapas that joined the oligarchs of that region in supporting the reformist government of Francisco Madero in 1910 because of their hostility to the new agricultural bourgeoisie of the lowlands of Chiapas (which had developed during the dictatorship of Porfirio Díaz). These forces were known locally as *mapaches* ("raccoons") because of their habit of provisioning themselves by requisition from the farms they passed by and because they often wore masks.

PGR. Procuraduría General de la República, the Federal Department of Justice.

Plan de Ayala. The proposal for a direct distribution of "land to the tiller," drawn up in 1911 by the original Zapatistas in Morelos to challenge Francisco Madero. Set the revolutionary standard for agrarian reform in Mexico from that day to the present.

plantón. A public demonstration in the form of a long-term "sit-in" or camp-in, complete with tents and barbecues, as a means of achieving visibility and being heard outside a government building.

presidencialismo. A widely criticized feature of Mexico's "one-party democracy." The president maintains control over the party while in office, and at the same time takes the lead in determining the actions of both the legislature and the judiciary, in addition to playing the primary role in selecting his own successor.

PRONASOL. Programa Nacional de Solidaridad, the National Solidarity Program. The Salinas government's program to carry out the traditional PRI procedure of dosing out tangible and visible benefits to specific regions, communities, or sectors of the population on the principle of "the squeaky wheel gets the grease." Financed during Salinas' time from the proceeds of the sale of publicly owned businesses, the PRONASOL program is a part of the PRI's "electoral clientalism." The communities that benefit are encouraged to provide labor and some additional funds and materials for the public works projects involved and to support the PRI. As always, the program was characterized more by much-publicized promises than by substantial benefits to the people.

"Revolutionary Laws"; "Laws of Women." Official EZLN documents promulgated in January 1994 to define the politics and purpose of the organization.

rocker in CU. Large portions of the UNAM's faculty and student body are traditional, self-righteous Marxist-leftists and provide little room for cultural dissent—especially of the kind that tends to come from youth in Neza (see above).

SEDENA. Secretaria de Defensa Nacional, the Mexican Ministry of Defense, which has responsibility for all of the country's armed forces.

SOLIDARITY. In the double-speak of the Salinas government, this refers to massively publicized public investments in local infrastructure and services under the PRONASOL (see above). One of the characteristics of PRI politics is massive publicity, including omnipresent billboards and wall-paintings. The SOLIDARITY logo can be seen throughout the country, in small towns as well as big cities.

Televisa. The enormous and powerful consortium of television and entertainment interests that operates on concessions granted by the PRI government in 1948 and works hand in hand with the government to maintain the status quo. Wields influence through a very tendentious nightly news program and flashy, morally bankrupt entertainment shows.

Tlalmanalco. Town in the state of México that was the scene of a 1994 PRD protest against a fraudulent mayoral election. The protest was severely repressed by the police.

Vale. Literally, "It's valid." As a parting expression, the Subcomandante uses it to mean "Okay," or, "You can count on it," or, "So there you have it," or just, "Be seein' ya."

zócalo. The central plaza of any Mexican city, with the principle church and government buildings on each side. Comes from the word *zoco*, which means the pedestal of a statue; it is a focal point for demonstrations.

—Leslie López and David Sweet